Escape with Honor

Brassey's
MEMORIES OF WAR
Series

Outstanding memoirs that illustrate the personal realities of war as experienced by combatants and civilians alike, in recent conflicts as well as those of the distant past. Other titles in the series:

Escape with Honor
My Last Hours in Vietnam

Terry McNamara

with Adrian Hill

An ADST-DACOR Diplomats and Diplomacy Book

BRASSEY'S, INC.
Washington, D.C.

First Memories of War edition published in 2003

Copyright © 1997 Brassey's

First paperback edition 1999

Map by A. D. McJoynt

Library of Congress Cataloging-in-Publication Data

McNamara, Francis Terry, 1927–
    Escape with honor : my last hours in Vietnam / Terry McNamara with
Adrian Hill.
        p.   cm. — (Brassey's Memories of war series) (The ADST-DACOR diplomats
    and diplomacy series)
    "An ADST-DACOR diplomats and diplomacy book."
    Includes index.
    ISBN 1-57488-693-2 (alk. paper)
    1. Vietnamese Conflict, 1961–1975—Personal narratives, American.
2. Diplomats—Vietnam.   3. Diplomats—United States.   4. McNamara, Francis
Terry, 1927–.   I. Hill, Adrian, 1943–   II. Title.   III. Series.   IV. Memories of war

    DS559.5.M43 2003
    959.704'3373'092—dc21   2003052229

Printed in the United States of America on acid-free paper that meets the American
National Standards Institute Z39-48 Standard.

Brassey's
22883 Quicksilver Drive
Dulles, Virginia 20166

10 9 8 7 6 5 4 3 2 1

For

Maj. Gen. Nguyen Khoa Nam

and

Henry Cushing

BOTH NOW DEAD BUT NOT FORGOTTEN

The ADST-DACOR Diplomats and Diplomacy Series

For the last 220 years an extraordinary group of men and women have represented the United States abroad under all kinds of circumstances. What they did and how and why they did it are not well known by their compatriots. In 1995 the Association for Diplomatic Studies and Training (ADST) and Diplomatic and Consular Officers, Retired (DACOR) created a book series to increase public knowledge and appreciation of the involvement of American diplomats in the events of world history. The series seeks to demystify diplomacy by telling the story of those who have conducted our foreign relations, as they saw it and lived it.

The role of a diplomat has changed greatly from the courtly days of earlier times. Nothing better illustrates this than the story told here of Terry McNamara's exploits in saving the lives of some 318 people as he led one of the last groups of Americans, together with Vietnamese staff and their families, out of the Mekong Delta on two small boats at the end of the Vietnam War. In doing so, McNamara drew not only on his experience of nineteen years as an American diplomat but also on his three years in the U.S. Navy and a tough Irish-American heritage. Though the Foreign Service officers who served in Vietnam did not wear uniforms and their record as fighters in that war is less well known than that of those who did, their contribution was no less eventful and heroic.

—*Stephen Low, President, ADST*
—*Joan M. Clark, President, DACOR*

Contents

Illustrations are after page 108

Preface

Shortly after my return from Vietnam in 1975, several friends urged me to write an account of my dramatic departure from that sad country as its badly weakened government succumbed to invasion from the north. Others were circulating distorted accounts aimed at covering the tracks of those who had fled taking helicopters desperately needed in the evacuation of Saigon. Honor and historical accuracy demanded that the full story be told.

At the time, I was still caught emotionally in the trauma of the U.S. departure and in the terrible consequences suffered by so many of those who had given us Americans their trust. I doubted my ability to write an account of such emotionally charged events.

A British pal, Adrian Hill, came to my rescue. He had served at the British Embassy in Saigon from 1969 to 1972, when I was in charge of the U.S. consulate in Danang. Adrian and I became fast friends in the course of his many visits to central Vietnam. Later, he was best man at my wedding. When I told him of my self-doubts about turning my story into a book, he offered to help.

We agreed that I would write a straightforward account of the events as they had occurred. He would then edit and revise my draft, putting it into a livelier form. Since that time, I have edited, restructured, and rewritten Adrian's text. In its final form, the basic story and responsibility for any errors or omissions are mine alone. Indeed, the story as told is as factual as I can make it.

The intent of our joint effort is a book with the ring of truth that also captures the strong emotions in play at the time. Readers may judge whether we have succeeded.

Acknowledgments

Adrian Hill merits special recognition for his help, support, and encouragement. Not only did he contribute to the writing of the book itself but his persistent encouragement kept my nose to the grindstone as I wrote a first rough draft. His novelist's touch enlivened my more staid prose style.

Another English friend who deserves my gratitude is David Martin, a veteran journalist and now publisher of the Zimbabwe Publishing House in Harare, Zimbabwe. David generously passed me his notes from a weeklong interview he conducted with me in Quebec early in 1976, less than a year after the evacuation took place and while my recollections were still fresh.

The fine photographs in the book were taken by Gary "Kass" Kassebaum, whose good humor and moral courage helped sustain us all throughout our nautical adventure. He kindly gave permission for the use of his photographs in this book.

Steve Low, president of the Association for Diplomatic Studies and Training, provided me with the generous organizational support that enabled me to finish the book and have it adopted as part of the ADST-DACOR Diplomats and Diplomacy Series.

The association's publishing coordinator, Margery Boichel Thompson, generously gave me her professional advice and deft editorial suggestions and, most important, found the right publisher for the book. It was at her urging that I undertook major surgery on the earlier text, without which, I am now convinced, the book would have remained unpublishable. Thanks also to Lale Üner, who kindly volunteered her assistance in the electronic preparation of the manuscript.

Brassey's editorial director, Don McKeon, is another to whom I am indebted. His intelligent editorial suggestions and his insistence on a change in the text from the third person to the more compelling first person resulted in a much livelier, more dramatic read.

I owe a profound debt of gratitude to the seventeen intrepid Americans who accompanied me on the downriver evacuation from Can

Tho. Each of them contributed, in his own way, to the success of our escape from a collapsing South Vietnam. The names of these faithful few (two of whom, Cushing and Odell, have since died) are:

> Florian Ajinga, *supervisor of the consulate general's local guard force*
>
> Averill Christian, *administrative officer*
>
> Henry "Hank" Cushing, *deputy consul general*
>
> Boyette "Steve" Hasty, *staff sergeant, USMC*
>
> Walter Heilman, *general services officer*
>
> Lee Johnson, *corporal, USMC*
>
> Gary "Kass" Kassebaum, *province representative*
>
> Larry B. Killens, *corporal, USMC*
>
> John Kirchner, *sergeant, USMC*
>
> Walter Milford, *CIA communicator*
>
> John Moore, *sergeant, USMC*
>
> Thomas Odell, *province representative*
>
> Terry Pate, *sergeant, USMC*
>
> Lamar "Mac" Prosser, *province representative*
>
> Andrew "David" Sciacchitano, *consular officer*
>
> Robert Traister, *province representative*
>
> James "Dave" Whitten, *political officer*

Above all, I wish to express my gratitude to my wife, Nhu De, for her unstinting support in all things great and small. Without complaint, she has cheerfully accepted the discomforts, the personal inconveniences, and the dangers of Foreign Service life with me. Her love and wise counsel have sustained me over an eventful twenty-odd years and continue to do so. The presence of our sons Terry and Marc has added a further dimension to a happy and fulfilling family life.

Thank you one and all!

—*Francis Terry McNamara*

Prologue

In 1975, when the events chronicled in this book took place, Vietnam had been at war for some thirty years, with only a relatively short respite from the fighting during the late 1950s. The Geneva Accords of 1954 had divided the country and led to the departure of the defeated French. Fearful of a more general communist takeover of Southeast Asia, America came to the support of a fragile nationalist regime in the southern half of Vietnam. This perceived communist threat was seen at the time in the context of the Cold War. Indeed, the U.S. decision to intervene in Vietnam was taken as part of a worldwide policy aimed at the containment of communism.

Responding to an increased communist challenge in the south, American commitment to Vietnam began to expand dramatically as an energetic Kennedy administration came to power in 1961 with an incautious engagement to "pay any price." As the war grew in intensity during the early 1960s and our Vietnamese allies appeared unequal to the challenge, that price became increasingly heavy.

The first U.S. ground units to be committed were sent wading ashore at Danang in March 1965. The initial mission of those Marines was to protect the major airfield on the city's outskirts. Once the earlier taboo on the deployment of U.S. ground forces had been broken, the arrival of additional U.S. and allied troops continued apace until by 1969 some 543,000 American soldiers were in Vietnam.

A grinding war of attrition was undertaken as the strength of the U.S. forces in the country grew. The objective was to gradually weaken the enemy's resolve and compel its acceptance a noncommunist regime in the southern half of Vietnam.

Hanoi's forceful response was a countrywide offensive mounted in 1968 during the Vietnamese holiday period of "Tet." For the communists, the immediate outcome was a military disaster. Communist losses were appallingly high, with little or nothing gained on the battlefield. Ultimately, however, the offensive proved brilliantly successful on the more decisive front of American public opinion. Indeed, this seminal event of the war led ineluctably to the final U.S. troop withdrawal in 1973 and the eventual defeat of an abandoned South Vietnamese ally two years later.

Faced with the withdrawal of its troops, the United States had to address the question of how residual U.S. interests and activities could best be sustained outside Saigon, the capital. The cease-fire agreement forbade the continued presence of U.S. military personnel in rural Vietnam. Eventually it was decided to adopt a suggestion I had put forward much earlier when I was in charge of the U.S. consulate in Danang. Under this proposal, consulates general were established in each of the four U.S. military regions in Vietnam to serve as civilian umbrellas sheltering all remaining U.S. activities. The scheme became a reality with the signing of the Paris Accords in 1973.

These four unusual consular establishments were situated at the seaport of Danang, for the most northern mountainous region; at Nha Trang, for the thickly jungled central highlands; at Bien Hoa, just east of Saigon; and at Can Tho, among the rich rice paddies of the Mekong Delta. The State Department named a senior Foreign Service officer to head each post.

On April 29, 1975, I was serving as consul general in charge at Can Tho. With a North Vietnamese army at the gates of Saigon and a massive American evacuation already under way from the capital, I was about to witness the fall of South Vietnam.

Part I

The Honorable Choice

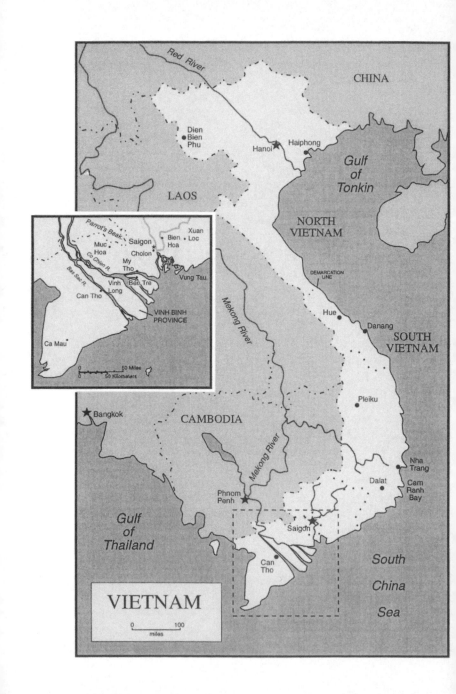

≡ 1 ≡

A Rude Awakening

A series of loud explosions awakened me. As I came to my senses, I recognized the deep boom followed by a jarring concussion to be rockets landing nearby. My stomach muscles tensed as I groped for my watch in the somber gray light. Two more explosions hit in rapid succession; this time the walls shook. Now fully awake, I jumped from my bed. In a few strides I was on the small balcony outside my second-story window. As I searched the horizon, Can Tho's wood and tile roofs obscured my view.

A few hundred meters away toward the waterfront, where a major canal met the Bas Sac River, a branch of the Mekong, dirty black smoke began drifting over the rooftops and the tall trees planted by a past generation of French colonials. I reckoned the rockets must have struck near the central marketplace.

My eyes followed the smoke as I listened for an answering thud of friendly artillery. None came. It should be easy, I reasoned, for the Vietnamese air force to put up some helicopter gunships and to direct counter-battery fire. The rockets must have been fired from across the river, in Vinh Long Province.

A radio set stood on the floor by my unmade bed. I brought it outside on the balcony for better reception as I tried to raise Boyette Hasty, the thin, keen, bespectacled staff sergeant who commanded the consulate general's six-man Marine security detachment. Hasty was probably out in a jeep trying to assess damage. The young sergeant would check the consulate's staff, official property, and finally the town.

Switching on the radio, I heard several of my staff members trying to speak at once. The Marines intervened to bring some order to the electronic chaos. Nobody seemed injured. Reassured, I left the radio switched on, listening to the distorted crackle of excited radio chatter as I hurriedly dressed. Judging from the snatches of conversation, Sergeant Hasty was indeed already driving around town. He reported no damage to the riverside complex called Delta Compound, which housed some of my staff and included a restaurant, a bar, a movie house, and a food store. These facilities were for the use of the American staff and official visitors to Can Tho. Delta Compound was important. Two of our evacuation boats were berthed there.

I suddenly remembered my watch. Strapping it on, I noticed that it was just after 5:30 A.M. I decided I should eat before driving to the office for what was liable to become a long day. Gloomily, I studied my gray hair and tired face in the bathroom mirror while washing and shaving. I was forty-seven years old, too old for this kind of nonsense.

Screeching tires announced Sergeant Hasty's arrival. I laid down my razor and went back outside to see what more he had discovered. Once again I leaned over the balcony, surveying the gravel drive that ran alongside the villa. Hasty sat behind the wheel of his jeep alone, upright, and alert, like a thin fox wearing glasses. He called up, "Everything is number one, Mr. McNamara. Your residence is not damaged."

"Oh . . . thanks," I replied. What else could I say?

"I just checked Delta Compound, saw Corporal Johnson, no damage there either. We think it was only a total of four rockets. Probably 122s."

"How about the town?" I asked.

"On my way."

Hasty rammed the jeep into reverse and roared backwards out through the gate. Again the wheels screeched as he stopped, turned, then floored the accelerator. I heard the jeep motor's growl stutter for a second as Hasty rounded the street corner before heading north toward the riverbank and marketplace. A few minutes later he reported over the radio.

"Mr. McNamara, two rockets landed on that island out in the Bas Sac just off town."

"Go on," I said, releasing the radio's press switch so that Hasty could talk.

"Second pair hit downtown near the International Hotel. No Americans hurt. There's an unknown number of Vietnamese casualties, some KIAed [killed in action], but no figures yet. Both fires are being brought under control."

"Good work. Where are you going now, Hasty?"

The radio crackled. Then Hasty's distorted voice said, "Back to the Marine House with your permission. Thought I'd take a shower and get some chow. We still have a lot of gear to pack in case of you-know-what." Hasty was alluding to the near certainty that within the next few days we would be ordered to evacuate.

I had no objection to his plans. Switching off the radio, I finished shaving and went downstairs for a quick breakfast.

Phuoc, my handsome, unflappable Vietnamese driver and body-guard, was waiting outside, the small white official sedan's engine running. I gave him a terse good morning. Phuoc understood without verbal instruction where I wanted to go. He sped the car along dusty, busy streets, expertly swerving to miss Honda riders and packed motor-scooter buses, rarely touching the horn, weaving under the shadow of huge trucks, until we crossed the yellow bridge over a large canal that divided the city.

Within a few minutes I was sitting impatiently at the gates of the consulate general, protected in front by a concrete wall three meters high with barbed wire strung along its top. A chain-link fence enclosed a parking lot on the south side of the building. The sleepy Vietnamese guard was startled when he saw the consul general at such an early hour. The gate swung open more quickly than most days.

Five white buildings filled the compound, connected by a maze of outside ladders and catwalks. The consul general's office was on the second floor in an old house, one of a pair that stood behind the others. I crossed the lobby and ran upstairs, two at a time, without bothering to give Phuoc any instructions. Phuoc, the recipient of an American Bronze Star medal for bravery while serving as an interpreter with a U.S. Army unit, unfolded a newspaper, not giving me a further glance as I hurried to work.

Once behind my desk, I began reading reports of the night before. Can Tho had escaped lightly; that first couple of rockets must have undershot, as there was no obvious target for them on the island. In the surrounding countryside among the endless darkened paddies, broken only by clumps of trees hiding small villages and cut across by thousands of tiny waterways, the night had been fairly quiet.

My tall, gaunt deputy, Hank Cushing, and I had developed excellent sources among the Vietnamese. All they were offering this morning was evidence that the Viet Cong propaganda mill was busy, spreading rumors of an impending ground attack on Can Tho City itself.

Disposing swiftly of the morning's reports, I joined Mac Prosser and Dave Whitten, two of my officers, in my outer office. Walt Heilman, the gentle bear in charge of building and equipment maintenance, was also among those gathered around the empty secretary's desk. As so many were present and I had work for them, I turned the little group into an impromptu staff meeting, asking Cushing to join if he wished.

For days, Hank had been orchestrating the movements and departure of potential Vietnamese evacuees, almost all of whom were local employees of the consulate general and their families. They were in danger from the communists because of their association with us, and many had already been sent to Saigon to join the general evacuation from Tan Son Nhut airport. Others were being gathered in Can Tho for eventual evacuation.

As on each preceding morning during the last few weeks, there was almost no news from Saigon; much of what we had learned in Can Tho came informally from Air America helicopter pilots, reasonably reliable sources. (Air America was the CIA-owned airline that then catered to all U.S. government business in Vietnam, both overt and covert.) It was this lack of hard information about the rest of South Vietnam—what was left of it—that I found most frustrating. While station chief Larry Downs* and his CIA contingent on the floor above managed to obtain some flow of news from their local sources, as well as from their Saigon headquarters, I was often skeptical of its veracity. Unfortunately, I had found frequent errors of fact, as well as a disquieting analytical weakness, in their reports. In any case, as a longtime Foreign Service political reporter, I thought it prudent to add my own network of informants to provide much-needed second opinions.

For some days, a variety of sources had been warning me that the enemy was preparing a serious attack aimed at cutting Route 4 and the canals that ran between the northern Delta and Saigon. This threat would be mounted from the Parrot's Beak, a dagger of Cambodian soil that stabbed deep into South Vietnam. The focus of the attack would be the point north of My Tho where all of the lines of communication converge to pass through a narrow corridor between the sea and the Parrot's Beak.

If the communists cut Route 4 and the canals, it meant serious trouble, for this was the capital's main supply line from its breadbasket

---

* In order to gain CIA clearance for this book, the author agreed to use pseudonyms for CIA personnel. Other published accounts refer to "Larry Downs" as "Jim D."

in the Delta. But the South Vietnamese forces in the Delta were still largely intact. Indeed, they had already reacted to this new threat by shifting the 7th ARVN (Army of the Republic of Vietnam) Division northwards astride Route 4 to protect it.

Our little group had hardly begun its meeting when, shortly after 8:30, Sergeant Hasty peered round the doorway, asking if I had any special orders for him. I instructed him to continue assembling evacuation supplies and equipment at our planned points of embarkation. As Hasty started to leave, he stopped suddenly. From inside my office had come the bleeping of the Emergency Action Communication (EAC) telephone used for direct calls to the ambassador and other senior mission officers in Saigon.

I ran through to my office and picked up the receiver, which stood on a small table near the cherry wood desk. I heard only the usual static. Annoyed, I replaced the telephone in its cradle. There was silence.

I returned to the outer office and perched on a desk. "Where were we?" I asked. "Supplies," piped Heilman, in his rich baritone.

Suddenly the bleeping resumed. Again I rushed next door, only to hear nothing on the line—the EAC telephone was malfunctioning.

At this moment, Larry Downs walked in from upstairs. Tan Son Nhut air base, he announced, had been rocketed and shelled early that morning. Two American Marines were killed. There was a second of silence.

Cushing wondered aloud how much material damage had been inflicted. Downs, who still managed to carry his air of physical toughness despite growing tired like the rest of us, explained what he had learned from Air America sources.

Some rockets had struck the Air America ramp. There was a possibility that four helicopters had been hijacked at gunpoint by South Vietnamese paratroopers. At that moment it was difficult to come by hard information. Downs would let me know at once should he learn more details. Leaving us, he hurried back upstairs.

I looked through to the long outside office, noticing a faint smell of burning paper from the code room. Some distant artillery fire shook the windows. It was this lack of hard news that was so frustrating. Thank God for the Air America pilots and their regular updates! Without them we would have been even more dangerously lacking in information from the rest of the country.

Turning to Prosser, I asked him to get Air Operations and find out whatever additional information he could from the pilots on conditions at Tan Son Nhut. Prosser nodded.

"My God," I grumbled to myself, "it's as if the capital were on a distant planet instead of only a hundred miles up Route 4."

The EAC telephone bleeping could have been caused by a technical fault. Or Saigon was trying to make contact. Not unduly worried, though not ready to risk a serious omission, I decided to dispatch Hasty to the Defense Attaché's Office. The DAO also had an EAC telephone with which Hasty could call Saigon.

Hasty thought for an instant. "Maybe the emergency radio is being overpowered by the CIA transmitters. We can open up an alternative station at Delta Compound. I'll have Marines monitoring it twenty-four hours a day." With that in mind, he left.

I glanced at my watch again. It was already quarter to nine. The impromptu staff meeting continued. Bob Traister, the consulate general's province representative in Vinh Long, had joined the circle. He now suggested that the ARVN interpreters who had accompanied him from Vinh Long the day before be quietly moved to Delta Compound and live on board the boats to ensure that no one interfered with them. As a mark of the high regard in which he was held by many Vietnamese, when Traister's friends in Vinh Long heard he was being withdrawn, they begged me to allow them time for a farewell party in his honor. That Saturday night had been a time of sad pride. Traister reached Can Tho the following day at two in the afternoon, exhausted from a night of hard drinking and soaked in sweat after his drive through dust and heat along Route 4.

I readily agreed to the compound move. "Good thinking, Bob," I added. "They can eat at the Delta Club." Finally, I admonished, "Be careful how you explain their presence to the cook and waitresses. We don't want word getting around that we are preparing to evacuate."

It was important to maintain an element of surprise in the evacuation. While most Vietnamese were aware that the Americans were likely to leave as the situation in the country deteriorated, a sudden, premature movement or unwisely obvious preparation could cause panic among the population or a bitter reaction from the ARVN.

Traister nodded, although he did not need reminding. "I've got a meeting organized at the boats for 0900," he said. "They don't know why. I want to ask my guys for the last time who wants to stay and who wants to leave."

Delta Compound was ten minutes away by car. Traister got up to leave. He stood for an instant and removed his thick-rimmed glasses, polishing them with his handkerchief.

"When you have finished, Bob, come straight back," I added as he turned to go.

Heilman was continuing to ready the boats for possible use. He had seventy-five Vietnamese on his staff, and many wanted to leave. But family problems had reduced this number to about twenty-five employees and their immediate relatives. Heilman's locals appeared calm about the situation, whether they wished to leave or stay. All were working coolly and efficiently, destroying records, servicing vehicles, checking the three boats—routine work that nonetheless had to be done thoroughly.

Prosser returned with word that an Air America pilot had confirmed via Air Operations in Saigon that considerable damage had been inflicted on Air America's terminal at Tan Son Nhut. Both hangars and the ramp had been hit, causing the total loss—or damaging beyond swift repair—of several of the company's fixed-wing aircraft and small Huey helicopters. Since the departure in 1973 of the U.S. military, these were the only aircraft left to the mission for in-country use. Moreover, the loss of Hueys could cripple Saigon's ability to carry out its evacuation plan. These small choppers were tasked to pluck people off designated rooftops and ferry them to landing sites, where they would be transferred to larger and heavier military helicopters for the flight out to the fleet at sea.

George "Jake" Jacobson, the evacuation coordinator at the embassy in Saigon, was still convinced that departure by helicopter was the only safe method for all remaining Americans to quit Vietnam. But I felt a duty, indeed a moral obligation, to bring out as many as possible of those Vietnamese who, during fifteen years, had loyally served the U.S. government. The damage done by the air strike on Tan Son Nhut reinforced my feeling that we were not likely to have enough aircraft available for evacuation from the Delta, especially if we were to take along our Vietnamese employees and their families. I was convinced that we could safely leave instead by water, sailing down the Bas Sac branch of the Mekong River to the open sea.

It was not an opinion shared by all my staff. Larry Downs and the CIA contingent were never convinced. They preferred to fly out by helicopter. But this would have meant that only Americans and possibly a few Filipino employees of the CIA would escape. As the situation worsened in the country, the prospect that a large number of helicopters would come to evacuate Can Tho became increasingly dim. Indeed, Jacobson had warned me when I visited Saigon a week earlier that we were "most unlikely to get any Marine helicopters coming to Can Tho at the time of a general evacuation from Saigon." Clearly, we were on our own.

It had been a week of arguments with Downs, though not every day. But the lack of trust was there on both sides, growing, and would not go away. Three days earlier I had, by the barest margin, managed to halt a CIA plan to suddenly evacuate their personnel by helicopter. Presumably, they would have left behind non-CIA U.S. personnel and the Vietnamese employees being gathered in Can Tho for eventual evacuation. God only knows what might have happened if the Vietnamese military had found out. One clear possibility was another premature collapse of the ARVN structure and widespread panic, as had happened during the evacuations a month earlier of Nha Trang and Danang. ARVN rage might be another reaction.

On my desk, a small upright calendar announced that today was April 29, 1975. At this point, I had lost interest in the calendar. I was focused on the black telephone on the desk. Silence. My watch told me it was almost ten o'clock.

I called to Cushing, who was working in his own office next door, checking military activity reports from the night before, "Do you think I should go over to DAO and call Saigon, Hank? The EAC ringing has me worried."

"Don't start a panic," said Cushing, gesturing with a lighted cigarette between nicotine-stained fingers. He ambled into the secretary's office where we were congregated. "But I think it would be wise."

Nobody else spoke. "OK," I said. "Let's give Hasty another five minutes to make contact from Delta Compound. After that I'll call Saigon. Perhaps my phone will work if I dial out."

"There's been no panic among our civil population," remarked Cushing. He seemed less strained, though his eyes were showing fatigue. Cushing added, "I agree. Wait five minutes."

That morning's rocketing of the city had lasted barely twenty minutes, but I could see it had further shaken many of the staff. The CIA contingent had been convinced for some time that the city was in imminent danger of being overrun. According to their sources, six enemy regiments, more than ten thousand men by their reckoning, were poised to burst into the streets of Can Tho City itself.

Cushing and I were skeptical. Our contacts in the ARVN, as well as other South Vietnamese sources, had no reason to minimize enemy strength, but they made no mention of large North Vietnamese Army (NVA) formations near Can Tho. They did say the VC were busy putting out scare stories, trying to push the ARVN off balance, trying to pin down South Vietnam's troops in the Delta. We judged that the communists could not hope to break into Can Tho, even if fighting as fully formed regiments—not against the strong ground and air defenses of the city commanded by Nguyen Khoa Nam, whom many of us considered to be South Vietnam's best general.

Suddenly, the telephone rang again. All heads turned; Prosser quickly grabbed the receiver. "It's for you, Terry," he said. Cushing's eyes fixed on the desk. I felt an apprehensive tightening in my gut. Hasty's worried voice came through from Delta Compound. "Mr. McNamara, sir, the EAC phone works here. I have just been speaking to Mr. Jacobson in Saigon. He wants you to call him, urgently."

Before hanging up I told Hasty to come back to the consulate general. Then I went through to my desk. As I dialed the embassy number, I remember my glance straying out the window. Spreading away from the consulate general's back fence were Can Tho City's roofs, many of them badly damaged from a recent fire, with those tall, elegant trees, trying to stay aloof from the town's unplanned confusion. Was I now about to leave it forever? It did not seem possible.

Jacobson's voice was perfectly clear. He could have been in the same room. His message was a shock, although I had expected it for some days.

"Terry, we have been ordered by Washington to evacuate. You must leave now." There was a pause in Jacobson's voice. The retired World War II colonel was one of the last people left in the Saigon embassy who had survived several ambassadorial regimes.

I could not prevent my next words. "No other instructions, Jake?" I asked cautiously.

Again, a slight pause. Jacobson sighed, then said, "We want you to go out by Air America chopper. Americans only. When you have finished, Terry, send the choppers straight back to Saigon. We're going to need them desperately in our own evacuation."

I thought for about two seconds. I did not wish to monopolize Jacobson's time, for I was quite aware that this day was a symphony of crises. But the destruction of some of Air America's precious helicopters was for me the final argument for going downriver.

"You know how I feel about taking the Vietnamese with me," I protested warily to Jacobson, then waited for a reply.

As the ambassador's coordinator of the overall evacuation, Jacobson was under great pressure, but I had to make my case this one last time. I could not bring myself to abandon my Vietnamese staff. This was it. Vietnam was collapsing. The Americans were being ordered to leave. I wanted our departure done with at least a modicum of honor. The welfare of a lot of people depended on me and on my judgment.

"Jake," I began, "if you are counting on our four helicopters to help with the Saigon evacuation, you're not going to get them quickly if we use them to evacuate ourselves."

There was another silence. I sensed there was hope. Then, to my horror, the line went dead.

The conversation was not enough to guarantee support. Jacobson, while personally sympathetic to my desire to evacuate Vietnamese, had always considered the river plan too risky. I wanted to be sure. For several minutes I used every means available to contact Jacobson. The line was cut. Clutching at any possibility, I tried to raise him via radio nets to the Philippines and to Thailand. These too failed. As a last resort, with fading hope, perspiring heavily, I picked up the telephone and again dialed his number in Saigon.

Jacobson answered.

"Thank God," I said, trembling with relief.

"We're running short on time, Terry," Jacobson reminded me sharply.

"I know, Jake. But there are problems. The four Air America choppers here in the Delta are still out on missions. If we use them to evacuate ourselves to the fleet offshore, there could be a long delay getting them back to Saigon. When we bring the choppers back to Can Tho, we've got to refuel them by hand. If they then go out to the fleet with the staff, it will be at least four to five hours before those choppers finally reach Saigon."

Silence at the other end. I knew this was the moment for one last pitch. I suggested, almost plaintively, "We have the boats ready and waiting. The choppers can be dispatched directly to Saigon. We honestly reckon the water option to be our best under the circumstances."

Again silence. Suddenly Jacobson said, "OK. Go by water. Send the helicopters to Saigon at once. We need them badly. And Terry—good luck."

I felt a great weight suddenly lifted from my shoulders. But I had one more request. "Can you alert the navy, Jake? We should make the mouth of the Bas Sac by dusk."

"Of course," replied Jacobson warmly and rang off.

I felt empty but greatly relieved. Apart from the little cluster of anxious Americans in the outer office, everything else appeared normal in the consulate general. I looked at Cushing and the small waiting circle of staff. It was hard to believe my own senses. After twenty years, we were about to run from the North Vietnamese Army. I hoped my voice would not betray my real feelings.

"Listen, everyone," I began crisply. "Evacuation orders have been given. We go by water." Most faces brightened, a few dropped. "Departure will be at 1200 hours. All boats go straight to the rendezvous in midriver. Hank, would you start checking every office in the ConGen to ensure that nobody is left behind and *all classified material has been destroyed?*"

"On my way," said Cushing. He rushed out to search the many rooms in the consulate general's rambling collection of buildings. There was now less than an hour remaining until our departure.

≡ 2 ≡

To Witness

I beckoned to two of my staff, Kassebaum and Prosser. "I want you both to come with me," I said. "We are going to see Larry Downs and his people. I'll do the talking. I want you along as witnesses."

Climbing the stairs, it was difficult for me to stop from reflecting on other, better times. I remembered my last tour, nearly four years earlier. Relationships with Agency people had been easier, perhaps because I had no direct authority over them at that time. This tour was different. I was responsible for them and for the other official Americans assigned to Can Tho. More than any others, the CIA contingent seemed to resent and resist this centralizing authority. Indeed, our relations had worsened each month. Now, as a consequence, I felt compelled to take two colleagues to witness a critically important direct order to the CIA.

Downs was talking on the radio when we entered his office, busily directing Air America's four helicopters on their now-final flights in Military Region IV, which comprises most of the delta of the Mekong River southwest of Saigon. A secretary was pushing documents through a shredder. Downs showed some surprise at the unexpected arrival of his three visitors. The last few days had been particularly harsh on Downs. The CIA's Vietnamese employees had a lot to fear. Intelligence agents were likely to be in mortal danger when South Vietnam collapsed. Moreover, Downs was being pressed by his American staff, who were concerned for their own safety.

I repeated the instruction from Jacobson. Finally I added, "Larry, *all* personnel will evacuate by water. There are to be no exceptions. Send the choppers back to Saigon at once. They are needed desperately for Saigon's own evacuation."

Downs, his deputy, Tom Franklyn, and several others were in the room. I watched their faces for any sign of disagreement. To my relief, there seemed none. Downs told me that he would take the CIA's own boats, which included a motor launch and two Boston Whalers. Satisfied, I informed Downs that we would wait for them in midstream, off the end of an island opposite Can Tho. Rendezvous time was noon. As we were speaking, the wall clock jerked past 11:15. Communications, I explained, would be by the "Bamboo Net," a local code for our walkie-talkie sets. Nobody dissented. Kassebaum, Prosser, and I left.

All staff members knew the plans. Swiftly, word was sent to everyone. Evacuation by river was set for midday. The Americans were told, as were those Vietnamese who had been selected by their supervisors to go with us, based on their vulnerability and their adaptability to a foreign country. As written in the plan, all must assemble on the boat to which they had been assigned.

I took a last look around my own office before going downstairs with Kassebaum to find Phuoc for the drive to my house. I had two things to do there: pack a few clothes and collect a young Vietnamese boy, Bao Gia, from Hue, who had been sent by his father to stay with me. Little time was left before I was due at Delta Compound. Our evacuation plan called for me to supervise the boat loading and ensure a quick departure. Cushing, as my deputy, was to bring up the rear, making sure that neither people nor classified material were left behind at the consulate general.

At the consulate general's front door, we met Downs and two of his colleagues dragging heavy mail sacks. The CIA men flung them with obvious difficulty into an official car. Abruptly, Downs ordered the driver out of the car, roughly pushing him aside. Downs's expression was odd.

Cushing had already begun his sweep through the offices. The job of burning and shredding papers had begun weeks earlier, but something could easily be overlooked. David Sciacchitano, the consular officer, had been dispatched, as planned, round the town, double-checking to ensure that American citizens and all those with American family connections knew of the order to leave Can Tho.* These were mainly children of American fathers and Vietnamese mothers. In the meantime, Vietnamese employees went to fetch their families.

---

* See Sciacchitano's own account in Al Santoli's *To Bear Any Burden* (New York: Ballantine Books, 1985), pages 11–17.

Outside the front door, Phuoc was waiting stoically, the white car's engine ticking over with that smoothness that only comes in tropical climates. An air of fragile unreality was already creeping into physical objects. It was as if the car was no longer made of metal, paint, and glass; the hard facts of human impermanence were beginning to register in my mind. I was reaching that mental gateway where the surrounding world becomes near enough to a dream. "Phuoc," I muttered, "we must go to the house." Kassebaum jumped in the other side and slammed the door.

It seemed a long drive. When we crossed the yellow bridge spanning the canal that bisects Can Tho City, I glanced anxiously at the tide. Dry banks above the gray water brought me relief; the water had not yet begun to recede. I unwound a little. We passed the gate of General Nam's house, its old "French seventy-five" artillery piece standing in the garden, the barrel gleaming in the growing heat of a midmorning sun. The entrance slipped behind as Phuoc drove past the high walls of Nam's garden. Not long now, I thought. Yet, I felt miserable; Nam was a friend. Like the physical things around me, people too were beginning to lose substance. Departure's fast-closing moment robbed everything and everybody of much of the value they had solidly possessed just minutes before.

The car swung into the narrow, dusty street where the consul general's residence stood. Again, I thought about the tide. I was starting to realize that it was longer since my navy days than I cared to admit. Thirty-one years had gone by from the day I joined the navy and volunteered for the submarine service; even more horrifying, it was twenty-five years since my Korean War stint. Still, my nautical experience had begun as a sixteen-year-old on a tugboat on the Hudson River and the Erie Barge Canal. I had also worked summers as a merchant seaman and had frequently operated a boat during my time in Danang. Thus, my nautical skills were not all that rusty.

Doubt disturbed my thoughts, imposing a cold message of danger. At Delta Compound, where two of the boats waited, the landing in front became a mudflat at low tide. We could be too late to catch the tide. There would be no way of launching a heavy landing craft once the water had receded. Somehow, I confessed inwardly, tides had not been sufficiently considered during the last few days of frantic planning! Thank God Jacobson had telephoned during the morning. By the afternoon it would be too late for a quick departure: the tide would have already receded.

Weeks ago, when Cushing and I first talked about a waterborne evacuation, we had decided to leave, if possible, on the turning of the tide. The ebb flow would give us a lot of extra speed on our way downriver to the open sea. We had thought in terms of leaving from the Shell Oil Company dock, where one boat now lay alongside the quay. It had deep water at all states of tide. Timing was critical only at Delta Compound. Finally, we had figured that two points of departure gave more chance of success in an emergency. As the person in charge, I had no choice but to take the most exposed departure point for myself.

My residence stood on a corner. Palm fronds from its taller trees overhung the neat garden. The house in its garden seemed tranquil, the freshly painted white walls and bright red roof tiles contrasting favorably with its squalid neighbors. A light breeze from the distant sea occasionally lifted the American flag from its mast. Apart from one of the aging guards, sitting on a stool in the shade while he watched the gate, there were few other signs of life. It was the hour of rice and repose. A Honda motorbike spluttered down the street trailing dust and fumes. I stared in both directions. Everything was quiet. It was exactly as one would expect in Can Tho on a Tuesday just before lunchtime.

Inside the cool house I found Bao Gia in the lounge, reading, sprawled out on the sofa, enjoying the air-conditioning. The young man was still exhausted from his escape from central Vietnam. Shocked, too; he had experienced some horrifying adventures since leaving his native city of Hue. But the quiet, intense young Vietnamese was regaining strength fast. I was relieved to see how much a couple of days' rest had done for him. He might soon again need reserves of stamina.

Walking back to the kitchen, I told the maids that we would not be eating lunch at home. This seemed to satisfy them, although I felt rather degraded. I was, after all, cheating them by deciding there was no chance of saying good-bye or thank-you. Both were widows, both had children, yet I had earlier faced the possibility that they must be left behind. Neither woman spoke English. To my knowledge, they had no other skills. How could they survive in America? I suspected, at the back of my mind, that if the local VC cadre knew them—and probably they did—neither woman was liable to be in serious danger from the communists. As housemaids, they had not performed politically sensitive work.

When the women had left, I said quietly, "Let's go, Gia."

The young Vietnamese gave me a thin, trusting smile, carefully marked his place in the book, rose silently, and went to pack his few remaining belongings. I climbed the stairs to my own bedroom. I could hear Kassebaum opening and closing drawers in the next room.

For a moment I was at a loss, my mind blank. Where does one begin? I had five minutes in which to choose two or three items that would be saved out of everything I owned. Postponing decision, I changed from office clothes to jeans and a sport shirt.

My overriding fear was that one of the maids might return unexpectedly and sense that it was the end. Vietnamese women have no hesitation about screaming in moments of duress. I could almost hear the weeping. The whole street would be alerted within minutes. There would be a spate of over-the-wall messages. Word would speed through the neighborhood. A mob might try to reach our boats. The prospect was frightening and not entirely unrealistic. Such things had already occurred in Danang and Nha Trang.

The more I brooded, the less I wanted to stay in the house. Sadly, I placed a large roll of piasters that I had kept ready for this moment on top of the chest of drawers. The maids would know it was for them. But they would also know I was gone. It was a shabby thank-you, I felt. Yet they would be able to help themselves to anything else in the house before the inevitable looters came.

Neither, more painfully, was I able to tell General Nam. Logic overruled honesty—perhaps *openness* was a less hurtful word to my troubled conscience. But how could I deliver my friend, who was under enough pressure, one further impossible choice? Nam had told me that he would never stop Americans from leaving or hinder the flight of Vietnamese women and children. But young men of military age were different. The general had warned me that, even at this eleventh hour, he would uphold his country's laws. Who really knew what might happen? Saigon was falling. There was no hope now. Yet the Delta, with its huge rice surplus and three mighty river outlets to the sea, could hold out for months. Nam did not anticipate that the recently appointed President Duong Van Minh would surrender—not without some kind of fight. So, the general would arrest all young men of military age who attempted to leave.

Nevertheless, I was convinced that my Vietnamese interpreters— many of them soldiers, attached to the consulate general from the ARVN—would be in real peril in a communist takeover. Admittedly, some might be VC agents, though I rather doubted it. Most were just young men with good educations who spoke a second language.

For similar reasons I had long ago decided that my driver, Phuoc, must also leave. He had loyally served both the United States and Vietnam for many years. Phuoc was not simply a driver—he was a bodyguard and a friend. From the VC's point of view, Phuoc had long since sold his soul. He was too far down the reactionary path to be worth even a short reeducation regimen. If captured and identified, which he would be, Phuoc was a candidate for execution or at least a long prison term. When I broached the subject of leaving with him, he did not argue.

Nervously checking my watch, I forced myself to move. I threw a few extra clothes into my favorite small bag. Before closing the closet, I stared at the neat row of suits. All would be left behind. It was depressing. The handsome carvings displayed around the house that I had collected during my earlier tours in Africa and the paintings on the walls must also stay. In short, the artifacts of a lifetime were lost.

My Gurkha kukri was another matter. Colonel Maitra of the Gurkhas had given the big knife to me years before, in that other unhappy country, the Congo (later Zaire). Perhaps it would be useful on the boat. I wrapped it in a cloth and put it in the bag. Later I would attach the knife to my belt. Last, I opened a drawer in my bedside table. Uncertain for a moment, I lifted out the snub-nosed .38 revolver, attaching its holster to my belt. I then slid the gun into place. Finally, I picked up my bag and went downstairs.

Kassebaum, Gia, and Phuoc were waiting in the hall. For a last moment I was again tempted to let the two maids know of our secret. Then cold reason prevailed. Without speaking, all four of us left the house.

Part II

Gathering Clouds

3

The Foreign Service Goes to War

In 1975, I had been a Foreign Service officer with the Department of State for nearly twenty years. A native of upstate New York, with service in submarines during World War II and further naval service in Korea during that war, I had become a specialist in African affairs since joining the Foreign Service. The first time I saw the flat green richness of the Mekong Delta was in January 1968, after volunteering for service in Vietnam.

A month earlier, the American commander in Vietnam, Gen. William C. Westmoreland, had confidently informed a joint session of Congress of his vision of "light at the end of the tunnel." Yet less than three weeks after I arrived in Vietnam, the United States experienced the sobering shock of the Tet offensive. Whatever has been written since by General Westmoreland and others explaining how the attack was expected, I still remember watching fighting from the roof of my Saigon hotel, followed by a hurried journey into the Mekong Delta to replace a dead colleague. There I was confronted by the smoking ruins of Vinh Long City, my new home.

Once Vinh Long's streets were cleared of rubble, the dead buried, the water and electricity repaired, my colleagues and I went about making some form of cursory security assessment. Gradually South Vietnamese self-confidence was restored, despite efforts by the Viet Cong to maintain the military momentum gained during the Tet attack. Vinh Long suffered a second attack in March. It was, however, of much diminished intensity and duration. Massive Viet Cong losses, coupled with the efforts of a hard-driving province chief, reversed the fortunes of Vinh Long. Within six months of Tet, GVN (Government of Vietnam) forces had taken the offensive and were regaining control of much of the province.

After eight months in the Delta, I was sent north to Quang Tri, in central Vietnam, the most exposed place in the country. There, I was assigned as deputy province senior adviser, second in command to U.S. Army Col. Harley Mooney, leader of a mixed civilian/military advisory team. I remember the dust and heat of summer, the damp, miserable cold of the *crachin,* that wind of winter that the French so hated. A few kilometers up the road from my office was the Demilitarized Zone (DMZ) and North Vietnam, with twenty thousand U.S. Marines in between, barring the way south.

An opportunity came to me near the end of this tour as an adviser. I was offered reassignment as officer-in-charge of the consulate at Danang, the great port that had become the second-largest city of South Vietnam. My bailiwick was to be central Vietnam, stretching from the DMZ down Route 1, near "the street without joy," to Hue, that unreal city that still held within its huge walls the calm of former days when emperors reigned in a somewhat reduced copy of the court in Peking. Danang came next, protected by mountains. The only way there was over the "Pass of the Clouds." After Danang came a broken, cratered, narrow plain of rice paddies, with clusters of wretched crumbling hovels that once had been prosperous villages. This wounded landscape went on for miles, hemmed in by mountains and the sea, southward through embattled Quang Tin and Quang Ngai Provinces.

Yet, looking back, it was my best time in Vietnam. Despite the American troop withdrawals that began in 1969, there was a feeling of optimism, of hope. Before I left in 1971, I saw the full scope of what improved security meant to the Vietnamese.

Put at its simplest, what happened was this: Viet Cong units that had previously been made up of local peasant boys had, because of heavy losses and a reluctance by the South Vietnamese farmers to part with their sons, become heavily dependent on North Vietnamese reinforcements. The sixteen-year-olds of 1971 were not so willing to die as their elder brothers. Life in South Vietnam was improving, despite unemployment caused by the American withdrawal. Few ordinary Vietnamese had great faith in the ARVN's ability to hold the field unaided. But there was a generally held assumption—albeit based on little evidence—that the Americans would return if South Vietnam's existence were threatened. In any case, the immediate Viet Cong threat had greatly diminished and the ARVN appeared to be holding its own. The most immediate concern of most families was fear of the economic consequences of a major reduction in American aid and presence.

Because I had spent eight months in 1968 in Vinh Long, Ambassador Ellsworth Bunker in 1970 asked me to return to the Delta to assess how the situation had evolved since I moved north to central Vietnam. The ambassador wanted a fresh but knowledgeable opinion.

I wondered if the changes in the Delta would be greater than those in I Corps, the five most northern provinces of South Vietnam. Apart from business trips to Saigon, I had not revisited my old territory.

Now I had the exciting chance to see Vinh Long again. I recalled its strategic position, lying astride the two main lines of communication to Saigon, Route 4 and the Mang Thit-Nicholai Canal. "I want your honest impressions of the province," said Bunker, and he reminded me, "It's already more than two years since Tet." The Vietnamese called the tall, silver-haired, seventy-six-year-old veteran ambassador "Mr. Refrigerator." He was nobody's fool.

Next morning I left for Vinh Long. Taking a new Ford Bronco, I drove south from Saigon along Route 4 into the rich landscape of the Mekong Delta.

It took some while to lose the houses and shacks on the western edges of Cholon, Saigon's ethnic Chinese sister city. But soon, Route 4 became a long strip of hot tarmac, running like a causeway over the flat land. On either side of the road stretched endless rice paddies. Here and there, the dark green splash of a coconut grove broke the golden desert of rice. Occasionally, under the palm fronds, hut roofs could be seen hiding in the shade. This was the delta of the Mekong, and it did not change, save for the great waterways that cut through it to the sea, from Saigon to the Bay of Cambodia. The land seems to open up and the sky grows wide.

I settled behind the wheel for the long drive. Traffic on the road was moderately heavy, with the inevitable Honda motorbikes, wildly painted buses, civilian trucks heavily laden with fruit and vegetables for Saigon's market, and, every so often, a military convoy. The roads throughout the Delta frequently cross bridges; waterways interlace the region. Each bridge had a guard, local militiamen, their uniforms charmingly incomplete. These peasant boys and the number of military vehicles on the move were the sole signs of war. It took me two hours to reach the ferry crossing the Co Chien branch of the Mekong. Vinh Long was on the opposite bank.

My greatest surprise was on the mile drive from the ferry to Vinh Long City. Gone were the signs of recent shootouts. There was no doubt that prosperity had arrived. Recovery from the devastation caused during Tet was virtually complete.

The day after my arrival, I set out on a tour of the province. To see things close up, I decided to make the journey by car and boat. My guides were waiting outside the freshly painted office of the Civil Operations and Rural Development organization (CORDS): a young captain of the U.S. Army Corps of Engineers who was now advising the public works department and, to my astonishment, my former secretary, Madame Le Thi Kim-Hue. Without wasting words, I made it plain that Madame Hue was not joining such a dangerous outing. I shook my head wearily. It was typical. She stood there wearing a lavender *ao dai,* as if she were going shopping.

"Look," I said firmly to both of them, "I have to visit the insecure areas, not just the safe ones."

Before the captain could open his mouth, Madame Hue replied with a smile calculated to calm me, "There are no more insecure areas! We can drive any place in this province in safety without guns." And she added coolly, "As a mother of four young children, you think I would take risks?"

But I well remembered Madame Hue's impetuous nature—which had not always kept perfect calm in the office. I was unconvinced. Only when the captain, supported by several old friends, assured me that she was speaking the truth did I begin to accept her word. A tremendous change had indeed taken place during my twenty-four months in I Corps. "See for yourself," she challenged.

I had been living in the worst region of the country. More soldiers on both sides were killed in I Corps than in any other part of Vietnam during the length of the war. By 1970, the war inside Vietnam's borders was I Corps's, with sporadic fighting along the Cambodian frontier. It was only when Cambodia itself became a battleground that I Corps sometimes appeared "quiet" and then for less than a year. As consul in Danang, a listening post on North Vietnam's doorstep, I was effectively isolated from the relative peace in the rest of the country.

The argument settled, we climbed into my new Bronco. First I drove through the growing heat of morning toward Vinh Binh Province, on the way passing over the spot where Fred Abrahams, one of my predecessors in Vinh Long, and three other Americans had been ambushed and killed in December 1967.

Later in the day, I swung the Bronco southwards, down the recently resurfaced Route 4. About midway between Vinh Long City and the ferry to Can Tho, I turned left onto a secondary road that crossed the center of the province. Two years earlier, taking such a route would have been foolhardy.

Few people were to be seen. I began to feel that familiar tightness in the chest. My hands became moist as I gripped the wheel. Yet the others seemed unworried. Did they not remember the basic rules? No people in sight means danger, ambush. Or did it? Was it really possible that no human activity meant villagers simply resting, escaping the noon heat, as they had done for centuries in this land? Two years before, they would have mounted a regimental-size operation to open this road, even temporarily. I was amazed.

We drove on, through almost empty, flat paddy, while clouds began to gather, darkening the sky, preparing to drench the countryside. It was nearing the end of the wet season and storms still came late every afternoon. To one side was a place where I had seen B-52 strikes devastate the earth. Now it was peaceful rice paddy. Finally, we reached the second artery of central Delta life, the Mang Thit-Nicholai Canal.

It looked the same: narrow, clogged with silt, overhung by foliage, a place of death. I felt the skin on my back cringe, ready for the deadly crack of an automatic rifle. There was boat traffic in the canal! I remembered full ARVN regiments battling day after day against some of the best VC main-force units in South Vietnam—big units, strong in heavy weapons—just trying to clear those banks. But on this afternoon, the only sound disturbing the peace was the chugging of outboard motors pushing heavily laden rice barges over the muddy water.

I visited all seven of Vinh Long's districts without hearing a shot fired. Perhaps the ultimate surprise came on the final evening. It was late and I had been writing up my notes of the day when I thought a walk around the compound would do me good. I stepped outside into the damp, fresh, warm air of night. There was something stirring beyond the compound gates. It sounded like a large military convoy on the move. As I opened the gate, I found a column of large trucks passing, their headlights sweeping the dark land. A never-ending stream of them grumbled through the night. In that direction on Route 4, I concluded, they must be going to Saigon. As my eyes grew more accustomed to the dark, I found, to my surprise, that the trucks were not filled with soldiers or military supplies. Instead, they were loaded with fruit and vegetables. It was commercial traffic, racing through the night to meet the opening of Saigon's great central market.

That was the moment when I finally recovered from the emotional trauma of Tet. Tet had made optimism difficult.

I duly returned to Saigon and made my report to Ambassador Bunker. Relative peace had returned to Vinh Long. Insurgency had been pushed back to a more primitive stage. Pacification, I thought, would continue as long as the United States provided the essential military and economic aid. If Vinh Long was a valid example, Vietnamization in the Delta was already well launched. My impressions seemed to confirm a mass of other optimistic information the embassy was receiving.

Having reported to Bunker, I set out to fulfill a long-held ambition. I wanted to drive from the Delta to the DMZ. Most people thought me mad. But I felt there was something worth proving. If it came off without incident, as I was now confident it would, my drive would bolster claims of considerable pacification success. No American had attempted such a trip since before the Tet attacks.

Before leaving Saigon, I attracted two traveling companions: one was from *Time* magazine, the other from the *Washington Post*.

Having left behind the Saigon hinterland of shantytowns, the huge sprawling American base at Long Binh, we took nearly all day to pass into gentler countryside, beyond Xuan Loc where the rubber trees tower in long lines like green armies. After climbing the twisting, winding road into the fir-clad highland, we reached Dalat, where we stayed one night in the old French hill station. It is a pretty town, small, yet full of hotels, an alpine village lost in Vietnam, boasting South Vietnam's main Catholic seminaries, chic boarding schools, and a military academy.

Leaving Dalat's rustic beauty behind, we descended on a winding mountain road to Phan Rang on the coast. Continuing northward, we passed the large naval installations at Cam Ranh Bay, arriving at dusk at Vietnam's most beautiful seaside town, Nha Trang, whose seafood restaurants are legendary.

Next morning, suffering from overindulgence, we called on Ted Long. A fellow FSO, Long was in charge of the Pacification Program in II Corps. Again I heard the familiar recitation. "By all means drive in our corps by day anywhere you wish," said Long. But, he added, " 'Anywhere' means keep to the main roads. Be careful. Do not be so foolish as to drive into lower I Corps. We hear that conditions there are extremely dangerous."

"Not so," I piped up. "That is part of my consular district!" I then explained to Long how I regularly drove those roads in an ordinary sedan with only my chauffeur for company. Perhaps there is a lesson in this, I suggested. Most American and Vietnamese officials we had encountered on this trip told us that it was reasonably safe to very safe within their jurisdiction. But, to a man, they were convinced the province or region next door was dreadfully dangerous. This had been the pattern all the way north. From province to province, until we reached the 17th Parallel, the advice remained the same.

Both my traveling companions wrote stories about the journey. The *Washington Post* man got his prominently displayed next to the editorial page. The man from *Time* was less fortunate. Perhaps our peaceful journey lacked the sensationalism needed to satisfy his editor's appreciation of what would catch the interest of his American audience. A bloody ambush might have sold better.

From this journey emerged a crossing point in the story of what later befell South Vietnam. My visit to Vinh Long, my drive north through the whole country, proved to me that most of the populated areas of South Vietnam were, by 1970, under the control of the ARVN, the local militia forces, or the U.S. Army. This pattern was widely apparent.

Control stemmed from two things: the VC became less and less effective as the North Vietnamese Army was withdrawn into remote border zones, Cambodia, Laos, or North Vietnam itself. Taking the war over the frontiers into Cambodia and Laos, though tragic for those two unhappy countries, had driven the North Vietnamese even farther from the centers of population in South Vietnam and disturbed a whole system of supply and support. Moreover, it would take years for the North Vietnamese to recover from the terrible losses suffered during and after the Tet offensive.

When I left Danang at my tour's end in mid-1971, I was guardedly optimistic. I Corps was relatively peaceful and enjoying the beginnings of prosperity. An extra division, the 3rd ARVN, was being raised to cover I Corps's long, exposed western flank as the U.S. troop withdrawals continued apace.

≡ 4 ≡

On Familiar Turf

Following a year at the Naval War College at Newport, Rhode Island, I was offered the job of deputy chief of mission in Cotonou, Dahomey (now Benin), a small francophone country on the Guinea coast of West Africa. Prior to the arrival of France in the mid-nineteenth century, the country had been famed for its amazon warriors, who formed the shock troops of the Fon Kingdom. Later, after independence, it became almost equally well known for bloodless coups. I was not concerned—I was going back to Africa, reestablishing myself with the State Department as an African specialist. If I was to have any chance at all of becoming an ambassador, it was likely to be in an African country.

While I was absent from Vietnam, much took place. The Americans completed their withdrawal. Emboldened, the communists' Easter offensive of 1972 broke like a brutal wave over the DMZ. The 3rd ARVN Division broke and ran. This time the North Vietnamese had come with tanks and large field guns in a blatant invasion mounted by a modern, well-equipped army.

Nevertheless, the North Vietnamese advance lost momentum as it was smashed from the sky by American air power and doggedly resisted on the ground by hastily reinforced ARVN units. A gradual stalemate developed. Bombing of the north was intensified. Finally, the aging, obdurate leaders in Hanoi decided to rid themselves of the American threat through negotiation. A cease-fire was signed in Paris. America agreed to withdraw its remaining troops, while thousands of communist troops were allowed to stay, ready and waiting, at bases well inside South Vietnam. Instead of real peace, all South Vietnam got was a shaky armistice that was to last only two years.

In August 1974, I had been serving for some time as chargé d'affaires at the embassy in Cotonou. Fresh orders arrived from the State Department. I was instructed to leave for Washington at once, entrusting the embassy to the nervous hands of a newly arrived administrative officer. After confirming the urgency of my orders, I departed for Washington.

Two weeks later, as a hastily frocked consul general–designate to Can Tho with responsibility for the Mekong Delta region, I stepped off an aircraft into the sweaty heat of a Saigon midnight; the rainy season was drawing to a close. George Jacobson had promised to be waiting in customs. I glanced around as I walked across the wet tarmac to the ugly, floodlit concrete terminal building at Tan Son Nhut. The noise level was much lower than I remembered. Before I left in 1971, American fighter aircraft were taking off in pairs, with their afterburners blazing, at all times of the day and night from the great twin runways.

The muddle at immigration was still the same. With quiet influence, Jacobson soon got me through with only cursory formalities and into a waiting embassy sedan. Half an hour after landing, Jacobson and I were being driven into the city.

I had already met Ambassador Graham Martin in Washington and had received quick briefings at both the State Department and CINC-PAC (Commander in Chief, Pacific) Headquarters in Hawaii, so I felt I wasn't going in cold despite the short notice. The embassy wanted me to attend a "principal officers'" conference the next morning before I headed southward to Can Tho. The meeting's purpose was to bring together the consuls general from all four military regions to discuss the circumstances in their areas and, in return, be briefed by the embassy on its view of the more general political, military, and economic situation in the country. Hanging over the meeting like a sword of Damocles was the question of continuing military and economic aid for South Vietnam.

I had much to think of that evening as we were driven through the snarled, frenetic traffic toward the center of town. Gazing out of the open car window, I saw the familiar slouching policemen as they watched the traffic confusion with studied indifference. The houses along each side of Cong Ly Street were shabbier than I remembered from three years earlier. If anything, there appeared to be more vehicles on the streets.

Yet they were older, seeming to belch even more noxious fumes. Or had I simply forgotten the material poverty of a third world country that had been at war for thirty years?

What distressed me most was the apparent absence of that peculiar Saigonese vitality. The "Pearl of the Orient" was tired, dowdy. She seemed to have lost her special jauntiness, which had always been present despite the war and the presence of yet-another foreign army. I came to the reluctant conclusion that joy had died in the hearts of the normally ebullient Saigonese. For all its unwanted disruption of traditional Vietnamese society, the American presence was a lesser evil than that of the communists. The Americans gave hope. They also brought prosperity. But the Americans now were gone. Even their economic assistance was drying up. The northerners, like vultures, were patiently waiting for the right moment to pounce on a weakened foe. Sadly, the South Vietnamese were the cornered victims awaiting the coup de grâce, not quite believing that they would be abandoned in their final hour.

Next morning, I went to the embassy, a snow-white fortress of concrete with a helicopter pad on its roof. It was in the center of Saigon, a stone's throw from the well-remembered brick Catholic cathedral. Half a mile away, in gardens at the western end of Avenue Dai Lo Thong Nhat, President Nguyen Van Thieu's Independence Palace sat like a bunker, blocking the city's central streets.

Having made my way through the embassy's spotless foyer under the sharp eyes of armed Marine guards dressed in their smart dress blue uniforms, I took the elevator and was sucked up three floors. I wondered how much the embassy had changed under its glossy surface.

What I found only heightened my earlier concerns. Ambassador Martin had been absent most of that summer in Washington, where he was attempting to induce Congress to grant what he believed were adequate levels of both military and economic help. Martin was still absent. In the end he never got the needed amounts of cash from Congress.

What disturbed me most was Martin's choice of a team. Most of the senior officers at the embassy, as well as my new colleagues from the other three consulates general, shared two qualities: little or no previous experience in Vietnam and prior service with Ambassador Martin.

I found the security and political briefings reflected none of the depth that comes only from years of studying a problem. For the most part, I was disappointed at being lectured to by people who seemed to have no more than superficial knowledge and understanding of Vietnam and the Vietnamese. The information being bandied about the room by the young man from the CIA, for instance, seemed particularly banal. The analysis offered was opaque. Its authors appeared unsure of what was going on outside the embassy, much less outside Saigon. I began to realize that morning, quite plainly, that the CIA and the embassy were not going to be much help in a crisis. My new colleagues and I had come to be briefed on the mission's overview, only to find that it had none.

That afternoon, I was cheered up by talks on more technical matters. The most exciting presentation was on rice production. Enormous advances had been made during the years I had spent in Africa. Burgeoning production in the rich Delta had brought rural prosperity. With the "miracle rice" strains developed by Ford Foundation researchers in the Philippines, the tough, hardworking farmers of the Delta managed, in the space of a few years, to quadruple yields. More recently, the introduction of simple, cheap Japanese-built irrigation pumps was making it possible to grow an extra crop during the dry season. The experts from the U.S. Agency for International Development (USAID) confidently predicted a national rice surplus for 1975–76, the first since 1964, with the possibility of exports to come.

This phenomenon has been christened the "Green Revolution." For once, prosperity was reaching down to the ordinary farmer. Land reform had freed him from the clutches of absentee landlords. Rural banks, another USAID innovation, were supplying him with money at a fraction of what the Chinese money lenders asked. One might never prove it, but I strongly suspected that, with rural prosperity, there was now less reason for farmers' sons to leave their land and fight for either side.

Promising oil discoveries had also been made off the coast. Given time and stability, there was now a solid chance that the Delta could lead a national economic recovery. Self-sufficiency in food needs, at least, seemed within grasp, if American support could be sustained during a transitional period. Greater general prosperity was a more distant but realistic prospect.

Late the following afternoon I drove to the airport with Lacy Wright, the calm and effective officer who had been standing in at Can Tho pending my arrival. We reported at the tiny terminal of Air America. It would take an hour of flying to reach Can Tho. On the ramp, a veteran twin-engine C-46 of World War II vintage awaited its passengers.

Five minutes off the ground we both stopped sweating, as the old silver bird, engines gargling contentedly, slowly climbed above tumbling clouds into cooler air. For a while, Lacy and I tried to talk. But it grew frustrating shouting over the engine noise. Wright was a friend. We had known each other since my stint in Vinh Long in 1968. He had been in the Delta for some four years and was well regarded by the embassy. Now Wright was going to the political section in Saigon. Over drinks the previous night, Wright had warned me that my counterpart, Lt. Gen. Nguyen Vinh Nghi, the Vietnamese corps commander, was an accomplished racketeer. He was also very close to President Thieu.

On Can Tho's small airfield, a car was waiting. The Delta is quite different from other parts of South Vietnam. Grass grows thick and spiky, deep emerald, even in the shadiest places, so rich is the soil and strong the sun. In the distance, I saw dozens of coconut groves, washed, almost sparkling, as the sun cleared away afternoon storm clouds. The fresh, clean air was a relief after the pollution of Saigon. I threw my bag into the car and wondered what I would find in Can Tho.

I had not been in Can Tho for nearly four years. My recollection was of a dusty, down-at-the-heels city of some one hundred thousand souls, its melancholy roofs huddled along the southern bank of the ocher Bas Sac River, one hundred miles south of Saigon. The French had built the place—that much did come back from the recesses of my memory—a market town, their administrative capital of the Delta.

From the city's river port, a web of canals radiated outward into the rich farmlands of the southern Delta. Other canals, as well as Route 4, ran in a northerly direction, toward the national capital and its teeming hungry mouths. There were farmers by the thousand in this region. Each tiny hamlet was a garden nestling under the trees surrounded by its rectangular rice paddies. Yes, I could visualize it all now.

I sat back, letting my eyes absorb the surroundings while the car swiftly transported us into the city. My earlier impression of the town was of a farmyard, dirty in the dry season, muddy in the wet. After today's rain, it was indisputably muddy. Yet the atmosphere was different now. Perhaps it was the cleaner air. Even the cars and bicycles on the road gave a feeling of purpose that seemed lacking in Saigon.

The previous day in Saigon had been exhausting. I looked forward to a bath, wondering what the residence was like. So far, Can Tho appeared to have changed for the better while I was in Africa. Perhaps I would change my assessment with closer inspection.

But once among its outskirts and driving along the road into town, I was even more pleasantly surprised. As we reached the first busy crossroads, it was obvious that the city was cleaner, less congested, with fewer army trucks and jeeps. Continuing eastward toward the town center, we crossed Route 4 where it turned southward past the big, open Ben Xe Moi bus terminal.

Next we crossed the first canal bridge. Can Tho, like Amsterdam, is a city of canals. Boats were moving with the concentration of insects over sepia water. The place was becoming increasingly familiar. From here on the town changed in style, as we entered the older French-built core. Large trees formed an avenue on each side of the busy street. It was the same in all these colonial towns, from Lao Cai on the Chinese frontier to Ca Mau on Vietnam's southern coast.

Up ahead, on the left, an imposing buff-colored villa was surrounded by a long, high wall. Only an open pair of green metal gates offered any clue of what lay inside. As we drove past, I glanced beyond the heavily armed sentry to see an old brass cannon guarding a spacious, lovingly tended garden. Farther back stood the villa itself. This was the home of the man who might give me trouble: the corrupt commander of IV Corps, Gen. Nguyen Vinh Nghi, that friend of President Thieu who had paid handsomely for his job knowing he would recoup it all during the first year in office. Wright smiled knowingly and nodded as the car moved past.

Almost next door to the good general was another reminder of the French past. A rambling series of old industrial buildings stretched back from the road. *Brasserie, Glacierie d'Indochine.* Its pride of manufacture was the formidable *Ba Muoi Ba ("Bière 33")*, whose yeast odor alone could inflict a long and painful hangover. Some of its victims claimed that one of the essential ingredients was formaldehyde direct from an embalmer's shelf.

Then I saw what I had been looking for since crossing the first canal bridge. Above the small shops and houses on the left, I picked out two long roofs reaching toward the Bas Sac River. This was Delta Compound. Wright told the driver to slow down at the open gate so I could study the inner courtyard. All seemed well cared for; the paved roadway between the buildings was clean, a good sign. After the briefest pause, the driver put his foot back on the gas pedal. Wright frowned, but I shook my head; Delta Compound could wait.

Past the imposing villa of the province chief, with its large gardens, the road swung right. Here, as I could now remember clearly, the road widened to become a grand boulevard. The IV Corps HQ spread along the west side, its parade grounds turned into truck parks, barracks, and storage sheds marching in rows parallel to the street.

To the east was the heart of Can Tho. Its business quarter had changed. The old French-style buildings were now jostled by ugly new construction. Cement had pushed stucco into history. On the waterfront, Wright said, the Vietnamese restaurants still produced some of the world's best duck and seafood dishes. In the Chinese hotels, the bed linen was still changed once a week; some things never change. I was again on familiar ground.

Tired, sweaty, sticking to the car seat, I was reassured. This was not Saigon. The capital could have been a thousand miles away from these bustling people. This was the Vietnam I remembered and loved. Contrary to my initial impression, the military *were* still everywhere. Uniforms were sprinkled liberally among the civilian crowds. Their trucks, belching exhaust, pushed through jams of small, aging cars and Honda motorbikes. Every few seconds, a trumpeting horn would signal the moment for humans, animals, and chickens to scatter from the path of an army truck.

I noticed another familiar sight: smartly dressed women being chauffeured round the town in military jeeps piled high with shopping bags and children. So the ARVN officers' wives and mistresses still wended their way from shop to teahouse, that daily ritual observed by privileged Vietnamese women, the last place being where business deals could be discretely negotiated.

In this part of Can Tho, the houses were tall, running deep into the back alleys; their ground floors contained shops opened to the street. The families lived two or three stories above, depending on the ratio of children to merchandise. On the sidewalks were the inevitable market women, often nursing small children, busy selling beer, cigarettes, bottles of gasoline, toothpaste, and cigars. It all retained that dirty, noisy, boisterous disorganization, that sordid youthfulness, that I had loved so much from the first day I set foot in Vietnam.

Minutes later, Wright nudged my shoulder. Surrounded by a high chain-link fence, situated on a back street corner, and guarded by an aging watchman who sat on a stool clutching an obsolete carbine, was a medium-sized white villa. The driver waited while the guard unlocked one of the two high metal gates in the fence. I could see a lawn and flower garden stretching for thirty yards in front of the two-storied house. The roof was steep, covered with red tile. The porch had been enclosed and converted into a bar. The driver pulled up alongside the house. Behind it I could see the servants' quarters and kitchen. Away from the distant street noise, it appeared to be a haven of peace.

Entering the house, I found myself in a large central room with a high ceiling. This, explained Wright, was the lounge and dining room. The wall of the outside bar stretched half the length of this main room. Plexiglas windows in the former porch (a precaution against splinters of flying glass) gave a view of the garden. Upstairs were two bedrooms. A small room next to the master bedroom served as a study. "It is quiet here," Wright said, "the only really quiet room in the house." I began to relax.

Foreign Service life is not everybody's choice. Where you lived could make the difference between happiness and misery. I noticed the furniture was mainly cheap and tasteless, probably bought in Thailand, where teak is plentiful. The standard was low, much below what normally went into the residence of an American consul general. When Wright showed me the modest Japanese dinner service and stainless steel cutlery, I confessed to being distressed. Whatever did the face-conscious Vietnamese make of all this strange austerity from these rich "long noses"?

As I soon discovered, both house and office were furnished by the U.S. Agency for International Development, an organization with few representational duties—unlike those of senior State Department officers. Making a mental note to improve what I could, I began to decide where I would hang my collection of African carvings and paintings.

Later, with the two of us perched on bar stools, I tried to profit from Lacy's final evening. His informal advice and assessment were infinitely deeper and more useful than anything given the day before at the embassy. There had been startling changes in the Delta while I had sweated out my stay in Dahomey. Can Tho University now boasted fifteen thousand students, many studying agriculture under USAID scholarships. Wright described the campus, a mixture of low French army buildings and modern concrete blocks, surrounded by neat, small experimental agricultural plots.

It all came back. I could picture those low buildings, standing on a flat open space among rice paddies at the side of Route 4. I remembered a group of modern villas, one of which was the home of Dr. Xuan, the rector. My mind went back to Tet 1968 when I first visited Can Tho on my way to Vinh Long. A VC battalion had to be blasted out of the campus. They were making a last-ditch stand in one of the dormitory blocks. I could see again the lazy circling and sudden diving of jet fighters, dark smoke slowly flowering over the roofs, the somber crump of bombs.

Lying in bed that night, thinking matters over, too tired for sleep, I tried building a mental picture of the American effort in Vietnam. At the summit of a hierarchical pyramid was Martin himself, then came his deputy chief of mission, then the heads of all the various agencies, including the defense attaché. The latter's role was mainly logistical, ensuring military equipment and supplies were in the right place when needed, but his office also produced military intelligence analysis. The DAO continued in an advisory capacity in that sense.

The role of the CIA was harder to fix. Indeed, the Agency still appeared to be operating in a world of its own, if the briefings in Saigon were any guide. Thinking it over, I concluded that, like the embassy's political section, the CIA's intelligence role had hardly changed, despite the withdrawal of half a million American troops. Intelligence work went on as before. The CIA's direct involvement in paramilitary operations, however, must have altered with the massive decline in our overall presence. I would watch this aspect of our activities carefully.

I was filled with foreboding that night. Nothing on the surface was wrong, yet I sensed trouble coming. There was a vast difference in our role in the country since my previous tours. Now Americans could only persuade or plead. There was no military power at my elbow.

Advice given had to be the best. In case of disagreement within the mission, would Martin defer to me when making decisions involving the Delta, choose my advice over that given by old and loyal colleagues, albeit with limited experience in Vietnam?

The four consuls general assigned to the region were like barons calling at court. But below their level, the pyramid broadened rapidly. From the middle down, there were many experienced officers in Saigon and in the provinces. Most were veterans of CORDS, which had teamed military and civilian advisers in provinces throughout the country. Others had served with the embassy's Provincial Reporting Unit, which assigned young political officers to roam rural Vietnam and report direct to the embassy. The latter had been the embassy's independent eyes and ears, unfiltered by any military or civilian hierarchy.

Collectively, former members of these groups had become known as "Vietnamese specialists." Many had years of service in the country, and, very important, most spoke its language. Thus, a richness of knowledge and experience was available within the mission. Was it being properly used by a much less informed top leadership?

My own most pressing task was to find a deputy. I would have gladly retained Lacy Wright, who had already spent six months as acting consul general. Much as I was sad to lose him, it was obvious that experienced hands like Lacy were needed at the embassy. Unfortunately, Wright was scheduled to complete his Vietnam tour in the next year.

In the event, it finished earlier and far more dramatically than either of us then imagined it would. Meantime, I was stuck with finding a deputy of similar quality. This would not be easy.

The deputy principal officer in a U.S. consular post traditionally is a State Department Foreign Service officer who holds a consular commission. But Can Tho was not a "normal post." The only FSOs then present in the Delta were junior officers on their first overseas assignment. It would have been both unfair and dangerous to pick one of these enthusiastic, but still green, young men for the job. All had plenty of drive. All were intelligent. All could speak Vietnamese. But none of them yet had enough experience to impress the CORDS veterans. Several of the latter were senior USAID officers who had lived in Vietnam for ten or fifteen years. Relations with Vietnamese counterparts also had to be considered. My deputy would have to deal with ARVN colonels, sometimes generals, very powerful men with great influence. Age is a key factor in the degree of influence one could exert in a Confucian society where longevity is greatly respected.

Providentially, I was to find the perfect solution right under my nose. Already present in Can Tho was Hank Cushing, director of field operations of CORDS, a former university professor who had been working for several years for USAID in Vietnam. Highly respected by all, he was the recipient of the State Department's highest award for bravery. Over the years Cushing had been a province senior adviser in several difficult places, from Chau Doc on the Cambodian frontier to the wounded landscape of Quang Ngai. To add to his escutcheon, Cushing had been forced out of Quang Ngai because of his unwillingness to acquiesce in building an unneeded road that the notoriously venal commander of I Corps wanted for his own purposes. Moreover, we had known one another for years, and I was sure we could work well together. How then to get the rules changed?

I was not in the least surprised when State's Personnel Office objected—USAID officers cannot serve as acting principal officer, no matter who they are or how capable they might be. That was the rule. While I understood this attitude, I could not accept such arbitrariness in these unique circumstances. I, therefore, appealed the case to Ambassador Martin, who supported me. The State Department bureaucracy, with characteristic lack of courage, folded.

Cushing's appointment demonstrated to our diverse team that Can Tho was a fully integrated post, where the management functions went to the best candidate, regardless of his agency of origin. I had heard of the chaos that ruled American field operations in Vietnam prior to 1967 and the formation of CORDS. I had long been convinced that only a fully integrated, united team could face the extraordinary stresses of war with such a wily ally. This judgment was shared by many others, including the widely respected former director of central intelligence, the late William Colby, who had helped set up CORDS and was its last chief before the cease-fire agreement in 1972.

The problem of a deputy settled, I was now ready to face the more substantive aspects of my challenging new job.

≡ 5 ≡

Settling In to a New Domain

The offices of the consulate general were located on the outskirts of town. Over the years, as new requirements arose for more office space, doors were broken through outer walls to connect with haphazard extensions. By 1974, it was an architectural nightmare, the archaeology of a war in tasteless layers, an odd dovecote of bricks and steel.

Behind an enclosing wall was the first row of three Vietnamese houses. Between the connected buildings was what vaguely resembled a patio. From it, dark narrow stairways led to upper-floor offices. This architectural abomination was America's face to the citizens of Can Tho. I surveyed the sad collection and sent for Averill Christian, a retired army colonel, who had made a second career as the consulate general's administrative officer. Poor Christian had the thankless task of being responsible for everything from the supply of beer to helicopter flying hours.

In principle, I am careful about using taxpayers' money. But if the United States was going to run a mission, anywhere in the world, there was a right and a wrong way to do it. To my mind, Can Tho's consular buildings had become a daily reminder of America's confusion about Vietnam. I told Christian to tidy the place up—and fast—suggesting he start by removing the hot dog stand from the main lobby. The next day, a small garden was planted at the front entrance. Soon painters were put to work on the buildings, transforming them all to sparkling white, set off with dark green trim—although the curious eyes of Can Tho's citizens probably never realized it, the colors would be familiar to anyone who has seen a Grandma Moses painting; perhaps another unconscious symbol of innocents abroad. As the painting progressed, the compound lost some of its strangely dismal aspect.

The lobby was next. I had it cleaned, painted, then furnished with some of the surplus furniture left by the departed hordes of Americans. I let Walt Heilman, the general services officer, design a curving concrete desk, which would offer protection to the Marine guards while adding tone to the reception area. As a final touch, I told Christian to install the prettiest and smartest young woman on the staff at a reception desk in the lobby with orders to wear the traditional *ao dai* dress at all times.

The rest of this part of the building was occupied by the small consular section and SAFO (Special Assistant for Operations) headquarters staff (the rump of the old CORDS advisory organization). They were hidden beyond doors that closed off the lobby and public offices. The communications room, with its teletype and coding machines, was on the ground floor behind the reception area. Although convenient to all the other sections, this arrangement was not ideal from a security point of view.

The other buildings housed various elements attached to the consulate general—the road-construction advisers, the agricultural specialists, the consulate general nursing staff with their clinic. Across the yard, in the remaining pair of houses, were the offices of the defense attaché's representative and his intelligence-gathering team. Next to them was the JCRC—Joint Casualty Resolution Center—still busily engaged in searching for traces of Americans missing in battle. The last building housed me, my deputy, and my immediate staff. A large room filled with young political officers and another crammed with busy Vietnamese typists and translators completed this section of the offices.

Most of the third floors of all the buildings were given over to a maze of offices used by the CIA. One large room in the upper floor of the reception building, however, had been transformed into a conference room. At its center sat a U-shaped table with room for twenty places, each equipped with its own microphone. An elaborate audiovisual system similar to those used at major military headquarters for formal briefings completed the room's equipment. I remained puzzled as to the need for such a lavish installation in rural Vietnam. Christian and his men were never able to give me a satisfactory justification for its presence.

Shock was my enduring reaction to my own office. That first morning, with Lacy Wright and Christian as my guides, I boldly pushed open the door. Inside I found a large rectangular room with walls painted a bilious green. Three wide Plexiglas windows looked out over a sea of wooden roofs that sheltered Can Tho's most crowded quarter. Just beyond the consulate general parking lot was a squalid bar-cum-brothel. The tight-fitted glass in the windows made the room almost soundproof. As I stood staring at the view, a heavily painted lady with long fake eyelashes spotted one of my American staff members emerging from the consulate general building, headed for his parked car. The woman's bright red lips opened to form the ritual greeting, "You wanna have a good time?"

More amused than censorious, my eyes returned to the room. A handsome cherry wood desk occupied a corner by the window accompanied by a matching leather-cushioned swivel chair. Behind the desk were two flags—an American flag to the right and my own consular flag to the left with its thirteen white stars and large "C" set on a dark blue field. A couch, several easy chairs, and a coffee table completed the room's furnishings. I found these last pieces especially exotic with their bamboo arms painted a slightly darker shade of the same objectionable green and cushions covered in muted orange. The whole effect was an interior decorator's nightmare. As my eyes adjusted to the color scheme, I noticed that the inner walls were covered with large maps of the Delta, a useful addition. I asked Lacy Wright about the two telephones. One was on the desktop; another sat alone, looking important on a small table.

"The one on the desk is the usual civilian-type telephone—maintained by the ARVN Signal Corps," Wright said.

"Is it reliable?"

"Absolutely," Wright grinned.

"And the other?" I asked, pointing to the table.

"That is your special restricted phone. You can use it to call directly to Martin and a small number of the embassy's other top brass."

Next stop on the tour of my new domain was Delta Compound, located on the main street coming into the center of town. It was only a couple of blocks from my residence, and midway between General Nghi's villa and the Vietnamese province chief's residence.

The complex had been built many years earlier by the Shell Oil Company. Their senior personnel had lived there until the U.S. government offered to rent it. Only the Shell regional manager, Troung-Dai-An, still dwelt within its walls, with his wife and young daughter. He retained the prettiest villa, located nearest the riverbank.

I had seen the compound briefly on my way in from the airport. It consisted of two long buildings facing each other across a paved roadway. At one end of the road was a high metal gate opening on the main street. The buildings ran back nearly a hundred meters, almost to the river. Just inside the gate, on the east side of the central roadway, was a staff restaurant and bar, guest rooms for official visitors, and the commissary. These were managed by an employees recreation association with a Korean manager in charge of daily operations. He had a staff of some fifty Vietnamese cooks, waitresses, maids, bartenders, and salesgirls. Membership was open to all American government employees. In addition, American and "third country national" employees of American firms were welcome to join as associate members.

The bar was said to be the longest in the Delta. Like the card room next to it, the decor was Gay Nineties. Waitresses, all of them Vietnamese, wandered among the tables dressed in abbreviated "Bunny" costumes complete with floppy tails. I was not quite sure what I should do about the Delta Club, but neither was I prepared to risk a mutiny by attempting to change the club's style. The overall effect (I eventually concluded), if not inspiring, was bearable. No doubt it was in keeping with the tastes of most of its clientele. Anybody familiar with American noncommissioned officers (NCO) clubs, or relatively affluent American Legion Post bars, would have felt immediately at home in the Delta Club.

The bar decor had invaded the restaurant next door. The dining room was large, easily seating two hundred guests. Yet there was space for dancing and a small stage. I was impressed to learn that three meals were served daily. While the restaurant catered officially to those who had temporary business in Can Tho, many others used its facilities, especially those who had no functioning kitchen in their quarters. The food was not imaginative, but it was wholesome and, above all, clean. Perhaps many years earlier the Chinese cook and his staff had possessed the culinary skills of which his race is justly proud. Sadly, their talent had long since disappeared, been destroyed, or perhaps simply withered through long years spent in too close association with American mess sergeants or military club managers. Only a single midday's experiment was needed for me to vow never to dine voluntarily at the club.

I well remember the first Saturday night function I attended at the club. It was protocol for a new consul general to put in at least a token appearance. In any case, I have always upheld the idea that senior officers, especially those serving at isolated posts, have a responsibility to take a visible interest in the welfare of their staff. Thus, I rarely refused an office party.

After years spent in some of the world's tougher parts, I thought little could surprise me. Yet when I entered the club dining room that night, I was amazed at the spectacle. A dance band and strippers had been imported from Saigon for the evening. The place was packed with members and their guests. The CIA contingent had invited some ARVN and police officers who, I guessed, had accepted only from politeness.

These Vietnamese gentlemen were now paying heavily for their effort to improve relations with America's version of an official Santa Claus. As the evening advanced, the Vietnamese found it harder to conceal their discomfort. None could eat the food, let alone enjoy it. Worst of all, in keeping with the general ambience, the strippers were not simply bad; they were boring. I rubbed my eyes more frequently as the painfully thin girls with oversized silicon implants continued their mechanical routines. One culminated her act by lying on the floor, naked, legs spread widely apart. For a moment I wondered whether I had wandered into a gynecologist's examining room.

Between the club and Troung-Dai-An's house were three small townhouses. Each had a tiny garden planted with flowers at its front. Hank Cushing lived in the first house, with the Bas Sac not far from his windows. In the middle was Averill Christian. Next door to the club lived Wendy Knowles, another retired army officer with long service in the Delta. On the west side of the compound was a long building with two floors. This had been converted into flats. It housed CIA personnel and the two defense attaché representatives. The ground floor also included a movie theater. Here films or TV shows were shown several times a week for the Americans and their guests. A nominal fee was charged to pay for the projectionist. Indeed, the club was entirely self-financing, despite a maximum price of fifty cents per drink.

On the river side was a small dock. When I first saw it I thought it might be useful for mooring pleasure boats or even landing supplies from river craft. I little realized how vital the existence of that dock would prove to be. For the moment, I saw a happy staff that liked simple entertainment, worked hard, and were probably saving a lot of money.

The CIA contributed roughly half those assigned to the consulate general in Can Tho and made up about the same proportion of the strength in the branch offices scattered throughout twelve of the sixteen provinces in Military Region IV. This large CIA presence would present difficult and continuing problems. While the Agency people paid lip service to full integration, they resisted it in practice. They were, after all, the rump of a once mighty autonomous fiefdom. It was hard for many Americans to accept their reduced importance in Vietnam. It seemed hardest of all for the CIA. But the ground rules had changed as the resources for American support dwindled daily. Influence on events was correspondingly in decline. Probably more good now could be done by reporting the rate of inflation and its very visible effect on Vietnamese morale than by talking to clandestine agents about politics. Manpower was scarce. So was money. With such reduced means, the need for strong centralized coordination was compelling. In the Delta this meant a single point of command—the consul general.

At first impression, Larry Downs, the recently arrived CIA station chief, seemed pleasant and competent. Yet I was always to feel uneasy about Downs. It was hard to isolate the reason. For one thing, though, it worried me that he had no previous experience in Vietnam. Rather, he and his deputy, Tom Franklyn, had both spent years in the CIA operations in Laos. Unfortunately, this was a bit like taking a sandlot baseball player and starting him against the New York Yankees. The VC and North Vietnamese were truly big-league foes. In Can Tho Downs had a very big job.

I was perhaps the only other person in Can Tho able to fully understand its complexity and strain. It was thus disappointing to find that Downs kept his own counsel. He would not, for unspoken reasons, try to build even a rudimentary bridge of friendship on which our twin burdens of responsibility could sometimes be laid down, even if only for a few passing hours. I knew that I could now and again lean on Cushing for support. Indeed, some kind of occasional unwinding with a friend was vital for balanced judgment. Downs's own deputy seemed to lack the intellectual depth needed to comprehend the problems Downs faced.

Downs looked the perfect secret agent. He had a tough, cool athletic outward image. I was therefore somewhat surprised when, at our first meeting, I discovered that he behaved almost the opposite of what I expected. In character, Downs seemed nearly the contradiction of his physical appearance. He was mild, with a forced bonhomie that struck me, perhaps unfairly, as not far short of a country club suburbanite. Though I tried hard with Downs in those early months, I never established anything more than a polite but almost formal relationship. I cannot say whose fault this was; it could have been either of us. But I suspected a familiar picture as I learned more about Downs, being myself, like him, an Irish American.

A product of a Jesuit college, Downs was most likely one of those young men the CIA recruited each year from politically reliable Catholic institutions. Downs was no doubt technically competent. If I had any quarrel, it was not about what we were all trying to achieve, but over the best way it should be done. Downs was now station chief in Can Tho. This was his first big job, and he was determined to succeed. If he did well in Can Tho, his career would be launched in a significant way. But if the hints of lack of self-confidence were real, they could foreshadow a risk. Even if he agreed with me and wanted to cooperate, Downs might do nothing that would risk upsetting his masters in Saigon or Washington.

Within the first few days, these grim forebodings registered themselves on my mind. Some problems were easy to solve—the picturesque hot dog stand was simply missing from its usual place in the central lobby when the staff came to work next morning. More serious matters, such as the CIA's relationship with me and the rest of the consulate general, were not so easy to resolve.

The CIA continued to run a freewheeling operation throughout the Delta while paying lip service to the principle of command unity and integration within the consulate general. When it came to its field operations, the CIA behaved as if it still had virtual autonomy. On the ground, this undermined work done by colleagues from other agencies.

Over the years, for example, the CIA people had paid bribes to ARVN officers and soldiers in return for routine information that should have been freely available to the DAO representatives and others on my staff. Once the poorly paid Vietnamese realized they could sell such information to naive CIA men, then only a fool gave it away to the defense attaché or to provincial representatives in the consulate general's branch offices.

In addition to its waste and corrupting influence, there was a more sinister hidden danger in this CIA practice. No intelligence source is worthwhile unless it is regular and offers prospects. Frequently lacking any real information with which to titillate their paying customers, the Vietnamese informants would simply make up news. Being clever people, they usually invented a story they assumed their benefactors wanted to hear, for such is correct etiquette in the East. Since almost none of the CIA men then assigned to Military Region IV (Mekong Delta) had significant Vietnamese experience, they seemed unable to detect any save the most outrageous fraud.

Obviously, false information could be highly dangerous, especially in a real emergency. The practice of withholding information from non-paying customers was equally troubling. Several times over the next few months, I was forced to protest on the DAO representative's behalf to the IV Corps commander and demand full military information be given him. It always came promptly. And the CIA? They denied knowledge of any palm greasing. This infuriated me. The practice undermined all our preaching to the Vietnamese about the need for probity in government. On the contrary, it further corrupted the Vietnamese. But this concept seemed always too subtle for Downs or his people in the Delta to take in.

A second problem was of greater urgency. Security was deteriorating dangerously in at least one vital province, which sat astride the main communication lines from Saigon to the central Delta. Some years earlier, when security improved dramatically, the adjoining provinces of Vinh Long and Vinh Binh were removed from the areas of responsibility of the regular ARVN divisions. Some of their local militia battalions were sent to other provinces where the threat of violence appeared graver. In those days, Vinh Long boasted the hard-driving Col. Doung Hieu Nhgia as province chief. Indeed, he all but eliminated the large-scale VC threat from his province. But that was back in 1970, when I made my last visit to the Delta. Since then a new chief had been appointed.

Reputedly he bought the job from the IV Corps commander, Lt. Gen. Nguyen Vinh Nghi, for a very large sum. He then was in a position to "squeeze" the farmers and merchants of his province. A private fortune soon began to grow. The pattern was classic. The district chiefs, and through them the hamlet chiefs, were forced to produce hefty payoffs. Nghi, of course, was implicated. So there was no fear of being disciplined—even as the province slipped unmistakably back into the waiting fingers of the VC. Thus was a web of corruption maintained, from President Thieu, who gave Nghi his job, down the chain of command to often corrupt and ineffective province chiefs, eventually wriggling its way into the offices of those at the very lowest levels of government.

Vinh Long was a blatant case. It was also a province of vital strategic importance. But I soon discovered similar patterns in other parts of the Delta. Doubtless, it was the same throughout South Vietnam. Corruption, of course, was not a recent import to Vietnam. Subordinates had long bought jobs. Regular payments were equally routine. Performance was not just a question of military prowess or skill at administration. Rather, a man was often judged by how much cash he could produce to keep the machine greased and running smoothly. Under such circumstances, institutional discipline was difficult—often impossible—to maintain. On rare occasions, President Thieu would sacrifice somebody to calm the Americans. Otherwise, he kept business moving, in some ways a prisoner of his own system.

General Nghi was well aware of what effect this practice could have on the "wrong" type of American. He knew that his master in Saigon would sacrifice him if an international scandal were to develop. Military and economic aid money was getting increasingly scarce; a major public relations disaster might be enough to stop the flow completely. A paradox had developed. While the Vietnamese were more independent of American advice, they were still completely dependent on the United States for material and economic assistance.

Long practiced at pleasing Americans, Nghi had become a statistical virtuoso, a numbers wizard. He insisted on lengthy and highly detailed reports from all subordinates, full of the quantified judgments earlier so dear to another McNamara's computer experts at the Pentagon. Nghi reckoned, with some justification, that impressive scientific management paraphernalia was exactly what many of his visitors from America hoped to see. Dozens of American generals, diplomats, and congressmen came and saw, leaving Nghi's office with a feeling of warm comfort. All were taken out to various parts of the Delta for carefully selected proof that Nghi's charts reflected reality.

The long-serving members of my staff were much less easy to fool. For a start, they knew what to look for when visiting rural areas. The average congressman was hardly well equipped to do so on his fleeting visits. Cushing, and other old-timers, had seen the tricks too many times before. An enterprising province or district chief could easily leave one with an impression of complete control over security during a short VIP visit. The area, which the visitors are asked to choose, is swept just before their arrival by a large force of troops. The force is then maintained just out of sight until the guests leave.

To General Nghi's chagrin I began dropping from the sky without warning, anywhere in the Delta, using one of our assigned Air America helicopters. When not flying, I traveled the roads in an unmarked car. Even more irritating to him were the province representatives that America had placed in twelve of the sixteen Delta provinces. Many of these men spoke Vietnamese, and most had been in Vietnam many years. Nghi's method of dealing with this threat was to flatter and soothe their superiors, particularly those visiting from Saigon and Washington, and ride out the odd flutter in that strange American temple called an embassy. The arrival of a consul general with significant experience in rural Vietnam meant that Nghi was going to be under more knowledgeable scrutiny. Like many in positions of authority, the general did not wish to hear bad news, and he certainly wanted to make certain that the complicated score system, devised by the Americans for measuring security in the countryside, always reflected a positive trend. This scheme was called the HES, or Hamlet Evaluation System. In the hands of a self-serving official, it was open to easy distortion.

The province chief of Vinh Long was doing just that—juggling the statistics. Thus, when he needed help desperately, there was no hope. He could not justify asking higher authority for the troops needed to rectify a worsening situation because, according to his own reports, nothing was wrong. In fact, I discovered, the man was unable even to muster a convincing argument for calling back his own province's locally recruited Regional Force battalions, which were still serving outside Vinh Long. What could the chief do when confronted with this dilemma? Rather than risk a loss of face, possibly even his position, by admitting his error, the province chief chose to emphasize the ceremonial and administrative side of his job, while ignoring the growing military dangers within the province.

A similar sad scenario, with a few variations, was being played out in neighboring Vinh Binh. Elsewhere in the region, security was not quite so dismal in late 1974. Two strong, well-led ARVN divisions held the northern regions of the Delta. These were the 7th and 9th Divisions. One of their main tasks was to sit astride the incursion routes out of the Parrot's Beak and the vast Plain of Reeds on the Cambodian border to the west. Both had long been used as sanctuaries and infiltration routes for large numbers of North Vietnamese troops. It was not unusual for whole communist regiments, two thousand infantrymen with heavy weapons, to enter South Vietnam through either region.

Recently, the two ARVN divisions had enjoyed some success. They cleared out a major VC base area at a place called Tri Phap, just south of the Parrot's Beak. The operation ensured that roads and canals in the nearby countryside could be safely used to carry merchandise and food to the capital. Three and a half million people lived in Saigon. If the Delta rice harvests were prevented from reaching their markets and shops, eventually they would starve.

Crucial to this was Route 4. Its most vulnerable stretch was where the road passed through Dinh Tuong Province. Here, all lines of communication from the Delta converged, near the border with Military Region III, at the last major river crossing; from there, Route 4 swung northeast to the capital.

On a map, the Delta looked like a big foot, holding up the rest of South Vietnam. The ankle joint was the point where the Parrot's Beak and South China Sea almost met in Dinh Tuong.

A little farther south, on the coast, was Kien Hoa, a traditional VC stronghold, a province of islands. Under a strong province chief, local government forces were holding their own. North of Kien Hoa, in the rich rice provinces such as An Giang spreading toward the Cambodian frontier, the Hoa Hao religious sect had a firm grip. It was fifteen years since the sect's private army was disbanded by President Ngo Dinh Diem. Nonetheless, nobody interfered in its backyard.

On the west coast was Rach Gia, a remote province, where strange islands rise from the sea and the shellfish are among the world's best. Here the government could control fishing villages, but could not pinch off infiltration routes that led inland. This was extremely worrying for me. Long ago, the Americans and South Vietnamese had recognized that supplies landed from the sea, usually at night on isolated stretches of coast, were as much a threat as weapons and ammunition being trucked down the Ho Chi Minh Trail. By 1974, the main traffic into the Delta came across the Bay of Cambodia to the Rach Gia coast or to the densely jungled region known as the U Minh Forest in Ca Mau Province, at the southern tip of Vietnam.

There were still government-held toeholds in Ca Mau and the U Minh, leftovers from the early seventies, that high-water mark of pacification. But these enclaves were gradually slipping away from GVN control.

It was this southwestern corner of the Delta that posed the third major threat; the VC and NVA were constantly trying to infiltrate from their forested base areas into the rich rice-producing provinces of Bac Lieu, Soc Trang, and the countryside south of Can Tho. The 21st ARVN Division was tasked to block this effort. A relatively ineffective unit, the 21st was based in Chuong Thien Province, just south of Can Tho. In theory, the division was spread across the province like a huge net that could be drawn tight whenever worthwhile quarry was caught within it. The trouble was that the 21st Division was understrength and poorly led.

Overall, while ground had fallen back into enemy hands since the peak of pacification success in 1972 when Gen. Ngo Quang Truong was IV Corps commander, the situation was infinitely better than when I had first set foot in the Delta during Tet 1968. Government forces still had relatively strong control over most of the central rice-growing provinces. Communist strength, however, was growing steadily. In contrast, South Vietnamese control was either static or slowly declining in strength. Nonetheless, the changes did not appear irreversible in the Delta.

I found it nothing short of amazing that the Vietnamese were able to carry on at all. Millions had been killed or permanently maimed in thirty years of fighting from 1945 to 1975. One wondered how much longer any society could continue such a cruel and punishing war without reaching the point of collapse. I knew what damage the years of bloodletting had done to the American military. Gone were many of the best and brightest officers and NCOs. Large numbers had been killed or wounded between 1965 and 1968 fighting Westmoreland's big-unit war of attrition. At the same time, some ARVN divisions were forced to replace themselves every two years. God alone knew what savage losses NVA divisions suffered in the fearful war of attrition. As for the local VC, they had all but disappeared from the battlefield after 1969.

It was not just the human losses that led to a decline in ARVN efficiency. The drastic fall in U.S. military aid resulted in combat soldiers being limited to a pair of hand grenades per month. Artillery support was also strictly rationed. Helicopter flying hours, including medical evacuation flights, were drastically cut back. It could be argued that the previous American-encouraged methods had been profligate in the use of ammunition and materials. Nonetheless, this sudden plunge from riches to survival rations had a very unnerving effect on an already fragile South Vietnamese self-confidence.

Many Vietnamese read it, with some justice, simply as further and increasing evidence that America was preparing to abandon them. In their propaganda, the VC reinforced these fears. Many a small post now fell to loudspeakers rather than fight against guns and mortars. They were all so isolated. VC propaganda teams would keep up the message throughout long, lonely nights.

Despite their many problems, however, the government forces were holding on to a large amount of very valuable ground. Most frightening in Vinh Long and Vinh Binh, the heart of the region, was that the steady loss of control was being quietly ignored. I determined that something must be done, and quickly.

Clearly, what was taking place across the frontier in Cambodia could not be ignored. Control of overland supply routes was a key factor in winning the Delta war. Most NVA replacements, orders, and heavy weapons came down the Ho Chi Minh Trail. The last leg into South Vietnam could be by land or sea.

When the Cambodian base areas were mauled in 1970, the fortunes of the VC declined all over the Delta. Only in the dense swamps of Ca Mau did the VC hold on virtually intact. But, as I lay pondering these matters during my first night in Can Tho late in August 1974, the war in Cambodia had gone catastrophically against Lon Nol's regime. The North Vietnamese once more had a free hand in much of Cambodia's southern marches. Their supply lines had been rebuilt. Now South Vietnam was far too weak for cross-border adventures. What could be done within the limits imposed by the present reality?

≡ 6 ≡

The Numbers Wizard

I had decided to try solving quickly as many problems as possible, referring to Saigon only those that were truly beyond a local solution. There was an obvious place to start this daunting crusade—General Nghi, the commander of IV Corps. But before doing so, I knew that Hank Cushing might well have wise counsel.

Cushing greeted me from the other side of a desk covered with papers. Each pile of documents—they varied in altitude—seemed to have its own character. Cushing was very methodical, perhaps because some of his formative years were spent as a Marine. I was always slightly surprised by the complexity of my deputy, who was not only tidy, but quite articulate, as would befit a former university professor. Cushing was also of Catholic origins, a graduate of the same system that had educated Downs, save that Cushing, after Notre Dame, taught English literature at Villanova.

Cushing gave his normal gruff good morning, then listened as I rehearsed my speech for Nghi. When I finished, Cushing nodded approval, but said nothing.

Frustrated, I remarked, "Is that all you have to say?"

"No," grunted Cushing. "He'll try to baffle you with statistics."

And later Nghi, facing me from behind his large desk, immaculately groomed, in a tailored combat green uniform with several rows of ribbons on his chest, did precisely that. In clearly pronounced English, he launched a blizzard of statistics in a textbook-style U.S. Army briefing, a performance aimed to send an American visitor home over-flowing with hope and confidence in Vietnam. I waited until Nghi had finished. Then, very politely, I told him that, according to my information, not all was well in Vinh Binh and Vinh Long Provinces. The general was nothing less than eloquent. Nghi had won victory after victory over American officials and reporters. He appeared openly shocked when his performance failed to sway a graying, midlevel American official.

Recovering quickly, Nghi counterattacked, turning on even more charm. Perhaps the general sensed that his visitor was no office-bound mandarin. Indeed, he already appeared to be fairly knowledgeable on the state of Military Region IV. No doubt the general had been made aware of my previous service in the Delta. He also may have been informed of my problems with the former I Corps commander, Hoang Xuan Lam, who never appreciated a nosy, independent-minded American consul in Danang who reported directly to Washington and to Ambassador Bunker in Saigon. For the moment, Nghi asked me to be more explicit, more detailed, then sat back in his chair and listened, with an expression of deep concern.

I began by drawing parallels between what I had discovered since arriving back in Vietnam and the situation in the same villages and districts during my 1970 trip. I pointed out, as diplomatically as possible, the Vinh Long province chief's failure to come to grips with a deteriorating military situation.

But information does not fall out of the sky. I knew that I must protect my Vietnamese friends in Vinh Long, as well as the sources of my province representative, Bob Traister, who was highly respected by both friends and foes.

Traister had spent nearly fourteen years in Vietnam. Few Vietnamese officials could fool this man who spoke the Delta dialects better than some of the city-bred Saigonese who had bought jobs to govern the local population. Nghi would guess that Traister had told me much of the gloomy news. But Traister's actual sources, the Vietnamese themselves, must remain hard to single out for revenge.

Nghi's response was to stand up in front of his wall charts and repeat his standard lecture. While the general's voice patronizingly droned for several minutes, I was forced to stifle impatience, sit quietly, then go through the whole argument again. Nghi had switched tactics. Now he was treating me like a keen, well-intentioned, but rather slow student who had asked for extra instruction in a fairly straightforward subject.

With a last glance at his charts, General Nghi eventually laid his pointer on the desk and resumed his seat. I still recall his bland face as he sighed and then, in a kind voice, inquired why I was so doubtful. "We all need to have faith," he said. "In a long, hard war there are bound to be periods when it is easier to despair. Leadership and courage are needed to show the way forward to better days."

Unmoved, I pressed my case as gently as possible, concluding that "if security goes on sliding back, the only better days will be those enjoyed by the VC."

After several more minutes of verbal boxing, Nghi reluctantly agreed to investigate, though adding politely that he doubted very much if my allegations concerning the security situation in Vinh Long would stand up to a thorough scrutiny.

Then Nghi reminded me of another reason for caution. His message to me was brutally clear—and yet, in its way, honest and fair. America might still supply money and arms. America might still have officials scattered the length of South Vietnam. But America had no fighting troops, no helicopters or bombers, no ships off the coast permitted to engage the common enemy from the north. I could urge or advise. The days when Americans gave orders were finished.

Frustrated but unbowed, I reported the encounter to Saigon. Somebody must take Nghi to task about the growing danger in the one place that South Vietnam depended on most for economic recovery. Only President Thieu himself had enough authority to order a corps commander to wake up and earn his pay. But no reply ever came from the embassy in Saigon.

Concerned that time was passing without any sign of change, I decided to drive to the capital in late September to see Wolfgang Lehmann, the deputy chief of mission who was acting as chargé d'affaires while Martin continued his quest for aid money in Washington. Lehmann had been consul general in Can Tho. He was, in fact, my real predecessor, Lacy Wright having held the job only during the interregnum before following Lehmann to Saigon. Indeed, I felt rather comforted that a key person in the embassy had recent experience in the Delta. This should ensure an understanding hearing of my problems.

To my surprise, I was smoothly dismissed by Lehmann with a pat on the back and advised "not to pay too much attention" to complaints from my colleagues in Can Tho. "You may find some of your subordinates to be unduly alarmist." And, the distinguished expert on German affairs continued, "Too many years of immersion in the politics of rural Vietnam breed that well-known Foreign Service disease, localitis."

I realized that, though too polite to tell me openly, Lehmann now included me among the afflicted. I had spent four years in rural Vietnam. Clearly, to a Europeanist, there was no counterbalance allowed for another fifteen years in Africa. It was a friendly parting, though a frightening moment. Smiling, Lehmann suggested that I listen to Nghi, adding warmly, "He is one of the most impressive generals I have ever met." Stunned, too surprised for a quick enough reaction, I had difficulty finding Lehmann's door. If Lehmann was puzzled, it did not show.

For months afterwards, I asked myself, should I have started once more from the beginning and forced Lehmann to hear the whole story through a second time? Or was my original reaction right, that there was simply no point in repeating fruitless arguments? I was now convinced that Lehmann himself had no intention of doing anything about Nghi.

I got back to Can Tho after a long, sweltering drive in the growing heat of Vietnam's dry season. There was only one person to whom I could unload my burden.

From long experience, Hank Cushing mistrusted the embassy. Thus, he was not surprised at my troubled state when I arrived back in Can Tho that evening. It took a strong whiskey and three minutes for me to explain what had taken place in Lehmann's office.

"He doesn't believe me about Nghi," I explained. "Not even the corrosive corruption. It's ridiculous."

"And what was OK four years ago is penal now," Cushing replied morosely.

"What do you mean, Hank?"

Cushing paused, then said, "Four years ago there was a lot of American money floating around this country. We still had over three hundred thousand troops and hundreds of civilian contractors. Just the sums of money they spent here—never mind USAID—were colossal. Corruption always was an evil feature of modern Vietnamese life. But, four years back, those involved were skimming the cream off a fairly affluent society."

I had no argument so far.

Cushing went on in his oddly slow way of talking. "Then we cut back on everything. We slashed economic aid by half. We stopped sending large quantities of ammunition and military equipment. Now the Americans, who have contributed to this corrupt pyramid, no longer supply huge amounts of largesse. Today, when our province chief in Vinh Long is asked to raise a certain amount of money, it bites into his people's real standard of living. Cash produced for services rendered equals somebody's loss of income."

"In other words," I said, "there is no more fat."

"And if the fat has all gone, Thieu and the whole spider's web are sucking blood out of ordinary people."

For a few minutes, neither of us said a word. The only noise came from the curtain, flapping in the evening wind as it blew off the river. In the street, Hondas and scooter-buses coughed and stuttered faintly as Can Tho went home for supper. I suddenly felt desperately tired. My mind seemed blank, empty of all thought, save perhaps despair. It was on this evening that I began to face the reality of total American retreat.

"What use are the consulates general, Hank?"

"Why ask me?" replied Cushing with a grin. "They were your idea."

"Was I wrong?"

"No," said Cushing. "There really is nothing else we could have done that would have been better."

"Maybe we should have just kept the embassy," I replied. "Americans won't give these people money much longer."

I studied Cushing's face, which appeared a dark tan in the amber glow from the setting sun. Cushing must have been going out for the evening because he was wearing one of his pencil-thin ties. Cushing noticed me smile.

"What's so funny?" he scowled.

"Why don't you chuck those 1950s neckties?"

This friendly insult signaled a sudden easing of my tension. I relaxed as Cushing replied in a good-humored tone, "That's all I need."

More seriously, he said, "You really got shook up today."

What could I tell Hank Cushing that, under the circumstances, was fair? Only one of us was consul general; there was no reason Cushing should carry an equal burden. Yet both of us were in too exposed a position for any other march of events. Lehmann was right in one very deep sense. We had been in Vietnam too long. We had developed an emotional commitment to the Vietnamese. But was that wrong in a war that Americans, at one stage, had fought boldly to win? Neither Hank Cushing nor I—nor any of those hard-bitten USAID men nor Larry Downs and his CIA contingent—could be faulted for trying to salvage as much as possible out of a situation that many regarded as hopeless.

Beyond the far riverbank, a swollen sun was slipping behind tall coconut palms, stabbing long shafts of canary light through their thick fronds. The Bas Sac, slowly changing into a sheet of platinum, slid past on its journey to the sea. I faced eastward into a cool breeze from the sea some seventy miles away.

"We have to do something about the spooks," I remarked.

Cushing sat staring across the river. At length he said, "It's duplication of effort. An autonomous and freewheeling organization within another makes no sense. The CIA still has its own logistics and a private club. Why not suggest they economize there for a start?"

"Well," I added, "apart from the cost of duplication, it's dangerous should we ever face a real emergency."

"They would resist. We would be attacking years of established custom and privilege."

"Didn't Lehmann object when he was here?"

Cushing thrust his hands deep into his trouser pockets. "Lehmann has spent most of his service in Europe. He's still assessing the situation out here. Trouble is, we don't have any time left for people to learn on the job."

The breeze was tugging ripples from the Bas Sac while its surface grew pale gray. The light had begun to fade. As I watched the river I mused aloud, "Theoretically, the CIA is under my control."

"Their real orders come from Saigon," Cushing corrected mildly.

"But I have the responsibility. As senior American in Military Region IV, I have to ensure their operations conform to U.S. policy. I am required to do that, to see that the total American effort is orchestrated so that we don't conflict with each other."

"And work toward the general goals laid down for the mission," Cushing finished the standard bureaucratic line for me with a sly smile.

"In short, Hank, my role is to ensure good management of our increasingly limited resources."

"Should we try talking to Larry again?" Cushing sounded doubtful.

"There's no way I can fulfill my responsibilities toward the CIA and the rest of the consulate general if the present situation continues," I insisted. "I don't know what they are doing. It's wasteful and could be dangerous. But suppose we do talk and he agrees. Could I ever trust Downs? He says that I'm now being informed of all their operations and that he takes orders from me, just like you and all the others assigned to Can Tho."

"Do you believe him?"

"At first I wanted to believe and trust him. Certainly, I have no wish to know the identity of his agents or the methods he uses to collect his information. These are legitimate trade secrets."

"That does not answer my question," replied Cushing.

"Let's say, Hank, that I'm suffering grave doubts. I most certainly do wish to be informed of any special operations he engages in, whether they be paramilitary or otherwise. I must know if that sort of thing is going on in our region. What really pisses me off, Hank, is that Larry starts an operation without telling us because he thinks we won't find out. Then, when the Vietnamese blow the details to us, we all look like fools."

"The Vietnamese don't understand why the ostensible leader is not aware of things being done by his nominal subordinates. Frankly, Terry, what you're trying to say is that you don't believe Larry."

"Not always; no. He has given me too much evidence to the contrary. Maybe Larry is simply following orders. Perhaps he has been told not to keep me informed."

"That's possible," agreed Cushing. "He could be under a lot of pressure from Saigon. So where do we go from here?"

"Try Larry Downs one last time."

"And then?"

"His chief, Polgar, in Saigon."

But nothing changed. Regularly throughout the dry season, we were to learn of CIA actions or operations from Vietnamese sources. Many were blown to us by agents of whom Cushing and I were "officially" unaware. Some of these CIA operations were to have a direct impact on overall U.S. policies in Vietnam. Others hindered daily work of the other sections in the consulate general. In fact, the CIA was verging on running a private foreign policy instead of simply gathering intelligence.

Having failed with Lehmann and Downs, I decided to try Tom Polgar. The CIA chief was my last hope, save Martin himself, who was still in Washington most of the time. Polgar arranged for me to see him at the embassy. Once again I took that long road, across endless miles of scorching paddy, punctuated with islands of gently waving palms shading gray-wattle village huts. It was by then early December. The temperature was well over 105 degrees as I drove at sixty miles an hour along the softening tarmac strip. Overhead, the sky soared to a powder-blue infinity. Now and then I would slow down, almost leave the road, to avoid the onrush of a military convoy, the green trucks belching black smoke from stove-pipe exhausts, their small ARVN drivers glaring through cheap sunglasses into the hard light. Small wonder, I thought, that there were so many deaths along this road. It gave me a jittery feeling.

Polgar greeted me with an outward show of friendliness. He was a short man, losing hair fast. Born in Hungary, Polgar still spoke with a thick accent. Normally he was rather silent at interviews. That day Polgar surprised me by purring, "Downs is under your authority, just as I am under the ambassador's." Further, Polgar promised that he would instruct Downs to brief me on all operations within the Delta. Not wholly satisfied, I asked that the CIA now begin full administrative integration. But Polgar declined to go that far, saying he thought it "premature."

While not fully satisfied, I was somewhat reassured. On return to Can Tho, I discussed the interview with Cushing. For the moment, there was no choice but to accept Polgar's word and watch events. If Polgar was not sincere, evidence of his duplicity would soon come to us through our Vietnamese contacts. There seemed little that the CIA did in the Delta that was not well known to a wide variety of South Vietnamese.

By November, the military situation was steadily worsening, and I considered General Nghi quite capable of losing large parts of the Delta. Then help came from an unexpected quarter.

≡ 7 ≡

A Welcome New Broom

Under daily rising pressure from his critics, most notably Father Tran Huu Thanh and his Anti-Corruption League, President Thieu was at last forced into vigorous action. Without warning, he sacked three of his four corps commanders—including my adversary Nghi—four members of his cabinet, and no fewer than four hundred senior army officers.

Thieu could do nothing less. Desperately in need of American support, the president was trapped. His army was starving for logistics support. His air force had no fuel. His country was on the edge of economic collapse. His own position—built on two foundation stones, acceptability of himself to the Americans and Vietnamese perception of his ability to keep on delivering vital American support—was shaky at best.

Thieu's trouble began with the gradual waning of American support after Tet in 1968. Now, even the principle of material support for South Vietnam was under widespread challenge in Congress. Thieu no longer dared to put down his critics with police truncheons. That was too dangerous. Yet, in Vietnamese politics, no action at all was a sign of weakness—and that would mean a dangerous loss of face.

It also might imply something much deeper. For many Vietnamese, it seemed a sign. The leader took no firm action against his critics, tolerating open challenges to his authority. He then gave in to pressure, sacrificing some of his closest associates. Could it be that "the Mandate of Heaven," the oriental version of the divine right to rule, was passing from Thieu's hands? Nobody was sure, but the seeds of doubt had been planted.

As in previous crises, Thieu was forced to name senior officials and key commanders on the basis of merit and qualifications rather than following his usual practice of extracting payment for the job from the highest bidder.

Early in November, the enormous burden of command in IV Corps fell on the slight, plump shoulders of Maj. Gen. Nguyen Khoa Nam, a veteran airborne soldier. Several years earlier, Nam had taken over the 7th ARVN Division, which guarded the northern Delta. Gradually he built it into the best division in the Delta. Some said the 7th ARVN Division rivaled the 1st ARVN Division for the honor of being the best in South Vietnam's army. For me this sudden appointment was the beginning of a deep, though tragically short, friendship.

The honor guard was dismissed. General Nghi stepped into the helicopter and was lifted in a whirl of dust and grit, clattering over the tin roofs of corps headquarters. Off the general went, high above the slender trees beyond the parade ground, to be flown for an hour until he reached a well-deserved pigeonhole in the Saigon military bureaucracy. A short, uniformed figure was left standing almost alone. Clad in the simplest of combat greens, with only two stars on his shirt collar giving away his rank, he turned and asked me if I would care to talk in the privacy of his office.

At our first meeting, Nam was something of a puzzle. My impression was of a soft, rather gentle, painfully reserved person—a personality more befitting a scholar than a soldier. The general was a bachelor and also reputed to be honest and austere in his way of living. Possibly this foreknowledge, combined with the obvious contrast with his predecessor, influenced my judgment. As we sat talking, I had the sensation of being with a monk in his cell. For despite the new set of miniature flags on the desk, a wall still covered by tactical maps of IV Corps, the parachute wings on his plain, though crisply starched, uniform, it was Nam's physical features that dominated the room. He was pale, with not a hair on his arms. I wondered, sitting there watching those child's hands rustle through some papers, whether this odd man ever needed to shave, so soft was his skin. His face, however, was strong, and in contrast to his arms, thick black hair was combed straight back over his scalp. It shone from coconut oil, a little affectation that seemed out of character.

But once we began to talk, Nam lowered some of his armor, allowing me to glimpse through small chinks the personality that lay below the surface. It was soon clear that he was extremely reserved with those he did not know well. I later concluded that this was often mistaken for shyness. His smooth skin and round face made him look much younger than his years, but in truth he was forty-two. His eyes were not soft. That was the earliest hint of the real Nam. I watched them change from one expression to another: sorrow, anger, sometimes hope. Nam, I suspected, could be harsh to the edge of cruelty with errant subordinates when it came time for discipline.

The room was hot. Sweat trickled down our faces as we talked. At first, we were both cautious, defensive. I had no wish to make a bad start with Nam. Our personal relationship might one day be a crucial factor in the lives of thousands, not to mention each other's existence. Nam, for his part, did not know me personally, only by reputation, though no doubt he had already questioned his chief of staff and others about me. He would want my support, certainly, but he was a proud nationalist and would accept help only on his own terms. Surprisingly, it was Nam who eventually broke down the barriers.

"You know," he confided in lightly accented English, "it is easy to be honest when one remains a bachelor."

By this reference to his bachelorhood, he was alluding to the legendary avarice of Vietnam's women. They had a well-earned reputation for acting as the channel of bribes for their husbands. Many well-placed women amassed vast family fortunes. Indeed, Madame Nghi was said to be exploiting to the full her husband's position and relationship with the president. In contrast, Nam had publicly vowed never to marry until after the war had been won.

"I heard about your promise to abstain from marriage," I said. "Are you going to keep to your deadline?"

"That is a military secret," the general replied with a smile.

Indeed, the general lived little better than his troops. He was rumored to sleep in a trailer and eat in the troops' mess hall. Rumor also had it that half his monthly salary—25,000 piasters—went to Buddhist charities. At first, I found this snippet of information difficult to accept. At the time, a Vietnamese general's official salary was less than most Americans paid their Vietnamese cooks.

"I do not entertain," Nam gently informed me, "but you are welcome on any day to share soup with my soldiers."

"I consider the invitation an honor, General," I answered.

The soft face frowned. "You are, I understand, not happy with security. I should like to hear what worries you about the AO [area of operations]."

There was a risk. Criticism that was too harsh might ruin what appeared to be the beginning of a cautious relationship. But I also had decided, if the opportunity arose, to speak out. Without honesty, however improved my personal relationship with General Nam, it would produce no more results than with Nghi. Mustering my courage, I gave Nam a blunt, though respectful, twenty minutes of grim news on the security situation in his corps's tactical zone. I took it point by point, district by district, province by province, finishing with my growing fears for Vinh Long and Vinh Binh.

When I had finished, Nam said quietly, "One does not worry about fallen arches when one has cancer of the stomach. MR IV has stomach cancer."

"We are preparing to draft a secret report on the security situation, General."

"For Saigon or Washington?"

"For both."

Nam pondered for some time without speaking. Was the general offended? I doubted that he was, but Westerners could never fully understand the mysteries of face. Cautiously, I offered to pass a copy of the report to the general.

"This report would be about Vinh Long and Vinh Binh?"

"Correct, General."

The dark eyes almost closed, and Nam said, "Show nobody else this report, Mr. McNamara."

There was no point in arguing with that stubborn face across the desk. "As you wish, General. We are here to help, not to criticize."

Nam relaxed. His eyelids lifted slightly. He said, "Let me offer you a sample of my vice."

"What's that?" The idea of Nam having a vice had not occurred to me.

"Coffee," replied Nam demurely.

Almost immediately following my talk with the general, I flew over to Vinh Long. The province spread northeast from Can Tho, between the Bas Sac and Co Chien branches of the Mekong River. Vinh Long City, on the Co Chien, is a ferry port on Route 4, some three hours' journey from Saigon.

The flight in an Air America Huey lasted only fifteen minutes. I was met at the airport by Robert Traister, the colorful and well-informed province representative. I spotted Traister without difficulty—he stuck out like a homing beacon. Chewing on a cigar, sweat stains under the armpits of his crumpled sport shirt, the belt stretched tight round his waist, glasses jammed on his nose, the Caucasian waiting at the landing pad could have been nobody else.

Traister annoyed some people. They did not take easily to his querulous, opinionated nature. His rapid, dogmatic style was often too near the truth, too brutally intelligent for some tastes. Nor did Traister ease matters with his practice of ramming right-wing political opinions down the ears of unhappy liberals.

None of these idiosyncrasies bothered me, although I did not share many of his political views. Traister had spent over a dozen years in Vietnam. He was part of the scenery, a living morsel of Delta folklore. Above all, he was treated by Vietnamese almost as one of them. Traister spoke their local dialect fluently. He could delight a rice farmer by telling him the coarsest jokes, employing the man's own accent.

Not many other Americans were able to speak to those peasant soldiers of Nam's kingdom using their own rough, earthy language. Later on, I was to listen spellbound for an evening while Traister, fellow guest at a Vietnamese dinner in our honor, poured out one story after another in flowing Vietnamese. What made Traister especially valuable was this gift of language, coupled with his chronic curiosity. He was, by late 1974, a very hard man to fool when it came to the security in a country district.

Once in the privacy of Traister's small, untidy office, I asked about the military situation in Vinh Long. Traister grimaced. He then told me frankly, in those staccato bursts of speech for which he was notorious, that it was worse. "That's all the change I can report," Traister finished morosely.

"Could you write an assessment for Nam's eyes only? And later, maybe another on Vinh Binh?"

"Sure, but what would the reports cover? Are we going to include why security is getting worse?"

"Everything. Report on everything."

"Jesus! Some people are gonna be upset!" Traister's glasses were suspended precariously on the end of his nose. For a moment I thought they would fall to the floor.

"As you wish." Traister shrugged and immediately began to discuss in his usual thorough style the exact terms of reference. His first question was, What must the paper assess? Not, What were Nam and I trying to prove? Traister would add his own recommendations for improvements.

Two days later, Traister came to Can Tho. He wore a cunning look as he closed the door of my office before placing a thick folder on my desk. It was a detailed report with colored maps showing his assessment of the state of security in each hamlet of the provinces. Side by side was another set of maps that the province chief submitted to Nam showing the security of each hamlet that same week. VC-controlled hamlets were marked in red. The amount of red that flooded the eastern and central portion of Traister's maps came as a shock. The strength of VC presence was even worse than I had thought. When I glanced at the province chief's map, the same areas stared at me complacently in the gentle greens and yellows that indicated total or reasonable government control.

Fixing Traister with a hard look, I asked, "Are you certain about this, Bob?"

Traister nodded slowly. "Absolutely."

Given my confidence in Traister's judgment on such matters, I lifted my telephone. Within a few seconds I was passed by the switchboard to General Nam's private number. The general would see us immediately. Pausing only to let Hank Cushing know where we were going, Traister and I set off.

Nam was waiting for us, his desk top cleared of papers. He read the report slowly, sometimes asking questions, raising his eyebrows when halfway down the last page. Traister stared at the floor. I guessed that Nam must be studying Traister's urgent recommendations for action: sacking the province chief and several district chiefs. Eventually the general laid Traister's folder on his desk.

Nam looked at us without changing expression. "Sadly, this assessment is correct. Your information agrees exactly with the report given to me this morning by Colonel Vinh." Vinh was a dynamic, tough young airborne officer whom I remembered well from Danang.

"Where do we go from here, General?" I asked with growing relief. At last, I had a man with whom I could talk and perhaps accomplish something useful.

Nam smiled like a benevolent Buddha. "Mr. Traister seems very good at this work. He must write a second report—this time on Vinh Binh."

"And Vinh Long?" I asked, feeling it was my duty to press for some kind of answer, even at the risk of causing resentment.

But Nam was not one to be offended by the truth. Neither, it seemed, would he be hurried. "I must think about it," he said in a voice that left no doubt the meeting was finished.

The next morning Nam summoned me to his headquarters. The general had a brittle, almost wild expression in his eyes. I had not seen him so full of energy and enthusiasm.

"I have decided to set up a special command for territorial security," Nam announced.

"That sounds good, General," I responded, not at all certain whether I was about to be disappointed or pleased.

"It will take over tactical control of all forces in Sa Dec, Vinh Long, Vinh Binh, and Soc Trang Provinces. That will give me direct control over all security operations in these four key, central provinces of the corps area. My senior officer, my territorial security commander, will have to be good, the best." Nam paused then said quietly, "I have decided to put Colonel Vinh in charge."

"That's brilliant," I exclaimed, breathing out slowly. "Your choice of commander is inspired."

Vinh had proved himself many times as a combat commander. But his career had been in the doldrums since he upset someone in the joint general staff with his unwanted frankness. Vinh would brook no slacking. He would be an aggressive commander, but one with a subtle tactical sense.

Nam smiled gently. "Vinh will have some regular ARVN battalions assigned on an ad hoc basis," he said. "He will have my authority to move Regional Forces over province borders anywhere within his AO, as he thinks fit."

I was elated by this unexpected good news. Crossing provincial borders would be a major departure for the locally recruited Regional Forces. Normally they were obliged to serve only in their home province. Nam saw my astonishment.

"We are in a crisis, Mr. McNamara. Extraordinary measures are required. With all available resources at his disposal, Vinh still has a most difficult, uphill task. But he will be able to concentrate his forces. He will be able to meet the greatest threat with strength. He will be able to launch a counteroffensive without bothering, or caring, for artificial province boundaries."

Obviously, Nam was referring to a well-known VC tactic of fighting along the borders of two provinces where they could jump from one side to the other, thus sidestepping uncoordinated defense efforts.

"Vinh will immediately organize his forces so that he can mount aggressive operations against the VC," Nam purred like a contented panther.

"They are well entrenched, General," I warned, "and heavily reinforced with fresh NVA replacements from the north."

"I have decided on other changes too, Mr. McNamara." Nam began to list further, welcome surprises. "There will be a new province chief for Vinh Long. A good man, a regimental commander, a proven combat leader, who has all the right qualifications. I am taking him from the 9th ARVN Division."

"What if he falters?" I asked candidly.

"Then he will have the toe of Colonel Vinh's jump boot for encouragement. But I do not think this is going to happen. I think he will do well. He is ordered to concentrate on military operations—a soldier's favorite work."

"Vinh Binh will remain as it is for the present," continued the general. "I know you would prefer it to be otherwise. But the present province chief has a good record from his previous assignment in Kien Hoa Province. We must be fair and, moreover, seen as such. I have many officers in my command. I must also pay attention to their morale. He will remain, shall we say, 'on probation.' If he fails, then he will be sacked. Meanwhile, do not forget, we have the good Vinh with his energetic staff looking over the province chief's shoulder. Though not ideal, I believe this is the right solution for now."

"I understand, General."

"Good," said Nam briskly, "for I have one more unusual request."

I was puzzled, even wary. Surely Nam was not going to ask for some personal favor? Not possible, I thought. The general would not even accept the gift of a diary for his office for fear it might be misinterpreted by the staff.

"Do not look so worried," said Nam, "although I will confess my need is not an easy one to satisfy. I want you to be very honest, with me, with us Vietnamese. I want you to prepare confidential dossiers. This time on all my province and district chiefs."

I could not prevent my astonishment from showing. "That's a very big order, General. I'm not sure we can handle it."

"I need a second opinion, like a doctor if you wish, on their performances. And if you think some are no good, then say so—and by all means suggest men who would make worthy replacements. I am sure you understand that this is a highly delicate task. It cannot be done, for obvious reasons, in my headquarters. Too many old friendships are involved. Your reports on Vinh Long and Vinh Binh have given me confidence in your understanding, in your objectivity. I am a patriot, Mr. McNamara, a Vietnamese nationalist. You know how much it costs such a person to ask for help from a foreigner. It is to bare my soul as a friend."

Swallowing to keep back my emotion, I nodded, touched by this unexpected show of confidence. "My provincial representatives and I will carry out the confidential evaluations." At this, Nam bent his head forward in a sign of gratitude before suggesting we take lunch together.

It was only a short walk through the bright sunlight to the mess hall. Nam said very little during our journey. As we entered the long, hot room, its low ceiling supported by exposed metal beams, hundreds of young soldiers stood as one. The benches on either side of each plain wooden table scraped on the concrete floor as the men rose and waited silently at attention for their general to be seated. Clearly the showman was coming out in Nam, yet I also saw that, in those serious, cautious stares, the respect was real. There was nothing phony about the soldiers' regard for Nam. He was the chief—the accepted natural leader. As the general bade all return to their rice and fish, the clicking of chopsticks once more began to merge with that singsong chatter of Delta Vietnamese.

A warm feeling of confidence swept over me. Whatever might be wrong with South Vietnam as a whole, in the Mekong Delta nobody doubted upon whose honest, capable, though frail shoulders the mandate of heaven had finally fallen. Unfortunately, the eleventh hour was about to strike.

8

Harbingers of Doom

I decided to remain in Can Tho for Christmas. We were then at the height of southern Vietnam's dry season: powder-blue skies, a bright sun burning the countryside. In the Delta this was a yearly compensation for all man's troubles. The clear weather would not change until April.

On my return from a brief absence in Hawaii, I went immediately to see General Nam. During our talk I presented him with an inexpensive gold-plated ballpoint pen. To my delight, Nam accepted, albeit with hesitation. Later I heard from a friend, an ARVN officer whom I had known in Danang, that the pen had caused quite a lot of soul-searching for the IV Corps commander. I felt guilty that my innocent gift had forced Nam to compromise his firm principles.

Long ago Nam had refused to offer the elaborate style of entertainment that important visitors expected as normal in Vietnam. Nam continued to live in his frugal way and so gained wide respect. He was a walking example of what "face" signified to devout Buddhists.

But my rising confidence in the situation, my hope for future prosperity, perhaps one day even peace, were constantly in the shadow of the war in neighboring Cambodia. Each day fewer boats passed upriver. There had been a time when river craft sailed to Phnom Penh as freely as boats ply the Mississippi. But those days were past. It now took a powerfully escorted convoy to reach the beleaguered city. Phnom Penh was slowly bleeding to death and, with it, all hope for Cambodia. The Khmer Rouge, with North Vietnamese support, steadily tightened its grip on the capital. Lon Nol's government was near collapse.

I felt sad for my friend John Gunther Dean, who had once been chief of CORDS in I Corps and was now American ambassador in Phnom Penh. The city's fall, I believed, was just a question of time. It only needed the river supply route to be finally cut; no airlift could feed Phnom Penh's swollen population. It was estimated that nearly half the people of Cambodia had fled inside the beleaguered city's defenses. In any case, the U.S. Air Force, even if it could supply enough food to satisfy this mass of hungry mouths, would not be allowed to do so by order of Congress. Once Cambodia fell to the communists, it would mean a long, hostile frontier opened on Vietnam's flank. The position of the Delta would become infinitely more difficult.

Yet I was not totally preoccupied with Phnom Penh. There was another problem zone closer to our northern border: the NVA controlled Parrot's Beak.

A week before Christmas, the North Vietnamese attacked a small province called Phuoc Long in MR III, seventy miles north of Saigon on the border with Cambodia. First, the NVA captured three district towns. Next the roads into Phuoc Binh, the provincial capital, were cut and its airfield bombarded by artillery and mortar fire. As Christmas week came, I began to read my morning message traffic from Saigon with nagging seeds of uneasiness. Phuoc Binh was in serious danger of falling to the North Vietnamese. Direct U.S. military intervention remained out of the question. Yet the ARVN too seemed dangerously ambiguous about defending or abandoning the town. It was as if they still thought American jets would mount a final rescue. In a sense, the government's bad judgment was reminiscent of the French at Dien Bien Phu.

There was nothing I could do in Can Tho about this distant battle. My task was to ensure, as far as I could, that all went well in the Delta. I could do this only by making certain that General Nam and his staff had the best American information, or advice, the consulate general could provide. I also had to ensure, to the extent I could, the smooth flow of the declining amounts of American economic and military aid.

The consulate general's Christmas party took place in my villa. It was a warm, clear night. Preparations for the bash were begun three days earlier under the careful supervision of my cook, Chi Lieu. One of those tufty Dalat fir trees was placed in a pot decorated with crepe paper to stand near the front door. All manner of Vietnamese and American Christmas decorations filled the house: stars of Bethlehem mounted on wheels of silver paper; long streamers of red, white, and blue; an enormous quantity of candies and colored lights for both house and tree; dozens of paper lanterns. Following another custom in Vietnam, the maids of my friends and colleagues had arrived earlier in the day to assist with preparations and to join in the revelry that extended to the kitchen on such holidays. To walk through the door into that hot, crowded, candlelit room was to imagine oneself in a part of southern France that was enjoying a freak warm spell in December.

I had, as was my own tradition, invited all the American personnel in the consulate general as well as many Vietnamese friends. Drinks were flowing. Swaying bodies moved more or less in time with the music booming from the powerful speakers of a Japanese-built sound system. Already the overflow was drifting out to the garden. Staring through the wire mesh fences, every so often caught in the glare of headlights from an arriving car, were a hundred small pairs of eyes. In a rare moment of reflection I noted the absurdity of big Americans jammed together with tiny Vietnamese. Most of my staff had by this time blended into a good team, working well together with little attention to their bureaucratic origins. Nonetheless, the CIA contingent remained isolated. This could not be blamed on Cushing or myself. Both of us had worked hard to smooth over lingering misunderstandings.

The staff was a collection of personalities, each in his own way likable or irritating; all blessed with a certain mad charm. In one corner, Kassebaum, known as Kass to his colleagues, was a slender figure topped by glasses above a neat goatee. He gave the impression of being a young graduate student, almost as if he were still a Peace Corps volunteer. Kass made up for his lack of physical bulk with strong-willed talk. Yet it was based on hard experience. Kass had spent much of the last four years in Ca Mau, a small forgotten town on Vietnam's southern tip, the most isolated province capital in the country. Kass was the only American in the place after 1972.

His father was a fighter pilot who retired from the U.S. Air Force as a colonel. Kass's mother was Jewish. Somehow, he said, each year his Jewish blood came nearer the surface—at least he felt Jewish more days than not. And he had a soft spot for children. This could have been Jewish too, or simply Kass. At the moment he was busy trying to converse with Walt Heilman, the post's bearlike general services officer who had the Marine Corps and the merchant marine in his curriculum vitae. Hasty, the Marine sergeant, bore less resemblance to celluloid Marine heroes than any other member of that elite corps that I could remember. He wore glasses, was tall and painfully thin. But when he opened his mouth, it was pure John Wayne. He was opening his mouth now, on the far side of the room, to a very pretty Vietnamese girl. They were shuffling at the edge of the dance floor. Hasty looked like a bright college freshman; he was only twenty-four. I recall wondering whether he had to shave that delicate chin with its barely tanned skin. Hasty sometimes made me feel over a hundred. The boy was bright and willing. He could produce the most incredible flashes of youthful courage bordering on the vainglorious. At times I found the young sergeant's enthusiasm terrifying, but his youthful weaknesses were far outweighed by his many virtues.

Hank Cushing loomed above most heads in the room. Even from twenty feet away, I could see his thin necktie contrasting with wider, more fashionable examples worn by the fresher members of the staff. Some of them had come in from the country just for this evening. Traister was holding forth to one of the CIA operatives with his usual intensity. For once, Traister almost qualified as well dressed. His shirt was uncrumpled and his trousers actually looked as if they had been run over with an iron. As I sipped a whiskey, I enjoyed the dim, warm lights and the happy spectacle. It was Christmas Eve with the war half forgotten and good cheer flowing in abundance.

Averill Christian, I thought, had put on weight. Strictly speaking, it was none of my business, except that health was important. I worried about Christian. The retired army colonel once suffered from heart trouble. He still showed signs of possible high blood pressure, which could be dangerous for him during a lengthy period of overwork. But on that evening, overweight or not, Christian was certainly relaxed and happy. Perhaps, I recall deciding, it was silly to fret over small changes in someone else's health or morale. People had to resolve their own problems. Yet I still worried. It was not in my nature to ignore such things.

New Year's came and the battle for Phuoc Binh, two hundred miles to the northwest, grew more critical. It seemed that President Thieu could not make up his mind whether the town was really worth defending. Some people thought Thieu was trying to frighten America into sending fighter bombers to win the battle for South Vietnam. Daily reports told of C-130 transports having to free-drop supplies from above ten thousand feet because of the threat from surface-to-air missiles (SAMs) and flak. In the end, the only reinforcements to reach Phuoc Binh were a couple of hundred airborne Rangers.

The garrison of about three thousand was encircled by nearly three times that number. Shelling was steadily reducing the city to a ghost town. Its population dwindled daily. Then, on January 7, President Thieu decided to abandon the town. The defenders slipped away as best they could. For the second time since 1954, a provincial capital had fallen. But this time, unlike Quang Tri in 1972, there were no forces left in reserve to mount courageous, if wasteful, counterattacks. Nor were there American B-52s to punish the invaders with a terrifying bombardment.

An atmosphere of gloomy resignation descended as the news trickled through. North Vietnamese troops were in control of the town center; they had hoisted a red flag. Throughout the war, Phuoc Binh had been a costly town to defend. It was forever being almost cut off from the next province. There was little military sense in clinging to such an island of government territory, miles from the capital, lost in the forests on Cambodia's border. But it was a part of South Vietnam. How many parts of western MR II and III (the central highlands), for example, could be likened to Phuoc Binh?

Very worried, Cushing and I concluded a few evenings later when brooding over the defeat that President Thieu was desperately short of troops. Apart from the airborne division and South Vietnamese marine division, Thieu had no strategic reserve. At the time, the marines were tied down in northern I Corps. Ordinary Vietnamese troops could not be moved far from the population from which they were recruited; this meant keeping even the regular army divisions within their military regions. In MR II, divisions were even restricted to their own half of the region. In any case, there was clearly nothing we could do about it here in IV Corps.

Within hours, there was a second shock: After five days without food and water a small ARVN company holding the summit of the Black Virgin Mountain, a vast green hump overlooking Tay Ninh City that rises a thousand meters above the flat countryside, gave up its position and struggled down the rough forested slopes. The citizens of Tay Ninh had lost more than a watchtower. The mountain also had great religious significance for the local Cao Dai, a bizarre religious sect that reveres Christ, Victor Hugo, and Buddha. The sect's dragon-pillared cathedral stands on the edge of Tay Ninh. Losing Black Virgin Mountain was a shattering wound to the city's fragile self-confidence. People began to flee toward Saigon.

Yet these shocks passed. Day-to-day life in Can Tho continued its even pace. I traveled about the Delta as frequently and as widely as possible. Normally I was able to visit at least one province each week. It was the only way to fine-tune my knowledge of local conditions in this large and diverse region. If time allowed, I went by car to get a closer feeling for the rhythms of everyday life on the ground. Otherwise, I climbed into a helicopter for a quick trip to several districts in the same day.

In January and February, the dry, hot season reaches its peak. Warm tranquil days flow one after the other, each one seeming longer than its predecessor. The sun takes its time rising. Then swiftly, the heat grows. By afternoon, a handful of ragged white clouds are navigating a vast sky.

It must have been early in February when I made my last visit to one of our most contested, most isolated districts. It was on the eastern edge of Vinh Binh Province, in the mangrove swamps near the South China Sea—a bad place to live. All we now controlled was the small district town. Our chopper touched down briefly in Vinh Long to pick up Traister before flying south.

Two thousand feet above the Delta, with the cool lash of rotor wash on my face, I relaxed in my canvas seat, staring at the land below. The geometric patterns reminded me of a vast silken quilt with green, brown, and gold patches. The young rice was still not ready for planting, and thousands of dry paddies lay bare, resting. The pilot, keeping clear of small-arms range, was following the huge, green Bas Sac River, which lay beneath the helicopter skids, slowly uncoiling as it moved toward the distant sea.

Suddenly the helicopter went into a shallow dive. People waved to us from small boats being poled along a murky canal. Then the helicopter was beating above the tin roofs of a small, sandbagged, stockaded town. Soldiers held back crowds of children; red dust flew away; the skids bumped to earth.

A small, tough man waited to greet me. Usually he was clad in combat trousers and undershirt. Sometimes he wore sandals. That day his bare, gnarled feet, with their splayed toes, were coated in red dust. It needed only a single look at the district chief to realize that this man (though an army major) was no transplant from Saigon, no well-connected city boy, as was the case with too many of his colleagues in more prosperous, safer districts, where civilization's amenities were close.

The district chief was a tough, rural type who possessed, in healthy proportions, both natural dignity and common sense. He reached out a rough-skinned hand to me. His grip was firm. When he spoke, it was with the harsh accent of a Delta fisherman. Taking me by the arm, he led me to his office. It was in an old thatch-roofed building. A wall of sandbags was built all round and capped with barbed wire. Patiently waiting were several supplicants. I wondered how the district chief coped. Already it was midafternoon and people were still arriving. Now I was about to steal another hour of the old major's time.

To my surprise, much of the crowd shuffled into the chief's small office. A ceiling fan was plunking laboriously, round and round, with no effect on the smelly air and no hope of reducing the temperature. Scores of flies attacked the guests. The office seemed to serve as a meeting place for the district's notables. Beer was ordered from a nearby ramshackle shop. Everyone sat on the floor. Soon a lilting discussion developed. The situation in their district was dismal. In a matter-of-fact voice, the chief briefed us, his guttural Delta accent giving his words greater emphasis as he told us that security was getting worse.

Government forces—a euphemism for the barefoot but relatively effective local militia—held the district town, plus a circle of farmland less than four kilometers around. Otherwise, the VC had taken over the rest of the district. The single road linking the district with its nearest neighbor, and, therefore, the remainder of Vinh Binh Province, was closed. It could be opened only by a battalion-sized clearing operation. The chief was a realist. He knew that too many other, more affluent, strategically important districts claimed priority.

Before departing, I promised to pass the major's message to Colonel Vinh and General Nam. It was all I could offer, not much, but he expected no more of me. At least he and his district were not completely forgotten. The purpose of my visit was fulfilled. Beer glasses were politely drained.

Outside, the flies were even more numerous and bothersome. The group set off on a rapid tour of the town, waving arms, beating hats in the humid air. But the flies seemed determined to follow yard by yard. The town population was no more than a thousand. I reckoned from the mob of children we attracted that most were under twelve years old. Piles of green sandbags festooned by barbed wire strung with empty beer cans marked strong points throughout the town. The buildings were scarred by pitmarks from bullets, many freshly made. I asked the chief, "Has the town been attacked recently?"

He spat a long, red stream of betel-nut juice into the dust before casually replying, "Mortar rounds hit the town most nights." Spitting another red stream, he continued, "Three nights ago we repulsed a big ground attack." The tough little man seemed resolved to face whatever his town's fate would be.

At each strategic point in the town, I asked a few questions, and Traister noted where the consul general's influence, or access to supplies, might help. After we had said good-bye to the district chief and the Huey was climbing, Traister sadly shook his head. No words were needed. We both knew how hopeless this chief's situation had become.

9

Recipe for Disaster

In mid-January, instructions arrived from Saigon to update the consulate general's evacuation plan. A routine Foreign Service inspection was to take place and the inspectors would want to see the plan, especially in a country as dangerous and as vulnerable as Vietnam. This was neither surprising nor worrying. After reading the instructions, I sent for Averill Christian, the retired army colonel who was my administrative officer.

Christian had long experience of operations in Vietnam. Without hesitation, he volunteered to draw up an initial version of a revised plan and make other preparations for the inspection. A short discussion ensued. I commented that "the present regime may rock along for years, in its peculiarly Vietnamese fashion, rising occasionally to a crisis. Or, it might collapse very suddenly, which has been the case quite often in Chinese and Vietnamese history. Scholars describe the latter historical phenomenon as 'the loss of the mandate of heaven.'"

"That gives us plenty of scope!" said Christian patiently.

Apologizing for my less-than-helpful analysis, I told Christian that we must have a practical, workable plan. It should, I insisted, take into consideration the possibilities that the Delta's many waterways afford. "From Can Tho, we have easy access to the sea. So when you draft the plan, remember to include water options. Do not simply rely on aircraft or road transport to Saigon. Don't neglect any viable possibilities."

Christian frowned. "OK," he said, although he could not hide the skepticism in his voice.

"When I organized evacuations in the secessionist province of Katanga during the Congo crisis in the early '60s," I continued, sensing that some explanation was required, "I learned some lessons. Airports can easily be closed and roads can be blocked with little effort. Large rivers, however, cannot be cut. And they are difficult to interdict for an enemy with no navy."

"I understand," replied Christian, although still without apparent enthusiasm.

Continuing, I insisted that we "include our Vietnamese staff with their families in the calculations."

Christian jerked forward in his chair. "But that's more than five thousand people. We don't have the resources to even consider evacuating so many people," he gasped.

"I know," I replied more gently. I then confirmed that I too had done my own calculations based on an average of five members per family and one thousand employees. I continued to further expose my growing concern. "Last month Phuoc Long Province fell. There was no American reaction. This may have been a testing of our will and intentions. I feel a very strong moral obligation to our local employees. If worse comes to worst, we must be prepared to do everything possible to get as many out as possible."

Christian glumly nodded as he gathered up his papers from my desk and rose. There was no need for further discussion. We both had been in tricky situations before, and Christian now knew that I was determined to include our employees in our emergency planning. Behind my insistence was an assumption that, if the Vietnamese lost one battle too many, no help would come from the United States to save them. The possibility of evacuation, therefore, had to be treated realistically.

When Phuoc Long was overrun, there were several days of popular apprehension in the Delta. Some feared that it was a forerunner of a much larger NVA offensive. Then an uneasy calm returned, giving way again to a resumption of normal life.

Yet this fooled neither Christian nor me. The North Vietnamese were almost certainly busy preparing a major offensive. Embassy reports, as well as information coming from our own Vietnamese contacts, were clearly pointing in this direction. Because of Vietnam's climate, particularly south of the central highlands, battles were often fought toward the end of the dry season. Sudden gains of ground made then could be held during the rains, when movement on the battlefields became difficult. Phuoc Binh had been a strong reconnaissance in force, a fierce skirmish compared with what might come. America had now given North Vietnam a signal that whatever happened, this time, no American bombers would strike. The sky would be empty.

Christian quickly got on with the complex task of constructing an evacuation plan. Not only did he have to provide for all the various elements of the consulate general in one workable scheme, but personnel from all agencies out in the countryside also had to be included in the intricate timetable of movements. This done, Christian's proposals had to fit in precisely with Saigon's overall evacuation scheme for the whole of South Vietnam. The latter requirement meant that all sorts of bureaucratic details had to follow clear, uniform patterns. Otherwise, there was danger of muddle and confusion. The five different evacuation plans, one for Vietnam as a whole and one for each of the four military regions, must be melded together using the same assumptions and criteria.

Christian finished a week later, appearing at my door clutching a heavy bundle of papers. He explained, somewhat short of breath, that he had managed to meld all elements—CIA, DAO, USAID, USIS (United States Information Service), SAFO (the rump of the CORDS' provincial advisory organization), and JCRC (Joint Casualty Recovery Command)—into the plan. I read it carefully. There was no doubt that Christian had painstakingly met every bureaucratic requirement as set forth in the instruction. Nothing had been forgotten. Nevertheless, drawing on my training as a student at the Armed Forces Staff College and the Naval War College, I sensed that something was lacking. After puzzling for some time, I realized that the plan conveyed no overall "concept of the operation." A reader could not picture how it would actually work with all the pieces fit into place.

I knew from my Congo experience that everyone being evacuated must have a simple understanding of how they fit into the complete operation. They must know why a move or a time is important. There must be no ambiguity—no excuse to say later that it was not clear to them why their particular job, or rendezvous, was vital to others. Everybody must be made aware that his or her role was a contribution to the group's safety as a whole. Should an evacuation from Vietnam occur, American and Vietnamese lives would be at risk. Plans never work out exactly as written. Nevertheless, they do provide a vital framework within which to improvise. While complimenting Christian on his good work, I gently pointed out his plan's major flaw. He dutifully went back to the drawing board.

I ate dinner slowly that evening, trying to work out solutions to the most daunting problems. For one thing, it was plain to me that nobody was going to provide airlift sufficient to evacuate three thousand to five thousand Vietnamese—not from the Delta. But how did you bring together thousands of employees and their immediate families from sixteen Delta provinces? It would require a fleet of helicopters with American troops to protect landing zones scattered over a vast area.

The largest U.S. helicopters could lift roughly fifty Vietnamese, more if safety rules were disregarded, but that still meant some hundred sorties. If only smaller Hueys were available, this figure for sorties could be quadrupled. I felt certain that, in a crisis, many large helicopters would be available from the fleet. However, a large number of calls would be made on these same lift resources from Saigon and from the other three military regions. In the event of a total collapse, with all government functions broken down, with no army or police, there could be small groups of Americans waiting for rescue all over Vietnam. The number of sorties called for could be colossal. On the other hand, even during a collapse, there might be a long-enough warning to implement an evacuation plan by stages. By road and waterway? I wondered. Possible, but only so long as conditions were still quiet. In a total disaster, would this be likely? Finally, would the United States be willing to commit the substantial forces needed to protect such an operation? It would violate the cease-fire accords. Political resistance in the United States against any reinsertion of American troops was likely, no matter what the reason.

I spent a restless weekend. After having puzzled for hours over the size of our workforce, I reluctantly concluded that Christian was right. We could not take everybody. At any rate, not under all circumstances. Besides, I had begun to question my own wisdom. Was it really desirable to evacuate simple people who would obviously experience enormous difficulty once they had arrived in the United States or elsewhere in the world outside Vietnam? Large numbers of our employees were charwomen, cooks, domestic servants. Others were clerks, guards, or laborers. The largest number were not employed on sensitive duties that were likely to put them in mortal danger from a triumphant VC.

It was tough for me to reach this conclusion. All the time, I kept asking myself, Are you just trying to turn necessity into virtue to salve your own conscience because you might have to accept loyal staff being abandoned? I was glad when first sunlight spread over the rooftops on Monday morning and I could get on with my regular work.

My worry stemmed almost entirely from what was going on outside the Delta. News had come daily in the cable traffic from Saigon but also from my close relations with ARVN Corps Headquarters staff, from General Nam down to majors and captains. Each week, I attended two or three American briefings on various subjects within the consulate general. And, without fail, I went to General Nam's big weekly briefing session every Monday morning. ARVN intelligence was generally good. The South Vietnamese had no need to exaggerate their plight. The picture that emerged was a comparatively stable security situation in the Delta, with some promise of later improvement. This was not the case farther to the north, in MR I and MR II.

Events were gloomy. The shake-up had brought Nam to the command of Military Region IV, but not all the other changes had been for the best. For instance, the president had appointed Gen. Nguyen Van Toan, whom he earlier had sacked from II Corps for corruption and inefficiency, to command MR III. I had known Toan when he commanded the 2nd ARVN Division in I Corps. His appointment in particular filled me with foreboding. Like many of my colleagues, I felt that the legendary John Paul Vann had lost his life near Kontum in 1972 trying to salvage the defense of that town, which, had it fallen, would have let the North Vietnamese into the middle of Toan's Military Region II. Many felt that Toan's ineffectiveness as a commander had resulted in this earlier near debacle and cost Vann his life.

For General Nam, it was bad news. A good commander in MR III not only kept Saigon safe; his troops also took a lot of pressure off IV Corps. The same effect worked in reverse. This had been the case during Do Cao Tri's time four years earlier. Tri had maintained good control over III Corps, keeping the VC on the run by keeping his own troops in constant motion.

Intelligence had begun to warn that a big communist attack was liable to hit MR I and MR II fairly soon. Whatever might be achieved in the Delta could be flung to the winds by a major failure elsewhere in the country. When I thought about my evacuation plans, I was more and more influenced by what was taking place in other parts of South Vietnam. Thankfully, I decided, there was no need to exclude evacuation through Saigon from any plans. Whatever befell MR I or MR II, distance could still mean plenty of warning. Saigon, after all, was two hundred miles south of MR II. Still, I recognized that total collapse in Vietnam was always possible. At that stage, however, nobody was forecasting such a gloomy picture, nor was there any evidence to warrant such projections. Christian could use only established facts while planning. Yet, my ideas were beginning to diverge from those in Saigon.

The DAO in Saigon and the embassy's administrative section were equally immersed in updating their evacuation plans. They worked from an assumption that all four military regions would be evacuated first before a final evacuation of the capital. The plan was a document four hundred pages long. According to later accounts, their scheme called for the evacuation of just under seven thousand Americans plus their families. Saigon, for the time being, was not thinking in terms of evacuating large numbers of Vietnamese. At some time early in February, I understand, DAO asked the CIA, presumably Station Chief Polgar, if the Agency wished to contribute to this planning exercise. DAO had begun to draw up a contingency plan for secretly evacuating Vietnamese who worked for the American mission or were high government officials. The CIA, it seems, did not see any reason to become involved, not at that moment.

As February advanced, the battlefields of South Vietnam grew quieter. It was difficult to judge from Can Tho what was really happening throughout the rest of South Vietnam. The highlands of MR II and MR I were several hundred miles distant. Even Saigon was a day trip to the north. Localized security problems and the rice crop were uppermost in my mind, with inflation a close third.

So my first choice of evacuation plan was fairly conservative. In extreme circumstances, helicopters with squads of Marines for landing zone (LZ) protection could pick up passengers from points around Can Tho and in the provinces and fly them directly to Tan Son Nhut airport in Saigon for departure from the country.

If feasible, personnel could travel by road to Saigon. All would then join the fixed-wing airlift out of the country that the embassy would be directing. Additionally, Air America's old C-46 fleet might be free to fly passengers from Can Tho directly to Tan Son Nhut.

Not forgetting my feelings of responsibility for the consulate general's Vietnamese employees, Christian and I hammered out priorities regarding our Vietnamese staff. At the top of the list were people whose lives would almost certainly be in danger from a takeover. I had not forgotten the dreadful massacre that had taken place in Hue following the VC occupation at Tet in 1968. Among those in gravest danger, I concluded, would be the CIA personnel.

There were also people married to Americans, or with Amerasian children, who would obviously have pride of place. Then came those with relatives in the United States. And so on. The consular officer was at last able to begin screening his lists of people for potential evacuees without giving any hint that a plan existed. At this stage, I insisted that my staff do their planning in secret.

Once we were agreed, Christian and I made evacuation of Vietnamese employees a firm part of our plan. Fortunately, the mechanics of lifting people out looked fairly straightforward. Helicopters could rendezvous with groups of evacuees at a number of small, widely dispersed landing zones. Many of the LZs could be used only once. With tight security—no careless talking—Christian and I were reasonably sure that public knowledge of the evacuation would come too late for dangerous interference.

All the same, we wrote a warning into the plan: helicopters should fly low as they went out to sea or toward the capital. Otherwise Can Tho Airfield's radar would pick them up. This could bring about an angry ARVN reaction, we warned.

I submitted our plan with a caveat that we wished to include Vietnamese employees. Disagreement might ensue, but I knew enough about bureaucracy to calculate that the embassy would likely acquiesce if I remained firm. It was a game of attrition. You just had to be obstinate.

For the moment, our plan was merely drafted, not accepted. Nonetheless, it contained an element of realism. Without being able to speak of evacuation with them, I assumed that large numbers of Vietnamese employees would want to leave with the Americans.

The draft plan completed, I gazed approvingly at the last page and said, "That's pretty good work, Averill. We really could make it happen. It's easy to follow, our concept comes over clearly, yet it contains all the required detail."

Christian, though pleased with this praise, still seemed concerned. "Ours is all right," he finally volunteered, "but there is still a lack of coherent policy from Saigon."

"I thought the embassy had a tight grip on things," I replied.

"It doesn't seem that way to me," Christian answered.

"Now I'm getting worried."

"If Saigon has failed to give clear guidance to us," said Christian, "then we must assume that others have received equally unclear instructions. Have they, for instance, decided yet on a system of priorities to deal with non-American evacuees?"

"Good Christ! Disorganization could lead to total breakdown during an evacuation."

"Thank God this is still just a paper exercise." Christian sighed.

Preparation for the inspection continued. To my list of problems to be presented to the inspectors I added a note complaining about the lack of CIA adherence to unified control and coordination. I warned that such a lack of unity in a real crisis could result in disaster.

The senior inspector, Ambassador William Bradford, agreed, saying that he would take up the problem with the embassy leadership in Saigon and would include it in his report. Some months later, after the evacuation, Bradford sadly confided to me, "Your description of the problem with the CIA and your warning of its potential dangers are in the inspection files here in Washington. Too bad others did not take it more seriously before it was too late."

Part III

The Collapse

≡ 10 ≡

The Beginning of the End

It was March 1. Outside, the first cloud fortresses were sailing grace-fully overhead, advancing inland from the sea, warning of the coming of the monsoons to the Delta. That morning's cable traffic on my desk contained little that was eye-catching. I shoved the messages to one side. Instead, I examined another pile of papers in front of me. Trais-ter and the other officers out in twelve of the Delta's sixteen provinces were required to report regularly, in detail, on events in all provinces assigned to them.

This meant Cushing and I were always struggling to keep up with our reading. The advantage of regular visits to the provinces was that a few hours on the spot brought everything into perspective. After trips to the field, papers came alive when being read. Thankfully, with six months in Can Tho, I no longer had to plough through old files or ask numerous questions to fully understand a current problem. I was rapidly acquiring an institutional memory.

Finishing with the provincial reports, I quickly read through the col-lection of cables from Saigon and elsewhere. The only interesting item that morning was the report of a small village under attack at a cross-roads outside the town of Ban Me Thout in the highlands nearly four hundred miles northeast of Can Tho. It did not look too serious. The building up of communist divisions around Hue and Danang seemed more ominous. And those cities were almost as far away again from Ban Me Thout.

However, by next morning, the messages told a far more serious story. During the night, attacks had been made on several outposts between Pleiku, one hundred miles north of Ban Me Thout, and the coast. The situation now began to shape into a possible threat to the northern city. Three days later, reports told of an ARVN convoy being attacked on the road from Ban Me Thout north to Pleiku.

At the ARVN headquarters for MR II in Pleiku, the commander, General Phu, was undecided as to whether the threat was aimed at Ban Me Thout or simply a ruse to disperse his reserves before a main attack. Phu compromised. He sent a regiment southward from Pleiku to a position twenty-five miles north of Ban Me Thout. From there it could reconnoiter the hilly country and find out what the enemy was planning. It was a sensible precaution.

Another four days passed. Then, on March 8, a whole North Vietnamese division blocked the road between the ARVN regiment and Pleiku. General Phu was then under no illusions about what the communists were planning. They had isolated the garrison of Ban Me Thout and the recently deployed ARVN regiment from the rest of Phu's army.

Orders were given to airlift a further regiment into Ban Me Thout. But not enough helicopters were available close to the highland city for such a task. According to later accounts, only a single large helicopter was serviceable at Pleiku itself. The Americans could not help with Air America, because it would have meant breaking the peace agreement. Perhaps this should have been risked. To have done so, however, would have invited retribution from an increasingly angry and skeptical Congress.

For me, the crunch came on the morning of March 10. As usual, I came to the headquarters for General Nam's weekly briefing. Arriving outside the briefing room, I met Nam in the corridor where we shook hands quickly. The general gave only the hint of a smile, leaving no doubt that he was troubled. He never ceased talking rapidly to his deputy, too fast for me to follow their words. A corridor was hardly an ideal place to question the general. So I followed Nam and his deputy, General Hung, growing more concerned at each step, into the large, low-ceilinged room where the meeting would take place.

As on every Monday morning, the staff of South Vietnam's IV Corps were already assembled to present their weekly account of events, in tedious detail, to General Nam. The air conditioners hummed noisily as the waiting staff officers rose from their places down both sides of the horseshoe-shaped table. For at least the next hour their corps commander would sit though speaker after speaker. In formal Vietnamese, they would report all military actions, by both sides, plus an endless list of police arrests, statistics on logistics, the price of rice, and the myriad trivia that occupied the days of his corps's administrative tail. But for General Nam, this was his chart and compass. From this briefing and his daily sessions with the operations and intelligence staff, the general would perceive patterns. He would use these patterns as clues to see into the enemy's mind to read his intentions.

The principal staff officers were again seated. Each was a full colonel—a high rank in the South Vietnamese army. I had a place of honor at the closed end of the horseshoe to the general's right. At Nam's left was his deputy corps commander, now shuffling a few papers, talking anxiously to some other officers. I was puzzled. For some as yet unexplained reason, the room was full of tension.

Behind the main table sat various junior officers who would do the actual briefing; they were seated in groups around smaller tables. Normally Nam's entrance was a signal for silence. Today, the whole room continued to buzz with nervous conversation.

In front, the lectern stood empty, a large-scale map of the corps area as its backdrop. Nothing on the map had changed in a week, not dramatically, yet the chatter went on without halt.

No sooner was the silent, serious Nam comfortable in his chair than the chief of intelligence (G-2) went to the lectern. He stared rather blankly at a sheet of paper in his hand. Then, in a hushed, anxious voice, he announced that North Vietnamese forces had attacked Ban Me Thout in the central highlands of Military Region II.

The colonel hesitated for a second, as if he did not wish to believe his own words, before continuing, "Reports are as yet confused. But it appears the enemy is in the town itself in some force and has engaged elements of the 23rd Division."

Sitting at the general's right, I watched the concerned faces down either side of the room. This was serious. A major communist initiative had been expected since the successful attack on remote Phuoc Long Province in western III Corps near the Cambodian frontier. That had been back in January. But war moved slowly in Indochina. Both sides took time to develop moves on the battlefield.

Even so, I did not like the way Nam's G-2 had put it, for the NVA had clearly broken into the town and surprised the 23rd Division. He stepped down and resumed his seat. The conference passed on to the series of junior officers reporting the number of outposts attacked, roads mined, artillery rounds expanded, draft dodgers arrested, plus a host of other minutiae—their normal weekly diet. IV Corps's zone remained quiet. There was no need to be alarmed on that score.

But when I got back to my office, I immediately sought out Hank Cushing and gave him a terse account of what had been divulged by Nam's intelligence chief. Cushing listened in silence.

"What worries me, Hank," I concluded, "is that they are all on edge. You know, that funny Vietnamese nervousness."

Cushing knew exactly what I meant. Still, Hank was not overly concerned by Ban Me Thout. Other parts of the country were now being attacked. "Have you seen the latest stuff from Saigon?" he asked.

"Not since yesterday," I replied.

"I'll get them." In a few seconds Cushing was back clutching a folder of cables. He handed over the top three.

"Fighting in villages from Quang Tri to Hue. Tam Ky isolated, all roads to the coast sealed off in Quang Tin Province. Tri Tam overrun, just outside Tay Ninh. This looks like the beginning of some kind of general offensive," I opined.

"Still," said Cushing with some hope, "it's early days."

"Nonetheless, Hank, my instincts tell me to watch this developing battle closely." I thought for a moment, remembering my session with Christian only a month before, then said, "I had a nasty premonition after Phuoc Binh. Whatever happens up north, we must assume that no help will come from the United States."

"We can't intervene anyhow," Cushing remarked in a flat voice tinged with sarcasm. "It would be breaking the Paris Accords."

"I was thinking more of a situation where Vietnam got itself into big trouble, in danger of losing part of the highlands, or most of I Corps. Under present political circumstances in the United States, I assume that we still would not help."

"It won't come to that," Cushing replied cheerfully.

But the news got worse. I began using my telephone to Saigon more frequently. Nobody could say much on the open line. Yet it was certain that some dramatic event was about to shake the South Vietnamese. Traister's reports and my own efforts to help tighten security in Vinh Long and Vinh Binh had lost their immediacy. Colonel Vinh and his special command might soon find themselves fighting pitched battles for survival.

Our own situation in IV Corps, however, remained relatively sound. It would take a very large force of North Vietnamese troops to invade and occupy the vastly more densely populated farmlands of Cochin

China than to seize a narrow coastal strip, as the communists had tried, and eventually failed to do, in Quang Tri in 1972. If there was a danger point in this area, it was the narrow neck of land threatened by Northern Vietnamese troops in the Parrot's Beak. A substantial North Vietnamese effort there could cut off Saigon from its food supply. Yet I knew General Nam had taken all possible precautions to safeguard against this obvious threat.

By Friday, it was still not clear what was going on at Ban Me Thout, save that the ARVN's lack of hard news in itself hinted at some kind of serious defeat. But towns had been almost overrun before and still the ARVN had fought back, cleared out the enemy, and restored GVN control.

Over the weekend I planned to prepare my house for a St. Patrick's Day party on Monday evening. I had long intended to give the staff a party to boost morale. Fragmentary news from the north was unsettling everyone.

That Friday evening, I spoke to Hank Cushing before going home. There seemed no point in asking Saigon for more information. No doubt they would send what they had as soon as it became available. In any case, I should have a full rundown at Nam's Monday morning briefing. Cushing and I decided to meet in the morning; on Saturday we routinely worked until noon. However, next morning passed without any further hard news, good or bad. So everybody not on duty went home.

It was the regular news broadcast on Saturday evening that gave the first warning of a disaster already under way in the highlands. While the South Vietnamese could refrain from informing the American embassy of their decisions, they could not hide the resulting physical action, especially if it were on a major scale.

On Saturday, March 15, reporters had discovered that an evacuation of Americans and other foreign nationals was under way from Pleiku. With the departure of most American troops by 1972, the Armed Forces Vietnam television and radio station had been shut down. I was now depending for much of my news on the BBC and the Voice of America. Details were sketchy. I remember my first reaction to the radio news of an evacuation from Pleiku was that the newsmen must have gotten it wrong. But when I telephoned Cushing, who had spoken to some of his Vietnamese contacts, I had to accept that something very dramatic was taking place.

On Sunday morning I debated with myself whether to call Saigon. At that stage, the full extent of the debacle in the highlands was still unclear. No one outside II Corps or the embassy in Saigon had reason to guess that the reported evacuation from Pleiku included *all* official Americans. Given the paucity of hard information, it was difficult to determine the extent of North Vietnamese advances. As I was to find out subsequently, even the CIA and DAO in Saigon no longer knew which towns remained in GVN hands.

Monday morning produced little further clarification. General Nam was obviously not at ease, although the briefings stuck to the Delta. When I pressed the general, after the meeting, Nam confessed he was not at liberty to say much. More worried than ever, I called Saigon. My colleague at the other end of the line admitted something was afoot in II Corps, adding, "The Vietnamese are keeping their mouths shut tight— so far." He assured me that I would be informed as soon as the embassy had hard information. The St. Patrick's party went ahead. Little did I realize that it was to be the consulate general's last social event.

As the week progressed, the full truth became clear. Without informing, much less consulting his chief supporters—the Americans— President Thieu had embarked on the most difficult and dangerous military maneuver of all: withdrawal while engaging the enemy. Cushing and I could hardly believe that Thieu would be so foolish. The ARVN was rooted in the regions. Soldiers served in divisions that, except for the airborne and marine troops, never left their native regions. ARVN soldiers kept their families with them, or, if that was not possible, they were never more than a long bus ride from home. To order these peasant soldiers to abandon their relatives, their plots of land, and their family shrines was to remove the main reason they went on fighting.

Badly planned, the withdrawal from Kontum and Pleiku to the coast soon plunged into a rout. General Phu's army, trapped on an old logging trail between steep jungled hills, encumbered by thousands of frightened civilians, then bombed by its own air force, began to fragment. For any military formation, this is the kiss of death, the prelude to defeat in detail.

Next it was the turn of Hue, situated roughly halfway up the coast of the old Vietnam. Both Hue and Danang were defended by General Truong, who was I Corps commander, widely thought of as Vietnam's finest combat general. Poor Truong had been fighting the president as well as the North Vietnamese. Saigon desperately wanted to recall the airborne and marine divisions, its strategic reserves that were then in I Corps. Yet without them, Truong would have only three divisions against five or six on the communist side. Then came orders from Saigon. Shorten your lines; if need be, abandon Hue.

Loyally, Truong did his best, but again the soldiers saw positions, families, and homes being left behind; the elite of South Vietnam's army began to crack. On March 23, the North Vietnamese struck from the mountains, cutting Route 1 south of Hue. By the following afternoon Hue's defenses had collapsed. Marines, soldiers, and civilians began fighting each other in the surf, east of the city, for places in the rescue boats sent along the coast from Danang.

On the morning of March 25, an official GVN bulletin was issued stating that Hue had fallen. Fourteen big Russian rockets hit Danang. The great port city, second largest in Vietnam, was crammed with four times its already swollen population. There were now over two million souls seeking refuge among its acres of shantytowns, where many houses were built from ration cartons or flattened jerricans, where children played in the dirt and puddles, condemning themselves as yet another generation that must live and die with worms in their bellies. Into this teeming muddle of humanity came what was left of Hue's garrison, plus the remnants of other formations that had withdrawn from southern I Corps. Added together under a tough commander, they were still a potentially strong military force, but sadly, Truong was at this critical moment unable to impose order on disintegrating units.

Soul-searing reports of chaos in Danang began to reach me as all order in the city disintegrated. Later, I was to hear of the heroic efforts of my colleague, Al Francis, and his staff to maintain an organized evacuation in the face of mass panic. Indeed, Francis was within an ace of being killed as he tried to prevent several frightened Vietnamese marines from commandeering a barge that Francis had reserved for civilian evacuees. Fortunately, Francis had the Vietnamese bodyguard whom I had hired when in charge in Danang. "Bucky" Nghia reportedly jumped in front of Francis as a Vietnamese marine prepared to shoot and fired first, killing four or five marines while suffering a minor neck wound.

Danang was to be particularly sad for me. I had opened the post in 1969 and spent two and a half years there as the officer-in-charge of the consulate. The Vietnamese staff had been like a family for me. Indeed, I still maintain close relations with them and with their children.

Shaken by the dreadful accounts of the evacuation of Danang, I knew that all my previous planning would have to be changed, rethought at top speed. Two factors had altered dramatically. First, South Vietnam had suffered a military disaster of major importance. Second, ARVN soldiers were becoming scarce, therefore more precious, so even if the Vietnamese wanted desperately to help Americans escape, they were hardly likely to have troops to spare. But the awful truth was, there was little reason left for them to feel sympathy for an American's plight. Throughout the last terrible weeks, both Vietnamese and Americans had heard the stories of the highlands, Hue, and Danang. It was the Americans who got out—and the Vietnamese who were left behind.

A Sailor's Choice

Early Friday morning, March 28, Averill Christian walked through the door of my office with his latest revision of Can Tho's evacuation plan tucked under his arm. He was anguished by the news from Danang. Communist forces had already begun isolating the coastal towns of Qui Nhon and Nha Trang in II Corps. Nonetheless, for us the most pressing practical matter had been developing a new workable and inclusive evacuation plan.

I had not slept much the previous night. My mind would not slow down. This accumulating tiredness made proper rest even more elusive. Feeling I had aged ten years in two weeks, I greeted Christian with an irritated stare. "I suppose you've come to tell me that our plan has gone to shit," I growled.

Christian sat down grimly, laid the folder on my desktop, and said, "We have to take another look at our plan, Terry. Implementation may not be far off."

"Sorry," I apologized.

"Can I ask some questions first?"

"Go ahead," I grunted.

"First, are we liable to have a C-46, or other larger aircraft for a Delta evacuation?"

"I'm not certain," I said. "Nor am I convinced it's so wise. You heard about those terrifying scenes at the Danang airport."

"Are we still going to take out Vietnamese?"

"Indeed we are," I assured him.

Christian passed quickly to his third question. "Are we still planning on feeding our people into the main airlift leaving from Tan Son Nhut?"

"Not if they would be thrown into a gigantic Danang."

"Then it's choppers."

"Probably," I said.

"We'll never reach them all, Terry. Helicopters can ferry only so many people during a short amount of time. If we can't get military choppers, we will be dependent on Air America's fleet. Theirs are small and limited in number. We will get what Saigon can spare, and the calls on their flying hours in a real emergency," Christian ended blankly, "are going to be impossible to meet."

"As you know," I reasoned, "our plan calls for the Marine and navy helicopters to take people out directly from the Delta. However, this may not be a realistic possibility."

"Then we must reduce the numbers of potential evacuees," Christian shot back.

"Will we have interference from the Vietnamese?" I asked.

Christian shrugged. "I was rather hoping you, or Hank, could answer that."

"I wish we could, Averill, but I don't want myself or Hank asking that kind of question publicly. We could start a panic. Perhaps the best way of handling it is for you to have a discreet chat with the airfield commander. Just pretend that you are taking routine precautions. I know that sounds ridiculous, but do your best."

Once more I spent a weekend brooding, filled with a kind of frustrated gloom, growing more certain that some still undefinable calamity was coming.

By Tuesday—April Fool's Day—events had begun to flow faster than the hours. Nha Trang was abandoned. The scenes were harrowing, as they had been at Danang.

Now time seemed to stretch. In my notes from this period, the events during a single day are recorded as if they had occurred over several weeks.

Cushing and I were still agreed that, for the time being, there was very little danger of a military collapse in the Delta. The morning after Nha Trang, we talked over all aspects of the crumbling South Vietnamese defenses in central Vietnam. We were clear about North Vietnamese intentions. "We have the largest slice of agricultural land in IV Corps and over half the people still ruled from Saigon," I reasoned, "and three fresh ARVN divisions. The NVA will try to tie down these divisions in the Delta. They won't want strong reserves from here being thrown into battles north or east of Saigon."

Hank agreed with this assessment.

"Which means we have time—some time at least," I concluded.

"Correct," Hank nodded, "we must make the best use of this breathing space, move out a few people."

"We cannot," I insisted, "take out a whole office from any province without risking a dangerous reaction. But we can start to extract those employees who would be in the most danger from a communist government. Tell them to take small bags and just get their families to Can Tho or Saigon quietly. We'll need some form of priority list."

"For Vietnamese only, or Americans too?"

"Vietnamese. For the moment, Americans will remain. Which brings me to an unpopular order—no moving American personal effects either."

Cushing whistled through his teeth. "Some people will not like that, Terry."

I was unbending. "Thousands are at risk in this situation, Hank, not one or two individuals with classy stereo equipment."

"Steady," said Cushing calmingly. "I'm on your side. The fact that we may have to be firm doesn't rule out tact."

"Some of the staff only understand firmness, Hank."

"OK." Cushing decided to let the matter pass. "How many Vietnamese?"

I reviewed the numbers and said I had concluded we would never be given enough airlift to evacuate five thousand Vietnamese. I explained that we would need to categorize people according to those who would be in mortal danger—category A—and those who could make it in another culture based on work skills, education, linguistic ability, age, and size of family—category B.

The third category would be composed of people who were not likely to be in mortal danger and who would have trouble adapting to life in a foreign country. Manual laborers, guards, cleaning ladies, and the like would logically fall in this last group. Their American supervisors would have to decide who fell into the various categories.

"That sounds good so far, Terry, but what do we do once people are separated into categories?"

"I know this may seem heartless to some of our colleagues, but I reckon we must be realistic. Numbers must be reduced. At all costs, we must get out those in gravest danger. As a practical matter, we should concentrate on evacuating those in the first two categories. In any case, I am not convinced that we would be doing those in category C a favor by uprooting them and sending them off to a strange country where they would have great difficulty in supporting themselves and their families.

"Next, instruct all of our supervisors to quietly approach those in categories A and B to find out whether they wish to leave, if conditions warranted an evacuation and we had the means to carry it out. Under no circumstance should our guys mention any of this to those people in category C. We will consider evacuating them only after people in the first two categories have been taken care of. Then, if they want to go and we have the means, we can include them. By concentrating on evacuating those in the two higher categories, we should be able to reduce numbers to a more manageable size.

"Lists should be submitted to you, Hank. We can then start moving some people to Saigon and into Can Tho. This system of setting priorities should be included by Christian in our revised plan and communicated to Saigon. If the situation gets worse, we will start closing offices and pulling in Americans from the countryside. But reading the battlefield so far, the communists have their eyes fixed on Saigon. I think they're going right to the center for a kill."

"And the CIA?"

"Sure, inform Downs immediately, Hank. I just hope his bosses in Saigon do not have him on too tight a leash. We must stick together. It's going to be vital. Many of the most endangered employees work for him."

"This luggage rule, Terry . . ."

"What about it?"

"Do you mind if I say that no personal effects can be packed or shipped without your personal authority? It may end up meaning the same, but it will sound better."

Grudgingly, I relented. "All right, we could even try increasing the number of Air America flights between here and Saigon. Nothing obvious though, Hank, just enough to get people moving."

"Larry Downs thinks we should boost the number of flights dramatically."

"That would be stupid," I snapped. "It could panic the population, maybe even cause riots at the airport. The whole structure might collapse. Tell him nicely, Hank, that apart from the practical aspects of whether Saigon could handle such a flood, there are other, equally sensible reasons for caution. We don't want to upset the airport authorities or alarm the already-shaky civilian population and the nervous military. The best method, to my mind, is filtering people by road, so long as our road link with Saigon remains open. So let's think in terms of sending people to Saigon by road and on the regular Air America flights. A highly visible exodus by air is simply not a good idea. But we could increase the number of flights by one or two per week and augment the number of seats by using a slightly larger aircraft. Offices in the countryside may have to close soon. We can send the odd American on leave, call others here for consultations, give somebody else a girlfriend in Saigon. Lots of plausible reasons for moving three or four young men without showing our hand."

"Sure, I understand. What about Vietnamese here in Can Tho?"

"I want you to do the canvassing personally, Hank."

"Certainly."

"Maybe 'counseling' is a better word."

"Obviously, I'll start with the high-risk people. First of all, I have to determine who really wants to leave."

I nodded gratefully. "That's fine," I said. "The Vietnamese staff trusts you, Hank. What concerns me is that all those top-risk categories be able to make the decision as calmly as possible."

"I'll start today. My latest estimate is that we are down to around eight hundred people to evacuate, including families."

"How many of those worked for the CIA or are related to CIA employees?" I asked.

"Roughly three hundred."

"Then Larry must start canvassing as well."

What I feared most was a repeat of Nha Trang. As those who escaped reached Saigon and were subsequently debriefed, it became clearer what had actually taken place, and the story was not encouraging. The ARVN abandoned Nha Trang without any apparent immediate challenge from the enemy. When the helicopters were called in to evacuate the occupants of the American consulate general, a mob broke through its gates, disrupted the evacuation, preventing many of those waiting from boarding helicopters.

It was a panicky, premature evacuation, even by a single group, that I was determined to prevent; one mistake like that could slam the door shut on all the others. If such an exit were attempted, the population of

Can Tho would know within minutes. Mobs of panic-filled Vietnamese could besiege the consulate general. This had happened in Nha Trang and, unknown to me at the time, was to happen again in Saigon.

Even after Vietnamese were placed into categories, the numbers of potential evacuees remained a nightmare. They simply had to find another means of departure. The numbers of helicopters likely to be available to Can Tho were not likely to accommodate enough people in a short time. Never before in my life had I found responsibility a burden.

It was one night during that awful week after the fall of Nha Trang, while lying awake, that I realized we could all go down the Bas Sac River. There were plenty of arguments against the idea. Christian and I had gone over them several times when drafting earlier evacuation plans. For one thing, it was a voyage of seventy miles, and for much of the distance, both banks would more than likely be held by the Viet Cong. Once discovered, there was no cover and we would be in danger for at least ten hours, maybe longer. A mechanical breakdown could spell disaster. On top of all this, the only boats available were the CIA's small speedboats, which, though fast, could accommodate no more than six or seven people each and would be dangerous in the open sea beyond the river's mouth.

On April 9, I chaired one of my consulate general's routine staff meetings. Often, I would think aloud on such occasions, hoping that it would encourage the younger members of the staff to criticize and put forward their own ideas. That particular morning I began speculating about whether the South Vietnamese would manage to hold on to their new defense lines that stretched across the highlands from Cambodia to the coast near Phan Rang. Most were optimistic that they would.

Playing devil's advocate, I then raised the question, "What if they fail?" Saigon might well fall, I warned. Yet, so long as the ARVN could slip surviving formations down that narrow neck around the Parrot's Beak and into the safety of the Delta, it remained possible that South Vietnam would not surrender. In that event, should we evacuate from Can Tho? Indeed, if the communists conquered the whole Delta, should not a few Americans stay behind? Their presence could provide some insurance, no matter how flimsy, for the population. At a minimum, they might serve as credible witnesses of whatever came to pass. Some American presence might soften harsher communist measures. The American might be prisoners for a time, but the communists were unlikely to kill them out of hand. American prisoners had proven too valuable as bargaining chips in the recent past.

I invited comment. Discussion was brisk. Some of my staff thought the idea quite reasonable. Others were convinced that it would be offering a gift of American hostages to the North Vietnamese. Finally, I decided that a majority opposed the idea, and I moved on to deal with more routine matters.

When the meeting broke up, a grinning Cushing remained in my office. "What's so funny?" I inquired.

"You scared the shit out of them—well, some of them, Terry."

"How?"

"That talk about staying behind."

"That was merely speculation. We've got to think of all sorts of possibilities—and the idea isn't so stupid."

"Is the staff getting edgy?"

"Some."

"In that case I'd better knock it off."

His smile gone, Cushing informed me that General Truong, the former I Corps commander, was on an inspection tour of the Delta. "Our sources at ARVN Corps Headquarters say the president wants to know if there is any realistic hope of holding on down here."

"Really!"

"Truong's buzzing around in a chopper right now."

"When did he arrive?"

Cushing lit a cigarette. "Vinh wouldn't say. But I got the impression that Truong had been down here roughly two days. Vinh sounded as if Truong were leaving tomorrow."

"No idea what he will recommend?"

"Reporting only to the president. Even Nam won't know. Vinh would not hold back, if he knew. It's too serious now."

"Then we had better assume a negative report and push ahead with filtering people to Saigon."

"Afraid so, Terry."

"I've been doing some calculations, Hank," I told Cushing as I paced the floor. "I don't believe we are going to have enough choppers for evacuating all our people. In an emergency we would have to accept what Saigon can spare. Frankly, I am coming to fear that we could be vulnerable to the kind of horror story we saw last week at Nha Trang. How does one play God? I don't want to try. I want a feasible evacuation scheme worked out that allows us both space for significant numbers and reasonable safety. Boats may be the only alternative that provides these features."

Cushing drew on his cigarette, exhaled, then said, "We'd need something big."

"But you don't think I'm crazy?"

Cushing grinned once more. "Not about the boats."

"OK." I laughed, feeling a wave of relief. Cushing's calm, hardheaded opinion was likely to be the best endorsement I could get.

"Could we buy boats?" asked Cushing.

"Have to be done very discreetly, Hank."

"Who would do it?"

"Leave that to me," I replied. "I think it's just the thing for Jim Tully and Paul Mendes." Both were with the JCRC (Joint Casualty Recovery Command). Mendes was still a captain with the army's Special Forces but in civilian clothes on temporary assignment. "I just hope they don't try stealing the river ferry." I laughed. Little did I suspect that it would be their first plan.

I went home on Friday night, hoping that the weekend of April 11 and 12 would bring some quiet.

Instead, Can Tho City was bombarded on the night of April 11. At home in my bedroom, I heard a heavy whoosh pass overhead. Then solid explosions rocked the house. Rockets. More explosions shook the house. These sounded different, harder, more like a loud, sharp crack, but very big. I grabbed my radio and ran downstairs to find my servants and their families terrified. I quickly hustled them into a corner of the living room away from windows and under the heavy concrete stairway. This seemed the safest place in the house. Only a direct hit was likely to harm them there.

The bombardment went on for nearly thirty minutes. A huge swish would pass through the night sky. Seconds later, the ground trembled from the shock of a booming explosion. I tried in vain to raise Hasty on the radio. Finally, the bombardment was over.

When Hasty got through to me, it was with a report that both rockets and artillery had been pumped into the city. Fires had been lighted and threatened to do more damage than shells or rockets.

I summoned Phuoc to get the car. I was going to the consulate general to assess the damage and send out a report to Saigon and to Washington on the bombardment.

Fires raged throughout the night among the rickety, closely packed wooden houses in the center of the town. Winds carried the flames toward the consulate general complex. I went to the rooftop to direct

Marines and other members of the staff spraying water on the roofs of the consulate general building. I ordered David Sciacchitano, the vice consul, to move a gasoline truck from the parking lot located next to the main office building. As the winds carried flames closer to the consulate general, the ever-keen Hasty volunteered to scramble to the pitched roof on the far side of the buildings facing the fire to hose the most exposed part of the roof. Others stamped out burning bits landing on the roof where we were standing before they could ignite the tarred surface. Raging fires were approaching the last line of houses behind the consulate general. It seemed doubtful that the office building would be saved. Providentially, the wind suddenly died and a soaking rain began to fall. The fires went out of their own accord, and the consulate general suffered no more than a scorched roof.

Tired Americans went below to my office to sip welcome coffee and to assess the damage, both physical and moral. Many people were killed, far more wounded, hundreds were homeless, and the entire population of the city was made very nervous. The ARVN reported that recently captured 105mm guns from Vinh Long were now being turned on their former owners from across the wide river.

On Monday morning, reports from Downs and his staff indicated they were convinced that the bombardment was yet further evidence to prove their contention that no fewer than six North Vietnamese regiments were in position north of Can Tho. The CIA believed an attack on the city was now imminent. Yet my Vietnamese sources, particularly Nam and Vinh, remained just as certain that the story was part of a communist disinformation effort, a rumor designed to keep ARVN reserves in the Delta while the main battle raged at Xuan Loc, a rubber plantation town about sixty miles east of Saigon. The bombardment was done with guns captured by relatively small units operating in Vinh Long incapable, without large-scale reinforcement, of posing any real threat to Can Tho. Besides, they would have been on the opposite side of an almost mile-wide river and hardly in a position to mount an attack on the city.

Polgar, CIA station chief in Vietnam, suddenly arrived from Saigon on Tuesday morning. He attempted to calm Downs and his staff. Polgar is said to have told them of a possible negotiated peace and to have raised the possibility of a truncated embassy staff staying in Saigon even with a change of government. Under pressure, Polgar is alleged to have agreed to Downs's evacuating some of the CIA's Vietnamese personnel to Phu Quoc Island off the southern coast. Following my orders, Downs had already moved his Americans into Can Tho from the countryside, with some sent to Saigon.

At no time during this visit was I aware of Polgar's presence in Can Tho. This was most unusual. Senior officials do not normally visit Foreign Service posts without informing the officer-in-charge. I can only conclude that Polgar wanted to hide his presence from me for some unfathomable reason. Whatever the outcome of his meeting with Polgar, Downs maintained his reluctance to share his troubles with me.

Information from Saigon continued to be scarce and frighteningly indefinite. On one hand, there was talk of the possibility of some sort of political settlement or armistice. Certainly I could not rule out such a possibility on the basis of the sketchy information that was then available to me in Can Tho. At the same time, there was talk of making a stand in Saigon. In any case, my planning for evacuation went ahead, as the NVA's offensive was temporarily blocked by stiff resistance from the 18th ARVN Division at Xuan Loc, almost sixty miles east of Saigon. It was obvious that I needed better information and clearer instructions.

After weeks of planning and worrying, Terry McNamara convinced the U.S. embassy in Saigon to allow him to evacuate the Can Tho consulate's Vietnamese employees by boat. On April 29, 1975, the loaded LCM (landing craft, mechanized) headed toward the South China Sea along the Bas Sac River.

A CIA motor boat races back toward the CIA compound. The CIA operatives in Can Tho would evacuate via helicopter, leaving behind many of their employees, who were rescued by McNamara and his crew.

The LCM's well deck packed with Vietnamese families.

Hank Cushing, deputy consul general, barks orders as tow ropes are tied from the LCM to the consulate's disabled rice barge. The passengers on the barge were later transferred to the LCMs.

Province representative Robert Traister behind McNamara, at the helm. As a joke, the consulate's Marine guards had given McNamara a helmet liner inscribed "Commodore, Can Tho Yacht Club," and he wore it to help keep spirits up.

Province representative "Kass" Kassebaum watches over the Vietnamese refugees on the LCM.

Commodore Thang (at right) speaks with McNamara. The Vietnamese navy had stopped the consulate's flotilla and held them for two hours. Because McNamara had earlier arranged for Thang's family to leave Vietnam, Thang allowed the boats to continue along the river.

One of Thang's sailors bids a tearful farewell to his father and returns to Thang's launch.

Walt Heilman, the consulate's general services officer, rests a moment during his tense, hectic day.

The Vietnamese devise makeshift shelters for their families as rain begins to fall.

Heilman and administrative officer Averill Christian (right) with the consular flag.

Nearing the mouth of the river, Marine Sgt. John
Kirchner fixes the consular flag on the LCM's bow.

CIA-owned Air America helicopter in Can Tho. During the U.S. evacuation, the CIA in Can Tho used these helicopters to evacuate themselves, rather than sending them to Saigon, where they were desperately needed.

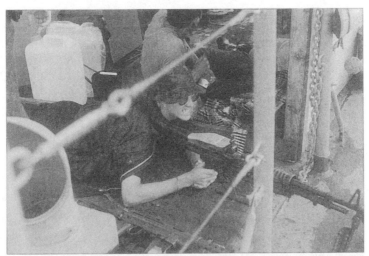

As the boats traveled along the Bas Sac River, they faced enemy fire. The Americans fired back—perhaps the last shots fired by Americans in the Vietnam War. Here S.Sgt. Boyette Hasty aims an M-60 as the LCM navigates a narrow stretch of the river.

Members of the Can Tho consulate staff on April 30, 1975, on the bow of the Japanese tug *Chitosa Maru* that would take them to a Korean LST (landing ship, tank), the *Booheung Pioneer.*

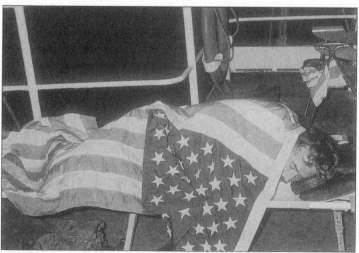

Aboard the Korean LST, an exhausted and cold Hank Cushing sleeps wrapped up in a U.S. flag.

After several difficult days at sea, the staff of the Can Tho consulate makes it to a U.S. Navy ship, the USS *Blue Ridge*. From left are Kassebaum, Heilman, and Cushing.

McNamara faces the press aboard the *Blue Ridge*.

Province representative Thomas Odell and consular officer David Sciacchitano on the dock at the Subic Bay naval base in the Philippines.

Most Vietnamese who wanted to leave Vietnam were not as lucky as those under McNamara's charge. From the safety of the *Pioneer Contender*, the Can Tho staff saw several refugee boats such as these still seeking rescue.

≡ 12 ≡

Preparations

On April 14, I was summoned to an urgent meeting at the defense attaché's offices at Tan Son Nhut outside Saigon. This collection of huge gray buildings set behind a high wire fence had been the military headquarters from which Generals William Westmoreland and Creighton Abrams had commanded half a million Americans. Now it was used by Gen. Homer Smith and his staff. I had the feeling of walking into a house without furniture. Gone were the hundreds of officers and soldiers who once had hurried down its corridors and filled the countless now-empty offices.

My eyes still adjusting after the bright sunshine, I walked into a refrigerated conference room. Jake Jacobson, mission coordinator, and the service attachés from the embassy were the only faces I recognized. Quickly I shook hands with the embassy's army and air force attachés. A navy commander, a Marine colonel, and an air force colonel from Thailand were also present. When I introduced myself, the naval officer and the Marine explained that they were from a fleet task force that was then offshore, just over the horizon, ready to assist in a final evacuation. It was a sobering moment.

Jacobson, as chairman of the meeting, worked through the Can Tho plan. Jake was still convinced fixed-wing aircraft were the best way to evacuate Can Tho. I was skeptical.

Bordering on the Delta was Cambodia, where, save for Phnom Penh, the country was occupied by Khmer Rouge and North Vietnamese.

Phnom Penh's expectations of survival could now be measured in hours rather than days. As the meeting progressed, all these factors were thrashed out. The air force colonel suddenly declared that he wished to make it quite clear that, until "Eagle Pull" was completed, all resources were being held in reserve.

"Eagle Pull?" I asked.

"Evacuation of Phnom Penh from the sky," explained the colonel.

Jacobson's first question was for me. "Before any further discussion—how many people do you have now, Terry?"

"On March 25, we had two hundred ninety-one Americans and third-country nationals. Subsequently, over two hundred have been sent out through Saigon. Averill Christian and Dave Sciacchitano estimate we will be down to thirty-six Americans and TCNs by the end of this month."

"That's not bad."

"My people have worked long hours. It's surprisingly hard to persuade some people they should leave. Those figures, of course, do not include Vietnamese," I added. Nobody reacted. However, the point was made, and for the moment I chose to bide my time.

Then those round the table began sorting out the technical details of an evacuation. The fleet representatives were still fixated on helicopters. A lengthy dialogue on helicopter loads ensued. Vietnamese are generally lighter than Americans. If fuel was kept low, then much larger loads could be carried. In certain circumstances the pilots were willing to risk almost double normal figures, which for a Huey could mean fifteen people instead of eight. Many more could be accommodated in the larger Marine choppers. There were questions about flight patterns. Helicopters should stay low so that bystanders could not guess precisely where they were going to land.

Communications were worked out. Frequencies being given were valid for the whole evacuation; we need only use the right one and every ship or aircraft in the task force would hear us. If radio failed, there were smoke grenades or even mirrors that could be used to send signals from an LZ in the countryside. Listening to the learned, professional discussion on communications was enough to convince me that I had only limited knowledge of such arcane matters. Of particular relevance, I had not been aware that to call the navy would involve knowing the fleet's frequencies for that particular day. The whole system sounded very sophisticated. To my relief, it was agreed that the assistant military attaché from the embassy, a Lieutenant Colonel Silva, would come to Can Tho within two days to assist us with our radio problems.

I then decided to raise the possibility of leaving by water. Jacobson would have none of it. Too great a risk to American lives, he argued. I pleaded that water evacuation must be treated as a serious alternative, reminding them of what had taken place farther north. Kindly, though firmly, Jacobson told me that he was not willing to permit evacuation down the river. He could not take the chance with American lives. I refused to accept this decision. Finally, after a long and sometimes heated discussion, Jacobson relented, at least allowing planning to start on a contingency basis.

Turning to the officers from the task force, I told them that I needed two things if we should go by boat: air cover and a ship at the mouth of the Bas Sac. While they could not promise the first, both officers thought the second request was not difficult to satisfy. A debate started about what type of ship could go close enough inshore. "How will we find the ship?" I asked.

"They'll see you on radar," came the confident reply. The Marine colonel then gave a firm promise that a navy ship would be off the mouth of the Bas Sac if a downriver evacuation was attempted.

My part in the meeting ended. After a last word with Lieutenant Colonel Silva, I flew straight back to Can Tho.

Phnom Penh fell that Thursday, April 17. With the American flag tucked under his arm, John Gunther Dean, last U.S. ambassador in a ruined Cambodia, was rescued from his beleaguered embassy by a force of U.S. Marines landed by helicopter in the garden.

On Sunday, April 20, in Can Tho, I gave firm orders to all agencies and section heads that they should now send Vietnamese employees to be evacuated to Saigon. As many as possible were to be sent by road, as long as the roads remained open. Christian and Heilman developed a plan to discreetly augment the number of seats on Air America flights by using a larger C-46 aircraft and increased the number of flights per week. Orders went out closing provincial offices on a staggered schedule. Their Vietnamese personnel in priority categories were told to leave quietly for Saigon or Can Tho. At all costs, nothing was to be done that might further undercut Vietnamese goodwill or panic the population.

Next day, the Xuan Loc front collapsed. Forty thousand North Vietnamese troops with tanks and artillery began moving down an open road toward the capital. No major South Vietnamese units were left to bar the way. That evening President Thieu made a two-hour speech on television. It culminated with his resignation.

The next morning, I summoned Christian to my office. The retired colonel gave a swift report on personnel movements out of our consular district. It was going smoothly and well.

"What about the CIA?" asked Cushing.

"They've drastically reduced their American staff," replied Christian, who was obviously very tired, "but cannot obtain approval for movement of their Vietnamese employees. Larry says he can't project his personnel strengths, because it has to be approved in Washington and Saigon."

"Let's sort this out, Hank," I said. "We're starting to run out of time."

Cushing and I asked Downs to come to my office. I informed him that Vietnamese were no longer to wait, the decision to hold back locals from evacuation had been reversed, and now he was to begin quietly moving high-priority Vietnamese to Saigon. I told Downs he could start immediately.

Christian and Sciacchitano were dispatched to Saigon the following morning. Their orders were simple: find out how the evacuation system worked at Tan Son Nhut. I wanted people leaving Can Tho to get through quickly. It was not selfish; it would help avoid clogging the organization the DAO had set up on the air base. That Wednesday was perhaps the worst day they could have chosen for a visit to the capital. With Thieu's resignation, the numbers of Vietnamese wishing to flee had doubled. Tan Son Nhut, and Saigon itself, were both charged with the ugly electricity of potential mass panic.

When the two men returned, nervous, upset, full of first- and secondhand stories describing the dreadful scenes in the last hours of Danang and Nha Trang, I decided that I must assess the situation myself. Taking Kass with me, I flew up to Saigon the next morning.

It was a windy but sunny day, with fragments of fluffy clouds scattered over the Delta. From the helicopter all below was lush, the rich, flat greens growing darker with the promise of monsoon rain. Four people were on board: a girl from the accounts section who was to collect enough cash from the embassy to pay all staff salaries in a last emergency, Kass, the Air America pilot, and me.

The flight had begun with an argument. I was in a hurry, but the pilot was worried. He would not fly direct to Saigon because of reports that antiaircraft missiles were being launched at airplanes and helicopters. So we went the long way round, over a thick brown Bas Sac River, past the tip of Kien Hoa Island with its deep swamps fringed by coconut groves, where the communists had landed arms for more than twenty years, out over an azure spray-flecked South China Sea, then inland toward Saigon. The Huey passed high above the oil storage tanks and the filthy hovels, brothels, and bars of Nha Be. Then I saw ships lying alongside the Saigon riverfront, five miles of rooftops stretching in hideous confusion, thinly wooded parks, and the old, red brick cathedral with its twin spires. We began to descend.

Down over the houses and frantic traffic we slid, skimming treetops, the bunkerlike facade of the president's Independence Palace approaching steadily as we flew level toward the flat roof of the embassy. The cathedral and its busy traffic circle flashed past on our right. Then I felt the skids settle on America's white concrete fortress. I slid open the helicopter door and stepped out into a blustery wind. With a last glance at the pilot, I led the way from the roof down into the embassy.

Jacobson's office was on the same floor as Ambassador Martin's, several floors below the roof. It was full of mementos. There were signed photographs on the walls of nearly every famous—or infamous—personality and politician who had been involved with Vietnam during the previous dozen years. Most of the bookshelves were jammed with plaques and miniature flags. I glanced round the room. Some of the Vietnamese and Americans in the pictures were people I knew. I noticed John Paul Vann's picture, serving perhaps as silent reminder that all too many in this portrait gallery were dead.

Within minutes, I realized that Jacobson and I were still in total disagreement over the water evacuation plan. In the friendliest way, he repeated his objections to the idea because of its risk to American lives. It was a question of judgment, he said. Finally, he advised me to see the ambassador. There was no rancor. We simply could not agree.

Martin, for once, was available when I asked to see him. Every other time, save one, during the past eight months he had been absent or busy when I had been in Saigon. There was nothing deliberate about this—it simply always turned out that way.

Eva Kim, Martin's much-respected personal secretary, ushered me into the spacious office. Quickly I explained my problem. "No Vietnamese?" The ambassador jumped up. "Let's go and see Lehmann." And he rushed, with me close behind, to the DCM's office next door. "Who told Terry he cannot take his Vietnamese?" demanded the ambassador before I could explain the problem to the bewildered deputy chief of mission. "Tell Jacobson that it's OK," said Martin. And with that, just as abruptly, he left.

Again I went over the whole story. Lehmann at last understood. He agreed a river trip was rational. He telephoned Jacobson, tactfully informed him that the water option was approved, then advised me to talk to the commodore of the Vietnamese navy in Can Tho.

"Buy his friendship, Terry," continued Lehmann, who while he served as consul general in Can Tho had become acquainted with Commodore Thang. "His goodwill could be very useful. He is unlikely to turn down an offer to quietly evacuate his family from Saigon."

The discussion over, I went back to see Jacobson. Apologizing for being so persistent, I recounted exactly what had happened, with both Martin and Lehmann. I respected and trusted Jacobson and would not have wanted Jacobson to think I had misquoted or misrepresented anything he had said.

I need not have worried. Jacobson had guessed the sequence of events. As I turned for the door, Jacobson warned that "Martin could still change his mind if circumstances were bad enough. In that case, it would have to be Americans only and by helicopter."

I nodded. My brain should have registered the warning, but it did not. I was too pleased at that moment. Downstairs, at the embassy's rear entrance, I found Kass admiring the sturdy old tamarind tree shading the rear compound. Its boughs moved gently, and its leaves rustled.

We got into a car I had ordered from the embassy's motor pool. It was now too late for a return flight to Can Tho. We would stay overnight at USAID's VIP guest house and leave first thing in the morning.

First, I drove Kass to a safehouse where Lacy Wright and Art Kobler were busy collecting people for evacuation. To my relief, I found that my faithful cook from Danang, Chi Lieu, was just about to leave with her children for Tan Son Nhut. I waded through a crowd of Vietnamese, deafened by screams of excitement, laughter, and some tears, to confirm all were safe and in reasonable health. I was so occupied talking and listening—time was very short—I almost failed to notice a Vietnamese doctor from Can Tho whom I had sent north by road to be evacuated. The doctor had his family and luggage ready in the yard. He was president—or had been—of the Vietnam-America Association of Can Tho. When I fondly kissed my old cook and her children good-bye, the doctor's wife was shocked to the point of horror. Imagine! Kissing one's servants! Lieu and her family were put into a car. I watched little Ha, rosy cheeks, gaps in her teeth from a fall, radiating an adult charm even at five, scramble onto the car's back seat for a journey whose length was beyond her young imagination. She had no fear—simply an expression of puzzled curiosity. Then Kass and I jumped into our car and headed the opposite way, back into town.

Curfew in Saigon was at eight in the evening. I drove hurriedly back toward the center of town and parked outside La Cave, until recently a fine French restaurant, now a shadow of its elegant past. Kass and I studied the sparse menu. Outside little traffic passed in the street. Very few people walked by the windows. Kass called over a jittery Vietnamese waiter.

Service was slow, but the well-cooked meal came as a surprise under the circumstances. When it was time to leave, the old Corsican proprietor, a relic of colonial days, opened his swinging door on to the hot street. He apologized for the slow service and bade me farewell with a sad embrace.

Next morning when we left Saigon, an atmosphere of tense gloom hung over the city. The dark clouds of the coming rainy season added a threatening sense of foreboding. Nobody knew who would pick up the burden of the presidency; neither did anyone know what was happening farther east near Xuan Loc. A whole country was being eaten alive.

Now the jaws were closing on its heart and head. Although I did not see many people on the streets, I was told that the city was full of refugees. Occasionally Kass and I heard the distant thud of gunfire. White-shirted policemen, visible symbols of authority, still stood on the street corners directing traffic and smoking cheap cigarettes, as they had done for years. It was a peculiar, ugly situation. Saigon was existing in a cruel form of purgatory, somewhere between life and death.

Both of us felt a wave of relief as our helicopter lifted off. Kass wondered aloud, as we flew southward, what the next few days would bring. I remarked curtly that the future was of marginal interest compared with the present.

In Can Tho next evening, I discussed the hourly worsening situation with Hank Cushing over drinks. We were now working nonstop, sometimes for eighteen hours at a stretch, but still with insufficient time to check and double-check each job, each move, each order, trying desperately to avoid that single mistake that could cause collective disaster.

"By the way," Cushing remarked, "I sent Warren Parker, Willie Saulter, and Jaime Valdez to Saigon now that we have closed My Tho, Muc Hoa, and Soc Trang. They were told to help the Vietnamese we are sending up from MR IV to get through the evacuation processing at Tan Son Nhut. Then they should leave themselves."

"That sounds great to me, Hank. It is just what is needed to get our people through that zoo at the airport."

Remembering an incident at the embassy the day before, I mentioned that Al Francis had offered to come down to Can Tho to advise us on evacuation planning.

"That was kind," Hank responded.

"Yes, it was. Nevertheless, I turned him down. The poor guy has been through a terrible experience in Danang. I doubt he could help us here. Danang was caught unawares by the suddenness of the NVA offensive. We have had more time to prepare. Our situation is not similar to that in Danang, as long as we avoid panic. I found out long ago that there is nothing more contagious than fear. I don't want people who were in Danang or Nha Trang coming here telling tales of the dreadful things that happened to them up there. That's what is now going on in Saigon, and they are scaring the shit out of many of the fainter hearts. I don't understand why Martin doesn't send them home now."

Cushing agreed, then added, "Did you know that Larry has some visitors who have come down from the north? I gather they are spreading just those kinds of horror stories and frightening the spooks shitless."

I exploded. "We're supposed to be filtering people out—not bringing them in! Moreover, I forbade all sections of the consulate general from bringing anyone to Can Tho who had been in other parts of the country. Having just seen Saigon, my forebodings were absolutely right. Many of these people are traumatized and are more likely to spread fear than give useful advice."

Adroitly changing the subject, Cushing asked what had taken place at the embassy the day before.

"I won," I said with a smile.

"No strings, no conditions?"

"Jake was very much against it. Martin overruled him; said we can take our Vietnamese and go by boat. Lehmann is in agreement too. But Jake is still not convinced. He thinks that Martin could change his mind. Even when I left his office, Jake warned again that we might have to face leaving by helicopter taking Americans only."

"Otherwise?"

"We are promised by the guys from the fleet that a ship will be at the mouth of the Bas Sac to pick us up."

Cushing almost cheered. We could now plan in the reasonably secure knowledge that means would be available to allow all Vietnamese employees who ought to leave to depart with us.

"Now, I have a surprise for you," remarked Cushing, cheerfully waving his glass. "Christian says we have two LCMs that were prepared to carry supplies to Cambodia. They were of no use to USAID after Phnom Penh fell."

As Cushing described them to me, the LCMs—an acronym that stood for landing craft, mechanized—were just over fifty feet long with a fourteen-foot beam and drew a little more than four feet of water. Most of the armored, slab-sided boats were taken up by an open well deck meant to carry trucks or even a small tank. There was a ramp at the bow. They were powered by a pair of 450-horsepower diesel engines. "Cliff Frink sent them to us from Saigon," Cushing added. "That means we can easily take five hundred people."

"This is great news!"

"To formalize the relationship, Christian 'leased' them from Cliff's USAID logistics setup," explained Cushing. "The boats really belong to Alaska Barge and Towing Company. In addition, Tully and Mendes want to purchase a rice barge."

"No objection to that."

Cushing and I continued to discuss the use and preparation of the newly acquired landing craft. Prudently, we decided to locate the boats at different riverside sites.

One LCM and a venerable rice barge were to be placed at the Delta Compound dock. The other LCM would be left at the deep-water dock next to the Shell Oil fueling installation. There it would be easily accessible to the American housing complex at "Palm Springs" and the CIA billeting complex across the road. Three guards would be watching each craft on a twenty-four-hour schedule. "What about supplies?" I inquired warily.

"Walt Heilman's sorting out the fuel, water, and food, mainly C rations, for all three boats," Cushing assured me.

Heilman was also pulling together other potentially useful equipment, such as flares, extra rope, and first-aid kits. Hasty and his Marines were busying themselves with more martial needs.

Christian had persuaded Cliff Frink to send two experienced Vietnamese crews to man the LCMs. Heilman produced two long-shaft outboard motors to propel the rice barge. He also found experienced boatmen among his work crews to navigate it.

Cushing and I were relieved to have real sailors with professional experience. "There was no point in taking LCMs without crews," Cushing said flatly. "Luckily, both Vietnamese LCM crews know the tricky channels of the Bas Sac. Later, we might even find ourselves on the open sea." Little did Hank know how prophetic his words would turn out to be.

≡ 13 ≡

The Final Hours

Now came the balancing act. Too early a withdrawal from the remaining provincial offices might collapse the whole South Vietnamese structure in the Delta, moving too late could risk loss of personnel. I continued to include in my planning an evacuation-by-air option. The warning time, if long enough, might permit a lift out by fixed-wing aircraft or large helicopters, if they were available. When Christian discussed the use of the airport for evacuation with the airport commander, however, the commander's reaction had been discouraging. The VNAF colonel told Christian politely, but bluntly, that he would close the airport to the consulate general rather than allow Vietnamese to be evacuated from his base. The argument in favor of boats grew steadily stronger.

The whole staff worked longer and longer hours. Gradually, the water evacuation plan took on substance, as well as definition. The boats arrived quietly in Can Tho. They had been refitted, for the dangerous supply run upriver to Phnom Penh, with a protective concrete collar around the engine room. I was assured that not even a B-40 rocket could penetrate the collar and knock out the engine.

The boats' fuel tanks were filled as part of a deal I had made with the Vietnamese Shell Oil manager. Our arrangement also provided for him to remain until the Americans finally left, to ensure control of gasoline supplies vital to the ARVN. In return, I had also arranged for his family to be evacuated earlier through Saigon. Finally, the manager was assured of a place with the last departing Americans.

The tide on the river worried me. This could be especially important at the Delta Compound, where the dock was left high and dry at low tide. The best moment to sail was as the tide began to ebb. This would give us a considerable increase of speed going downriver. Yet we had no assurance that Saigon would order evacuation at the right time of day.

A further deal was made with Shell's Vietnamese employee in charge of the petroleum storage tanks. This man lived next to the Shell dock, next door to the consulate general's Palm Springs apartments and across the street from the main CIA living quarters. There was a double advantage in berthing one LCM at the Shell dock; not only did it have deep water at all times of the day, but in an emergency many potential passengers would have only a short walk from their homes to the boat. I quietly informed the tank farm manager that, providing he kept quiet and upheld his side of the bargain, there would be space on the LCM for him and his family. The manager accepted the offer without question. Practical necessity demanded that such deals be concluded.

Boat assignments were included in our planning. I would be in charge at Delta Compound, where the tide risk was greatest. *Delta Queen,* the rice barge, would be in the capable hands of Hank Cushing and Walt Heilman. The Shell storage-tank man and his family, the CIA personnel, and most of the Vietnamese personnel and their families who had come to Can Tho from the provinces and were now lodged at Palm Beach would leave from the Shell dock. This boat was under control of a former lieutenant commander from the Vietnamese navy, who was the senior person among the boats' Vietnamese crewmen.

The second LCM at Delta Compound would carry the remainder of the American staff, who would have last-minute jobs destroying papers and equipment around the consulate general, most of the Vietnamese staff of the consulate general at Can Tho designated for evacuation, plus all stragglers. No matter how detailed our plans, somebody inevitably would be late, forget, panic, or rush back for somebody or something. The five Marines also would be with me at Delta Compound, divided between the rice barge and my LCM.

The number of people involved was now much clearer. The consular officer, David Sciacchitano, had worked long hours to trace local residents with U.S. passports, relatives in the United States, or others with close American connections. In particular, he searched out Amerasian children of American fathers. This activity was a straightforward case of giving an American, or dependent relatives of an American citizen, normal consular help. I had now come to the painful conclusion that there was never going to be sufficient space, not even on three boats, for several thousand evacuees. My decision to concentrate on evacuating those in A and B categories had to be upheld. No special effort would be made to evacuate those in C category unless there was enough extra room and they could be easily accommodated on the boats. However, they would be paid in full before the Americans departed.

The CIA remained a headache. Larry Downs's staff now insisted that an NVA division was poised south of Can Tho and other strong forces were threatening from the north, ready to sweep through the city on short notice. This kind of talk spread fast. A nervous CIA officer even appealed to me for immediate evacuation "before the communists came pouring into Can Tho." At the time, I was convinced the city was in no imminent danger of being attacked, much less overrun.

Fortunately, ARVN corps headquarters remained calm and fully informed. Nam had a strong staff, Vinh was especially cool and steady—courageous, considering the dreadful news coming daily from other parts of the country. Nam did not accept rumors—which the local CIA were inclined to believe—about the communists being poised to take over the region's main centers, the province capitals, the district towns, and Can Tho itself. Indeed, the CIA operatives in My Tho, the Delta's second-largest city, abandoned their compound, fleeing in panic to Saigon after hearing rumors of an impending "human-wave" attack.

Because of the reassuringly calm attitude of the ARVN leadership, I agreed to leave Traister in Vinh Long over the final weekend. The deputy province chief had begged that Traister be allowed to attend his own farewell party. I agreed but did not relax until Traister arrived in Can Tho, even though I was convinced that I had made the right decision.

There were, however, lighter moments. Toward the end, I called in Sergeant Hasty and explained that evacuation probably would be down the river. The Marine sergeant's eyes brightened. He announced sternly, "It sounds dangerous, sir, but no guts, no glory!" My mouth dropped open as Hasty did an about-face and marched from the room.

Other moments were far less amusing. Cushing came to me one morning looking extremely agitated. By accident he had learned that the CIA was not sticking to my rule concerning the packing and shipping of personal effects. Indeed, they had largely ignored the instruction, even ordering special Air America fixed-wing flights from Saigon for their belongings. This was being noticed by nervous Vietnamese, who had brought it to Cushing's attention. Disgusted, I prepared for another disagreement with Downs. I did not want it, not at such a crucial time, but I had to challenge Downs's unauthorized change of policy on flights, especially in light of Christian's conversation with the airport commander. I could not allow a breakdown in discipline.

At 9:00 A.M., Sunday, April 27, Jacobson telephoned from Saigon. As usual, Jake came straight to the point. Did I know anything about a mass helicopter evacuation from Can Tho? Admiral Benton, the officer in charge of the naval aspects of the general evacuation, had asked Jacobson about a CIA request to position a ship off South Vietnam's east coast to await large numbers of evacuees from the Delta.

I knew nothing of any such plan. It came as a complete surprise, I told Jacobson. I then asked whether Jacobson wanted me to look into it. He did. For obvious reasons, only Saigon could order evacuation, and Jacobson added that, for the moment, he was grounding all Air America helicopters in Saigon. Pending resolution of this mysterious plan, Jacobson advised me to ground the four Air America helicopters then assigned to the Can Tho consulate general.

I immediately telephoned Downs to ask if he was planning any special "air ops." Downs denied vehemently that he had any such plans. Unconvinced, though without revealing my hand, I informed Downs that, on Jacobson's advice, I was grounding all Air America helicopters then operating in the Delta. I then put Cushing in the picture before ordering the grounding.

Within the hour, Downs was standing in my office. He admitted there was a plan to move two hundred of the CIA's local employees by helicopter to a ship offshore. I ordered Downs to stop all such unauthorized flights at once. The conversation grew heated. Downs threatened to appeal to Saigon to override my order, saying, "The admiral in Saigon considers your plan to go by boat very dangerous" and had agreed to a heliborne operation. Under pressure, however, Downs confessed that the admiral had said the helicopter operation could be implemented only with the consul general's approval.

I found it difficult to control my temper. Hank Cushing, sitting in the next room, could not help overhearing the dispute and readied himself to intervene. Cushing and I assumed that Downs shared our view of the danger involved in any sudden, premature evacuation. The three of us had previously agreed that such a move would almost certainly panic the city's already-nervous population. It was deep concern for all our employees that made me refuse to relent: the operation could not start. Downs stormed out of my office.

Fuming, I telephoned Jacobson in Saigon. Jacobson patiently listened to the full story. He then told me to leave it to Saigon. Jacobson himself would take action to stop the operation.

But I remained worried. The ARVN was breaking apart—except in the Mekong Delta. It was South Vietnam's last chip in its desperate final catastrophe. Nothing should be done, least of all by so-called responsible Americans, to jeopardize this single major bargaining counter left to our allies.

My mind made up, I picked up the EAC telephone and called Lehmann. The embassy's deputy chief of mission answered almost at once. Briefly, I described the morning's events and the CIA's plan. Lehmann asked if it was only a plan and therefore would not be carried out. I assured him that it had gone well beyond the planning stage. Jacobson, I said, could confirm this. The CIA people had actually begun to take action. Lehmann said Jacobson would deal with the matter.

Then I asked that the CIA group in Can Tho be withdrawn. Lehmann was not sure if this could be done but said he would look into it.

I told Lehmann that I had lost confidence in the ability of the CIA group in the Delta to produce reliable intelligence and, based on this latest irresponsible action, doubted that I could trust them in the future. Their panicky, inaccurate reports of imminent mass attacks were frightening others and could cause dangerous overreaction. We were, after all, trying desperately to reduce the number of Americans in the country to an absolute minimum. Under present circumstances, I felt the Can Tho CIA's departure was fully warranted.

Jacobson was next on the telephone. At 11:30, he asked for my personal judgment on whether such a mass evacuation by helicopter, if carried out, "would panic the population of Can Tho." I told him that I believed it would and that it could put all Americans who remained in grave danger. It could also preclude further evacuation of non-CIA local employees and their families.

Jacobson agreed and said he would pass my views to higher authority. This could only mean Lehmann, possibly Polgar, or even Martin himself. Nothing more was heard from Saigon.

Next morning, still no word had come from Saigon concerning the foiled CIA evacuation plan. Time was passing, and I began to doubt that any clear decision would come from Saigon. In any case, I still had responsibility for all employees attached to the consulate general, including those who worked for the CIA. Given more time to consider the situation, I decided to go ahead with the CIA-planned helicopter evacuation but under much tighter control, to reduce the danger of the local reaction we feared. I called Jacobson in Saigon, who did not object. I then asked Downs to come to my office.

A night's rest had cooled emotions on both sides. A truce had to be patched together. On reflection, I suspected that Downs may have acted under pressure from above or perhaps from below. Whatever the reasons behind Downs's actions of the previous day, I had to persuade him that teamwork was vital if all our employees were to stand a chance of leaving. Hoping to build on areas of common interest, I decided to keep the recriminations short.

I explained that I still considered what he had done irresponsible. Nonetheless, whether either of us liked it or not, I was responsible for all personnel in MR IV, including those who worked for the CIA. We must work together, I told him, to ensure the safety of all, regardless of our personal feelings. We shook hands as I silently prayed that this slender olive branch would be strong enough to get everyone safely out to sea.

I then told Downs that I would allow helicopter evacuation on certain, carefully controlled conditions. The lift must be straight out to sea, and landing zones must be found in surrounding countryside— not in the city—where choppers could rendezvous with batches of evacuees. No landing zone was to be used more than once. The choppers were to fly low to avoid ARVN radar at the nearby Ben Thuy Air Base; Vietnamese air force reaction was the last thing we needed. Downs could begin at once, provided these conditions were met. He agreed.

Downs informed me on Monday, April 28, that the CIA would complete evacuation of its Vietnamese during the following day, although the exact time was uncertain. I decided that we could then begin evacuating other Vietnamese consulate general personnel and their families still in Can Tho by the same means after the CIA had finished. Most of the remaining CG personnel were not considered to be in mortal danger from the communists, but were in my category B.

With luck, all Downs's Vietnamese would be safely out at sea on board a ship by the following evening. If Downs completed his task by midday, I could commence flying out the Vietnamese who had come to Can Tho from the provinces, as well as some of the remaining Americans. The province representatives had already moved or were moving their category A and B staffs either to Saigon or to Can Tho. Those put in A and B had been discreetly taken aside and told that if they wished to leave, help would be available from the U.S. government. Not all chose to go, but most did. As the American officers closed down their offices, they brought their Vietnamese with them, sent them to Saigon, or arranged to contact each other in Can Tho. Thus, by April 28, the bulk of the Vietnamese and American personnel from the provinces had been sent to Saigon or were waiting in Can Tho.

By the final weekend, only one of my Americans was left in the countryside outside Can Tho—Traister. I made a note, a reminder for myself, that I should check around midday Sunday, when Traister was to close down his office in Vinh Long. He would then drive straight to the consulate general. He should make it by 2:00 P.M. with his own Vietnamese evacuees. I jotted down a further reminder. Traister could begin arranging for the evacuation of our interpreters who were members of ARVN to start on Wednesday, April 30.

That done, I steeled myself for the hardest job of that Monday: my regular attendance at General Nam's weekly briefing. The general, I hoped, was not aware of our evacuation of Vietnamese but only that we had gradually withdrawn Americans from province offices in the countryside. He might have learned that some Vietnamese employees had been sent to Saigon. I reckoned that Nam would accept the evacuation of Vietnamese women, children, and old people. It was Vietnamese males of military age whom he might stop.

After the briefing on Monday, we sat in the general's office drinking his rare luxury, good coffee. Nam was deeply saddened by the turn of events. Nothing that had come to pass could be blamed on him. The general seemed resigned, almost as if his uniform was an embarrassment, reduced to playing out his part of the last major commander whose troops were still in the field and holding well.

I told him honestly that I wished to stay as long as the Vietnamese were willing to put up a fight. In Saigon, Gen. Duong Van Minh, known as Big Minh, had taken over as president. Neither of us had a clear idea of what Minh's next move would be. Nam gave me the impression that he thought, or perhaps it was simply wishful thinking, that Minh would fight while talking peace. The alternative was total surrender. At length, I commented, "No doubt you are aware that the force of events elsewhere in Vietnam has already compelled me to evacuate a large number of my American personnel."

"I was aware," Nam answered softly.

"We will keep a small residual group here until the position in the Delta becomes untenable or we are ordered by Saigon to evacuate." I searched the general's face, but there was no hint of bitterness.

In a quiet, affectionate manner, Nam began to talk. "I am very grateful," he said, "and I understand and greatly appreciate all that you have done and tried to do to help me and my country. You are a good friend of Vietnam." For a second Nam paused. Then he said firmly, though not unpleasantly, "If you have to go suddenly, please do not attempt to evacuate any military—particularly officers. Now, let me give you more coffee," and Nam poured me a third cup of the hot black liquid.

When I had finished my coffee, I rose to leave. In retrospect, I believe that Nam knew it would be our last meeting. The general had far more information about South Vietnam's collapsing defenses than I did and had to be aware that the end was near. In a rare, uncharacteristic show of affection as we shook hands, he held my hand for some moments. When he spoke the word "good-bye," Nam wore a sad smile.

Outside, the headquarters was carrying on as if it were business as usual. Yet there was a sense of gloom in the atmosphere. Soldiers went here and there on the host of mysterious errands that only the military fully comprehend. A jeep raced by with some urgent message for the general. At this point, I almost went back. Should I risk disclosing to Nam more of the details concerning the evacuation of our employees and their families? Maybe I would tomorrow. For all I knew at the time, I might well be calling on the general the following Monday morning. Instead, I got into my car and told Phuoc to drive back to the office.

On a sudden impulse, I asked Phuoc to stop. Again I considered going back to Nam's office to tell him of our plans for evacuation. But he had warned me very precisely what would occur if soldiers or young Vietnamese men of military age tried to leave with the Americans. Nam would monitor our evacuation. There was danger that word could get to subordinates who might try to seize the boats. It was a hard choice. Yet my duty toward those in my charge did not allow for the emotional luxury of purging my conscience. Giving too precise information on our evacuation plan could jeopardize the whole enterprise.

"We go now?" asked Phuoc patiently.

"Just a moment," I said. I knew I should get back to the office, but Hank could manage for a while longer without me. I wound down the car window. For a minute I let time stand still and watched the soldiers hurrying from building to building. I saw Major Duc, the general's aide, walking briskly toward the operations staff's office. Duc looked far too young for his heavy burden, like a boy playing soldier—not part of this cruel war. As I sat forward, leaning slightly out of the window, I took in my surroundings carefully. Overhead, the noontime thunderheads had begun to climb, alps of clouds, rising higher and higher, slowly building themselves until they could blanket the sun. A wind was gathering. Now and then it swayed the palms or blew dust across the compound. I watched two determined-faced, bandy-legged soldiers placing sandbags to further fortify the entrance to the headquarters.

Sitting there, watching, I realized how much I had grown to love this slightly crazy oriental land. Africa was fascinating, but somehow Vietnam had a much stronger emotional pull on me. From the first, there had been something special about Vietnam. I found it difficult to stand aside and make the kind of uninvolved appraisals for which diplomats, political analysts, and the press were employed. America was at war. Bit by bit the land and people had sucked me further into their spell. I thought, too, of the friends I had made over the years—of General Nam, of Hank at that very moment guarding the office, of others too. That craziness had touched them all in its way.

≡ 14 ≡

Perfidious Spooks

Tuesday, April 29, 1975. Just after 10 A.M., Jacobson, the evacuation coordinator in Saigon, had called me to order our evacuation by helicopter—Americans only. But in the course of a hurried conversation—briefly but frighteningly interrupted—I had reminded him that the four helicopters then working in the Delta would be badly needed for Saigon's own evacuation and had thereby persuaded him to let us go out by boat, taking our local staff and their families.

A shock wave rolled through the consulate general as word spread that evacuation by boat was imminent. The clock reminded people of their tasks.

Traister and his group of sergeant interpreters had been guarding the boats at Delta Compound. I called over the radio asking him to try to start the engines on the LCM. Traister replied that he would try—but could not promise success. The day before, the Vietnamese crew of that LCM had jumped ship, leaving us to struggle with it on our own.

Traister clambered out along the old wooden jetty to the floating dock and climbed up into the LCM's bridge in the rear. It was raised above the open well deck and covered by a makeshift wooden roof. He studied the controls. There was a pair of starter buttons. He pushed one. Silence. He pushed both, harder, but his only reward was the sound of water smacking against the hull.

Traister then decided to try the engine room. A hatch led below into a cramped, oily space jammed full of machinery, mostly taken up by the massive bulk of the twin diesels. Leaving the hatch open, Traister lowered his awkward body down onto a narrow strip of oil-blackened deck plate that ran between the engines. After only seconds of searching, he found what looked like a master switch for power. He turned it on, then scrambled back on deck.

The armored coxswain post was set on top of the engine compartment. Traister climbed back up and began to check the controls once more. With a silent prayer he pushed both buttons simultaneously. A deep cough shook the deck. He tried again, this time keeping his fingers pressed hard, listening nervously to a long moan from the starter motors as they began to revolve both shafts. The engines were heavy, capable of moving the boat at over nine knots, fast considering she weighed fifty-five tons without fuel or cargo. There was a slight jar, followed by a solid bang, then both engines burst into life. Gradually the sound strengthened. Once it had settled into a throaty gargle, a contented Traister wiped his dirty hands on a scrap of cloth that he had found on the afterdeck.

About eleven o'clock, as I drove with Kass, Gia, and Phuoc the short distance from my house to Delta Compound, I was becoming impatient. The tide worried me. When we arrived at Delta Compound, the LCM and rice barge were well afloat. There was no sign on the shore of even a faint line of wet mud. But I knew the tide would soon turn.

My LCM and the rice barge could easily carry three hundred people. By this time, the Can Tho evacuation list had been further reduced to about five hundred people. Even then, many on the list had already departed for Saigon. Moreover, the CIA had taken out a significant number of its people by helicopter in the past few days. With the other LCM, plus the CIA's speedboats, there was plenty of space for those earmarked for evacuation. Nonetheless, one had to allow for the unexpected.

As planned, Christian stood at the gates controlling entrance to Delta Compound. Relieved at hearing the drumming engines, I took up my own allotted post near the entrance to the dock, steering families toward the LCM or rice barge. I presumed that Downs would be preparing the CIA's boats for the downriver journey. As agreed, the Agency's Americans would leave in them. This could present a problem once the sea was reached, but I decided to cope with that problem when it arose. Gradually, more Vietnamese and Americans drifted into the compound. Time was slipping by. I waited a few more minutes, then climbed up to the LCM's bridge.

I stood leaning over the top of the bridge's armor shield, trying not to appear concerned. In my bag, dumped nearby, was a blue painted helmet liner upon the front of which the young Marine guards had painted a single gold star, and below this, inscribed in large yellow letters, "Commodore, Can Tho Yacht Club." At first, I had been undecided about bringing along this sudden gift. Finally, I concluded that the Marines had gone to some effort and my going along with their joke might help to keep spirits up. At the time, I thought the liner would be of no practical use; it didn't even have a harness inside to hold it in place.

My eyes passed over the rolled flags from my office in the consulate general that I had placed in the coxswain's steering compartment. I was not going to leave those behind for some North Vietnamese general to hang as trophies on his office wall.

Suddenly I heard a fast-moving boat's engine. Round a bend in the river came one of the CIA's motorboats. I could see Carl Kachikas of the Defense Attaché's Office manning a machine gun mounted forward. The small boat careened past, heeled round in a tight half circle, then sped off over the oily brown water back toward the CIA compound. Did this mean their boats were already heading downstream? As the sound of its engine faded, I began to worry that the CIA might already be waiting for us in midstream.

Traister, on the stern, also watched the boat roar out of sight.

"That's odd," remarked Traister.

"What?" I asked.

"Carl was here only ten minutes back. He got into the boat with some of the CIA people. I thought they were going to meet us in midstream."

I glanced at my watch. We were fast approaching our planned noon departure time. I then looked at the gates and received a nasty surprise. A jeep was standing across the street. Although not certain at that range, I had an awful suspicion that its front passenger seat was occupied by Colonel Nghia, the province chief from Soc Trang. Were we being observed? The jeep started forward and disappeared.

I relaxed a bit as I turned to ask Traister how he had managed to start the motor. Traister replied vaguely, "I pressed different switches in the engine room. One worked by chance."

The risk grew as the tide began to ebb. The rice barge was almost filled. I gave the order for the few remaining passengers to clamber on board the LCM. Still more families drifted in through the compound gates. They were urged to hurry up, not so much that they would panic, but enough to move them a little faster. Every few minutes I spoke to Hank Cushing over the walkie-talkie. There was no further sign of the CIA's fast motorboats.

At that moment, several American CIA officers arrived at the compound escorting Vietnamese families. They shepherded the Vietnamese down to the boats and helped them board. When I asked one of the Americans who the newly arrived passengers were, I was told the newcomers were agents, or the families of agents, whom the CIA had not been able to lift out by helicopter. This struck me as odd. While I was urging people to hurry on board, I encountered Major Duc—the personal aide to General Nam.

Duc saw the surprise on my face. "It's all right," he explained. "This is my wife and children. They must go, but I return to the general. I could not let them leave without saying good-bye."

Still feeling my shame, I asked Duc to say farewell to the general on my behalf. "Tell the general how grateful I am for all his help over the months, not to mention his personal kindnesses to me. I wish you both good luck." I then urged Duc, "Get yourself and Nam out by boat if the situation becomes hopeless."

"My place is by the general's side," Duc shook his head, "and the general is resolved not to leave."

I nodded. "We'll look after your family. And Duc—good luck."

The major turned quickly, got into his jeep, and drove out of the compound. Not once did he look back. I could not blame him. I only wished somehow that both Duc and Nam might yet escape. But I knew Nam would stay at IV Corps headquarters to the end.

Hardly was Duc out of sight when another jeep roared into the compound. It was filled with armed soldiers. This time there was no mistaking, it was Colonel Nghia. The Soc Trang province chief suddenly slowed, took one long look at the boats, told his driver to turn, and the jeep roared out of the gate leaving a cloud of dust.

Nghia's sudden appearance made up my mind. It was time to leave. But Cushing was still at the consulate general. Once more I looked at my watch. It was already five to twelve and the tide was now noticeably ebbing. At this point Cushing came on the radio.

Earlier, at eleven o'clock, Cushing had gone to the front door of the consulate general with me. Shortly after, he had helped some of Downs's staff carry boxes and heavy bags to their vehicles in the parking lot. After I had left, Cushing came back inside for one final circuit of the offices, to make sure no sensitive papers had been left behind. As he worked his way through all five buildings, he discreetly urged the last Americans and those Vietnamese selected for evacuation to depart. His route took him via the hot, stuffy lobby, filled with worried Vietnamese.

Some were lined up to see the consular officer, David Sciacchitano. Others were waiting for their pay or to be evacuated. Cushing was anxious to separate the first two groups from the last without letting his motive become obvious.

The line waiting for Sciacchitano was politely told that the consular office was closing for lunch. Cushing next went along to one of the administration offices where he began signing vouchers—many of our local employees had not been paid for their last few days' work. Partly it was camouflage, designed to calm those being left behind; perhaps it was also hard for Cushing to come to terms with such a final moment.

Around 11:40, his signing finished, Cushing discovered the ubiquitous Hasty in the CIA's communications vault. The Marine sergeant was feverishly working a bolt cutter, ripping the tops off burn barrels used to destroy classified materials. His assistant was the CIA's communicator, Walt Milford, although Cushing realized at once that the situation was actually in reverse: something had gone badly wrong with Milford's destruction program and Hasty was lending Milford a hand. No one else from the CIA was left in the consulate general. They had rushed off, leaving Milford alone to do the critically important destruction of the super-secret coding machines and remaining sensitive files.

"Shit!" Hasty stared furiously into a barrel. "I've never seen one of these burn barrels before. How do they work?"

"Fill them," intervened Cushing, "Just ram the stuff down. We'll figure it out. Walt must know how to ignite them."

"Mr. Cushing," Hasty immediately suggested, "you and Walt do the barrels. I'll load files into the regular incinerator."

Sweat streaming down their faces, pouring down their backs and arms, the three men worked with only an occasional curse to break the steady crackle from Hasty's walkie-talkie, which stood on the floor near his feet. Milford packed cipher components into burn barrels while Cushing started securing their covers.

An increasing amount of noise was coming from the lobby. Cushing went out to investigate. When he returned, both Milford and Hasty noticed that Cushing, while his usual cool self, was not quite so relaxed. "It's getting tense out there," he said. "They know something peculiar is happening. Perhaps word has already gotten out about our evacuation."

After another five minutes, Hasty took a look at the lobby. He soon came back. "There's more people comin' every minute," he said. "They're getting increasingly excited. We'd better get the fuck outta here." All three worked a little faster.

Hasty lit the incinerator. He regarded the first licks of purple flame with satisfaction. As Cushing later described the scene, suddenly my voice spluttered over the radio. "Hasty, I want you over at the boat dock immediately."

"We got a snag in the C&R vault, Mr. McNamara," Hasty replied. "I'll send Sergeant Kirchner with Mr. Sciacchitano. It could get a little difficult here, Mr. McNamara."

"Who is coming to the docks?"

"I'm gonna send Sergeant Kirchner with Mr. Sciacchitano." Hasty paused while Cushing told him to tell me that they would be leaving shortly.

"OK. But hurry."

Hasty acknowledged my order, then spoke briefly on the radio to Sergeant John Moore. He told Moore that after dispatching Sciacchitano and Kirchner, he was to muster all remaining Marines at the boat and start loading the weapons, radios, and other equipment that had been stockpiled for the trip. Hasty went out to make certain his order was being carried out, but he need not have bothered. Sergeant Moore had already told Sciacchitano what was required.

The vice consul finished his current interview, then announced to those waiting—there were quite a number filling the lobby with a nervous chatter—that he was going to lunch. This seemed to satisfy curious minds, at least for a while. Sciacchitano closed his office. He collected a few documents and his seal, gave his stamp to Walt Milford to destroy, sent several Vietnamese whom he had been processing for visas to Delta Compound, then jumped into his Scout with Kirchner. After searching in town without success for a Vietnamese woman with an American child, they drove to Sciacchitano's quarters, where he collected a few belongings and paid his maid. John Kirchner, who had discreetly removed the American flag from the lobby, was put straight to work on their arrival at Delta Compound. I told him to keep out of sight but watch the gates in case a mob tried to rush through.

When Hasty came back to the vault, the barrels had still not lighted properly.

Milford asked urgently, "What the hell are we going to do about these cipher components?"

"No sweat," said Hasty with a grin. "I'll get some incendiary grenades from my office."

Cushing lifted his eyebrow, wondering what effect incendiary grenades would have on their lungs in such a confined space. However, as Hasty was returning with the grenades, the barrels finally shot out flames. Satisfied that the needed destruction was now accomplished, they moved toward the vault door.

"Let's get to my driver," ordered Cushing, "but walk slowly and look relaxed." Dumping the grenades, they went out and found Cushing's car and driver at the front entrance. They left without incident. There was no looting or panic in the compound, although Cushing saw signs that an early disintegration was likely. Milford was not sure what he should do. His CIA colleagues had long since left the consulate general. Cushing told him to get into the vehicle. "Everyone will soon be rendezvousing in the middle of the river," he reasoned.

Cushing and his two companions left the consulate general at exactly noon. Several minutes later, after driving through the quiet lunchtime streets, they reached Delta Compound. The LCM was at the far end. Cushing switched off his walkie-talkie. From now on, he and I would be within earshot of each other. Stopping in his quarters only to collect weapons, Cushing hurried down to the dock, where, having spoken to me, he found Walt Heilman and Florian Ajinga, head of the local guard force, helping local employees with their families onto the rice barge.

Heilman explained that he and Ajinga had been there for twenty minutes. Only two of Heilman's Vietnamese staff had reported, and Heilman wondered whether such short notice was too sudden for them to comprehend. When given the warning an hour earlier, some of the Vietnamese appeared traumatized, wishing him well, yet not really seeming to understand what was happening. Others simply picked up their personal belongings and went home—whether any of these would return with their wives and children for embarking, Heilman was beginning to doubt.

Dave Whitten, one of the young political officers, had driven into the compound via his apartment. After visiting both boats, Whitten grew increasingly worried about the Vietnam-America Association's staff members, who were also to be evacuated, although they were not employees of the U.S. government. Several times he left his post trying to make contact over the telephone. There was no answer. At one point during the loading an American CIA secretary drove into the compound, but left almost immediately, later causing concern, for nobody was quite sure where she had gone. As it turned out, she had gone to join her colleagues at their compound.

Milford was concerned for his Vietnamese fiancée. He wanted to collect her, but had been prevented from doing so by the difficulty of destroying his communication equipment. Milford had not even been able to alert the girl. Normally rather quiet and mild, he suddenly lost his cool. Cushing persuaded him to come to Delta Compound, but he did not find the girl there. For a time Cushing thought that he would have to forcibly drag Milford on board the boat. Then a shout came from the LCM. She was there!

Several bizarre incidents had occurred shortly before Cushing arrived. No sooner had I been told on the radio by Hasty of a snag at the consulate general than the deputy commander of the Vietnamese air force's Air Division in the Delta arrived in the compound in full uniform, accompanied by his wife and children. At the time, I was distracted by Hasty's radio transmission. I then stepped ashore, thinking that would make it easier to deal with late arrivals. I did not see the colonel strip off his uniform and follow his wife and children over the gunwale, to lose himself among the crowd in the well deck. Since we now had extra room in our boats, I simply assumed that he was putting his family in reach of safety before returning to his duties, as Major Duc had done. Later I was to learn that this had not happened.

The arrival at the quayside of a very pretty young woman dressed in a handsome, close-fitting *ao dai* caused another stir. At first, I thought she was the wife of a Vietnamese officer. As she approached the boat, I recognized her as the mistress—perhaps common-law wife—of a CIA officer. Tears rolled down her cheeks. Did we know the whereabouts of her lover? She must not be left on the quay. On the other hand, there was no time left for collecting lover or luggage. And so, with the clothes on her back for riches, wiping her face, she jumped onto the LCM.

Alarmed, I began seeing growing patches of mud along the shoreline as the tide began to ebb.

A woman's scream rent the air. Somebody in danger—were the VC in Delta Compound? Had some ARVN soldier arrived to stop the boats from leaving? Running hard toward the dock came Hank Cushing's cook, great shrieks and wails bellowing from her open mouth.

There had never been any intention, once heads had to be strictly counted, of evacuating domestic servants. Although a tough choice, especially when it involved abandoning maids or cooks who had become, over the years, a second family, there was no doubt in my mind that we had no other alternative. But Cushing's cook, who lived in the Delta Compound, had been watching for the last hour, tears streaming from terrified eyes, so shocked by what she had seen that neither words nor deeds would come. At the last minute, she screwed up her courage and, risking rejection, ran out to plead for a space on board.

"OK," I sighed, "on board you go."

But the woman remained immobile, rooted to the quay. She must collect her son from school.

"OK," I groaned, this time looking for an object on which to sit down, "but you must be on the boat within five minutes. We can wait no longer."

Fortune, they say, smiles on the righteous. At that moment, the awaited small boy strolled through the front gate. Complete with schoolbooks, the bewildered little fellow was hustled onto the boat, with no idea of what was happening. Cushing jumped aboard after him and crossed to the rice barge. It was now almost 12:30.

I had a last look around, then forcefully told the stragglers to climb on the boat and the Marines to prepare for getting under way. As I walked down the rickety jetty to the small floating dock, the tide was going out fast. Sergeant Hasty was waiting for me at the gangplank. "After you," I motioned.

But Hasty stood still, gesturing that I go first. Feeling a little foolish, I shook my head, determined to be the last one to leave Vietnam soil in the Delta. With some reluctance, Hasty boarded the LCM.

Our flotilla was already in trouble. The propeller blade on one of the rice barge's outboard motors had been broken in the mud, and the rice barge was moored against the LCM. Thus, my LCM was sandwiched between it and the jetty. I told Heilman to cast off and move into deeper water, otherwise the LCM would soon be stuck fast on the mudflat. Or worse, people from the town would get wind of what was afoot, break into the compound, and overwhelm the boats before we were able to leave. Either eventuality would be a disaster.

I climbed back up to the bridge where I studied the engine controls and the steering. Traister watched over my shoulder. If Traister could start the engines, I thought, I could maneuver a boat with two motors and a flat bottom. I asked Traister whether he knew how to operate the controls. "No," came the reply, followed by a nervous giggle. Traister then gave an excellent demonstration of how the throttle levers worked for both engines. Two throttles, therefore two propellers, thus more maneuverable. It was easy! My previous nautical experience was coming in handy.

With a final glance at Delta Compound, I yelled, "Cast off!" The Marines started untying the lines that held us alongside the old jetty.

Suddenly, Hasty shouted, "Hold everything!" He leapt over the side, landed hard on the jetty, and ran back up the planks toward the compound. Some twenty people were struggling toward the river.

I slipped both engines back into neutral watching, yet again, as CIA employees—this time six Filipinos with Vietnamese wives and children—rushed along the catwalk, loaded with sacks and suitcases.

One of them started to explain, tripping over words in angry relief. His American boss had neglected to make provision for them. That morning, at work, they heard about the evacuation. When time passed and no orders came from their supervisors, they decided to race back to their homes, collect their families, and then dash for the Delta Compound.

"What would we have done, Mr. McNamara?" he stammered. "We Filipinos? No way we look like Vietnamese." Hasty and Moore were helping these poor, frightened new arrivals, handing women and children up toward outstretched sunburnt and brown hands that, lifting them over the boat's gunwale, delivered them to momentary safety. Unfamiliar Vietnamese were now coming through the gate. The boat shuddered. She was aground.

Hasty and Moore were pulled back on board. I shouted at the Marines up forward, "Chuck the remaining lines over the side." Turning to Traister, I urged,"Let's try to get her off the mud, Bob."

Frantically, with Traister's help, I threw the engines into reverse: no effect. I tried forward, as Traister jerked the rudder from side to side. I sensed movement. "Get it together, Bob," I growled, half rebuking poor Traister. Walt Heilman stood with Cushing in the crowded rice barge, listening to the racing engines, swearing, and noise, watching carefully, certain the LCM was not aground. But Traister and I could feel that unrelenting solid deck beneath our feet. "This time, Bob." I spat the next words, "Ready—now!"

I pushed the port engine control to full ahead. Traister slid his starboard engine to full astern. At the same time I spun the rudder hard to port. The boat began to pivot on its own axis. It was also shifting, gently easing off the bottom, swinging round until the stern was pointed toward the open river.

"OK, Bob, let her rip!" And we rammed home the throttles to full astern, swinging the rudder to amidships. The LCM surged backwards, both powerful engines churning the khaki water to foam while it plowed its way into deeper water.

Hasty then picked up something on his radio. "What is it?" I shouted over the roar of the engines.

"LCM at the Shell dock," called Hasty. "They're loaded and proceeding to the rendezvous. Will see us off Can Tho City in a few minutes." Hasty asked, "You want me to say anything, Mr. McNamara?"

"No. Good news needs no comment."

The sergeant grinned. His radio crackled once more—a distorted voice, which sounded like Franklyn, the CIA deputy station chief. I caught something about "received permission from Saigon to use the helicopters as Air America choppers no longer needed in Saigon." I listened more carefully with growing confusion. Next the voice said they "were departing immediately by helicopter." No question of asking permission? What about my direct order not to use helicopters? Why should Saigon not want the helicopters anymore? Surely the evacuation from Saigon was not finished already? Who in Saigon had given "permission" to use the helicopters? I began to wonder if some terrible disaster had taken place in the capital. "Did the consul general wish to send any Americans with them," the voice crackled again, because they had "plenty of room." No doubt they did, I thought bitterly, staring at the Filipinos and their huddle of wives and children on the deck and at the forgotten CIA communicator, Milford.

Today I wish I had spoken to Franklyn. But at that moment I was overcome by anger and concerned with getting the boat under way. Had I taken the radio mike, I am sure that I would have exploded, that all my deep resentment, my feeling of being failed by members of a team, might have poured over the airwaves in a salvo of abuse. It would not have helped the morale of those trusting faces in the well deck, already wearing puzzled expressions. They could sense by the Americans' faces that something was going wrong. No. My principal concern had to be the welfare of my charges. This now meant meeting the other boat and heading downriver for the sea. Any moment the Vietnamese navy or the ARVN could discover our flight. "Hasty," I called, "ask Mr. Cushing to deal with the chopper on his radio. I am too busy handling the boat."

Hank Cushing took up his radio. First he told Franklyn that the consul general's order stood; the CIA did not have authorization to take the helicopters. They were to go by boat—"CG orders this at once." But Franklyn insisted again that Saigon had approved, carefully avoiding the question of who in Saigon had "approved." So Cushing looked over at me and shrugged. It was too late now to argue over chains of command. The tide was more important. Moreover, clearly visible on shore, a crowd was gathering in Delta Compound.

Hasty suggested to Hank Cushing that he ask Franklyn how he planned to transfer people from the boats to helicopters in the middle of the river. I quickly added, "Forget it, Hasty. Just ask Mr. Cushing to tell

Franklyn that it's a bit late for such offers. There's no way we can transfer people now in midstream." And with that came the steady beating of a chopper, low over the water. It came fast, a silver Huey that clattered deafeningly above our heads, flying swiftly in the direction of the sea.

"There go the CIA," growled a Marine, "in full flight."

Watching that helicopter fade into a speck above the brown surface of the Mekong was like observing a symbol of all that went wrong for America in Vietnam. I only had to look at the faces of my Vietnamese charges in the well deck. It was in their eyes. I was ashamed. These simple human beings were staring with an odd mixture of fear and contempt at the helicopter, as though watching mercenaries abandon a battlefield, running for safe haven with no thought spared for what has passed. Unknown to those sailing downriver, a price was to be paid by hundreds of Vietnamese trapped in buildings in Saigon awaiting planned rooftop pickup by Air America's Huey helicopters.* Instead, four of these precious birds were flying off, never to reach Saigon, where they were desperately needed.

Wasting no more time on recriminations, I gave my attention to a far more immediate matter: the rice barge was still in trouble. It was only crawling over the water and could not keep up unless we all slowed to the same speed, or we took her in tow. The latter seemed the only sensible thing to do. I did not like the idea of spending more time within full view of Can Tho. We were then off the central market, and such a lot of activity would be seen without fail. Tow ropes were passed and, under Hank Cushing's direction, made fast. The long haul commenced. Seventy miles of river lay between us and the open sea.

---

* See: Frank Snepp, *A Decent Interval* (New York: Random House, 1977), p. 486.

☰ 15 ☰

Commodore Thang Keeps a Promise

I admired my little convoy, struck by how picturesque and peaceful it all seemed. We were rounding the end of an island, which still sheltered our boats from the full power of the Bas Sac, at Can Tho an expanse of water almost a mile wide. Gradually the convoy worked its way out toward midstream.

The other LCM came into sight, her squat, friendly hulk sliding into line ahead so her captain could lead us through the meandering river channel. Unfortunately, the little convoy would not include the fast, armed CIA boats that Downs had promised would escort us downriver. As we slid past, I noted the province chief's house—no signs of life. Then came naval headquarters. Several sailors were languidly working on small boats, but none paid us more than glancing attention. Perhaps after fifteen years of American presence, most Vietnamese had drifted into philosophic indifference to the curious ways of those large, sweaty people with their long noses.

As the boat turned, moving steadily down the center of the river, I began to have a better feel for the steering. On reaching the main channel, I sensed the boat surge forward as the fast-flowing tidal current exerted its push. A light cool wind was lifting off the lazy ocher water, pulling mirrors of sunlight from an otherwise empty Bas Sac.

A traditional helmsman's wooden wheel moved the rudder. Speed was controlled by a pair of large bronze levers immediately to the right of the wheel. I now made a closer study of my surrounding protection.

The coxswain's post was high on the boat's stern, surrounded by thin armor plate.

Speed was increased simply by pushing the throttle levers forward. To reverse the engines, one pulled the levers backward. You could also use the engines when maneuvering in narrower waters. By varying the speed on either side, you could assist the rudder in turning the boat. By reversing one engine, the boat could be spun in a circle. While this could not be done with a tow, it might help, should we be forced to avoid shooting from the banks later on downriver. I also examined the rows of gauges and switches. I could only guess their roles. The boat seemed to be sailing smoothly, making over twelve knots; both engines sounded healthy. Were the dials honestly going to be that vital? I pushed up the speed a bit, checked that the pair of tow ropes were holding, then pointed the boat's flat nose straight down the center of the Bas Sac River.

Tension began to lift. It was as if some unseen force was removing a heavy weight from my shoulders. Hank Cushing was actually grinning, waving his cigarette in the air, signaling relief and satisfaction. Why not? We had managed to take on board nearly three hundred locals with no trouble from the South Vietnamese military. Half a mile of water stretched to either side. Watching the other LCM ahead, my own loaded with Vietnamese families, I experienced a surge of elation. So far, the evacuation had gone without a serious hitch. Then, again, I brooded about the CIA. What a tragedy they had not trusted the boats. Even from that distance, I could see the leading LCM was by no means full. Another two hundred or more people could now be sailing downriver. Those chopper crews should have been over Saigon all afternoon, rescuing people from rooftops.

I then started a mental check of those on board. All our remaining employees, with families, in the two top priority categories were down on the deck, or at least all those who wished to be evacuated and who were still in Can Tho. Some had not wished to go; the consulate general cashier, for instance, decided not to leave. Other people in lower categories took the spare places. On the rice barge astern, I could see Walt Heilman's hardworking car repair and building maintenance crews with their families. Some Vietnamese employees of the CIA were also on the boat. I assumed that some others with them were agents or the families of agents. The Agency's Filipino employees seemed quite happy now—rather a change from the frightened faces of some minutes before. Above all, not one of my American staff members had been lost.

I allowed the other LCM to slip ahead. Its captain knew the river well. The Vietnamese could sail this route blindfolded. Secretly, two weeks before, I had managed a helicopter trip to reconnoiter the river. At the time only Cushing knew of my flight. I remembered a few difficult stretches.

It was pleasantly warm on the bridge, and my thoughts began to wander. *Rirrrp! Rirrrp!* Jolted back into reality, I searched the left bank for a machine gun. More bursts tore the air. Then I saw them: a small flotilla of three RVN navy gunboats fanning out across the river up ahead, barring the way. More shots puffed from their bows. Spray exploded across the bow of the LCM in front.

There was no chance of outrunning the patrol boats. The landing crafts were too slow, and the rice barge was a further drag. Moreover, we were heavily outgunned. The RVN navy boats sprouted long black barrels of 20mm and 40mm cannon. Guns of those calibers would open the LCMs' sides like tin cans. As we closed, I spotted sailors cradling M-16 rifles and manning machine guns. My boats were full of women and children. Crossfire could turn it into a massacre. I grabbed Traister's radio and ordered the leading boat to stop.

The Vietnamese flotilla, guns trained on us, lay in a menacing half circle blocking our path downriver. The sailors looked to be in an ugly mood. I reduced engine speed gradually, running the LCM alongside its sister.

The nearest Vietnamese boat crew signaled me to keep our vessels in position, at the same time declining to come alongside either LCM. An officer motioned that somebody would be coming to talk. I stared blankly at Cushing on the rice barge. There was nothing to be done, other than remain calm and very patient.

As we lay under their menacing guns, I wondered whether Colonel Nghia had reported our departure to General Nam. Did Nam tell the navy to wait until my boats were out of sight of Can Tho, then arrest us, without fuss or interference? I was not sure. Half an hour dragged by, with no sign from the sailors other than a silent hostility. The patrol boats rocked gently as their engines held against the current. I maneuvered my own boats on cue from our sister LCM's Vietnamese captain, as the ebb tide picked up speed. We were wasting valuable time. But despite a growing unspoken pressure from my charges, there was nothing sensible I could do but wait. I became aware of dozens of eyes watching me—that sudden avoidance of a direct glance, the message of sympathy on Cushing's face reminding me of my loneliness.

Hasty called from the stern. Four more patrol boats were approaching from upriver. Now we were surrounded. One boat slowly came alongside. An officer was standing forward, ready to jump. I recognized Lieutenant Commander Quang, the deputy chief of staff for operations at the Vietnamese navy's 4th Riverine Area Command. Quang did not jump on board. Instead he spoke urgently to me in an apologetic but insistent tone. General Nam had ordered us stopped and brought back to Can Tho.

I refused politely yet firmly to turn about. But the young Vietnamese had his orders. Then I suggested, finally insisted, that he radio his commanding officer, Commodore Thang. I hoped Thang would remember the promise he had given me in return for the evacuation by air of his wife and children the week before from Tan Son Nhut.

Quang was very nervous, caught between pressures that, at his age, were still a mystery. Reluctantly, he agreed to call the commodore and disappeared into the patrol boat's cabin.

One glance around my boat warned me of another danger. Nearly every one of my Vietnamese males was still armed with an automatic weapon of some kind. Quietly, I gave an order to disarm all the Vietnamese in our boats. One desperate man could get us all killed. My American personnel who spoke Vietnamese went round the deck, moving slowly through the crowd, politely but firmly gathering an amazing variety of weapons. I had sympathy for my passengers' plight. Prospects for many Vietnamese were grim if they were made to return. General Nam would be quite within his rights to treat males of military age harshly, which could even mean a firing squad. If they were thrown into prison, the communists eventually would deal with them in their own pitiless way. All were desperate. And it says a great deal for those few Americans that these people, at such a moment, still trusted them enough to hand over their guns. For from then on, all were defenseless, relying entirely on me and my American colleagues to bring them and their families to safety.

From my point of view, one danger was now past. No longer was there any risk of a shootout between South Vietnamese with dozens of helpless women and children trapped in the crossfire. It had been a tricky job—even for Americans whom these men knew well—but of one thing I was certain: those men would never have voluntarily surrendered their arms to other Vietnamese. The job complete, I placed two Marines on guard over the stack of guns on the stern behind the bridge.

After what seemed an eternity, yet was actually no more than a few minutes, Quang returned. His flotilla was to wait. The consul general was not to move his boats. Commodore Thang was on the way. We were still held under arrest, but news that Thang was coming seemed promising, almost an omen. I felt the tension reduce—on both sides.

I decided to use the delay to advantage and further reduce hostility. I found that there was enough space in the two LCMs for all those in the rice barge. So, having cleared it with Quang, I transferred the barge passengers onto the LCMs. Not only was its propeller damaged, but if we were attacked, the wooden sides of the rice barge afforded scant protection to its passengers. The LCMs, on the other hand, had armored sides. They would never stop a heavy shell or rocket, but small arms could not penetrate. Moreover, with its round bottom and shallow draft, the rice barge would not be seaworthy on the open ocean. The transfer done, I offered the barge to the sailors of the naval flotilla. This seemed to please them enormously. Tension further relaxed.

For the moment, the boats wallowed and rocked in the Mekong current. Quang stayed on deck. He had spoken English so far. In this improved atmosphere, Quang allowed himself a conversation in Vietnamese with Whitten, whom he knew, for Whitten had served on an earlier tour as an adviser with the Vietnamese navy. But Quang was not talking solely for pleasure. He told Whitten that General Nam had given orders that no military personnel or civil servants could leave. The navy, he assured, had no wish to cause problems. Nonetheless, he asked Whitten who all the Vietnamese were that we had on board. Whitten told him that they were all employees of the consulate general and their families. Quang said Commodore Thang would arrive in less than an hour. The Americans could then continue, but any Vietnamese military, civil servants, or males of military age would have to disembark.

At about that time, having refueled, the last Air America helicopter left Can Tho carrying the remainder of the CIA contingent. Flying out over the river, the helicopter soon passed above the collection of river craft. A radio message came down asking if assistance was required. I instructed the CIA radioman to tell the pilot that the Vietnamese navy was stopping the boats. Could he call for U.S. Navy air cover—which earlier had been promised me to protect us as we proceeded downriver? I assumed the CIA people in the helicopter relayed my request, but no help arrived from the U.S. Navy.

Two hours had passed since we had been stopped. The wind died. The sun beat down. Sweat stuck my light sport shirt to my back. Traister gave up clearing perspiration from his glasses. Metal burnt fingers when touched.

Cushing, who had joined us on the shaded bridge, leaned over its side, peacefully smoking. Nobody spoke much. On the open deck, scraps of cloth and fans were wafted patiently by the women trying to cool their dozing children. Hasty and his Marines kept watch.

A small, French-designed motor launch came into sight. After the longest fifteen minutes I can remember, it chugged alongside. On its bridge was Commodore Thang. Declining to board, Thang told me, in low and serious tones, that General Nam had got word that some "senior officers" were aboard the boats and had therefore given orders that all vessels were to be brought back to Can Tho. I took a long breath to steady my nerves while remaining silent. Then, without warning, breaking out in a beautiful smile, Thang added dryly, "Under the circumstances, I will not obey the general's order."

In a louder voice, Thang asked, "Do you have any military men, civil servants, or Vietnamese of military age in your boats?" I replied that I had only consulate general employees and their families aboard. "That being the case," he declared, "I do not believe it necessary to enforce General Nam's order."

It was hard for me to keep a straight face. Thang was well aware of the kinds of people who were in our boats. Indeed, Thang's aide, Lieutenant Lich, was actually standing on the stern of my LCM speaking to Whitten. He could see clearly into the boat's well deck where the Vietnamese passengers were huddled in frightened family clusters. If Thang had seriously wanted to verify the identity of the passengers, it would have been simple for him to have done so. Instead, Lich explained quietly to Whitten how sorry he and the commodore were that the incident had occurred.

Thang, in his sharp singsong Vietnamese, called forward a young soldier in his motor launch. The boy jumped on board the LCM. For a moment, I thought Commodore Thang wanted the youth to go with us. But then I heard Thang say something different, in Vietnamese, about "your father" and "farewell." An elderly Vietnamese in the LCM embraced the boy. Tears ran down the cheeks of both. If there was any animosity left in the atmosphere, it melted then. Some of the sailors stared at the water, visibly moved; I felt my eyes prickle, even after all that I had seen over the years, as the soldier jumped back onto Thang's launch.

"What are you going to do, Thang?" I asked quietly.

"Stay and fight—if the war is to be continued."

"And if it is not, Thang?"

"Then I will lead my naval force down the river."

I then offered him my hand. "Thanks for turning a blind eye. Thanks for everything. Good luck. I hope we meet again, Thang."

Three hundred pairs of eyes watched the little naval flotilla, now including the rice barge, break from encircling us and slip into line behind Thang's motor launch. Both groups waved to each other as Thang and his boats turned to begin the slow voyage upriver. What was going to happen in Can Tho during the next few hours? What possible use was that rice barge as their country collapsed around them? I pondered the strange situation. No matter, I thought. We can do no more for them now.

16

With Any Luck

I looked at my watch: 2:50 P.M. I pushed the throttles forward and felt the boat surge beneath me. A hundred meters ahead, the other LCM threw a wide vee of wake across the river's surface. Seventy miles down the Bas Sac before we would reach the sea. The tide was still running out fast. Judging by the speed with which we were passing landmarks on the shore, I reckoned we were making from twelve to fourteen knots. At that rate, the lost two hours would be recovered. The boats would still reach the sea before dark.

The sun was already less fierce. Its warmth spread across the Bas Sac. Directly above, a few puffy balls of cloud drifted in the dome of blue. Farther ahead, though, low on the horizon, were dark clouds—rain squalls, and not so far distant either. At this point the river's best deepwater channel ran closer to the north shore. My tiny fleet drummed along, with the Marines keeping constant watch on the thickly foliaged riverbanks.

There could be VC on either side of the Bas Sac from this point on until we reached the river mouth. In the narrow channels between the islands farther downstream we would be especially vulnerable to fire from the banks. This was likely to be the most dangerous part of the journey.

A great roar suddenly swept over our heads. I looked upwards to my right. Every face in both boats did the same, most full of fear. At about ten thousand feet, passing directly above, was a U.S. Navy F-4

Phantom. As the big jet fighter flew away from our little boats, the sun caught its fuselage. Its pilot made a barrel roll before he continued on a course toward the west. I felt sure it must have been the navy air cover I had requested.

"Try to make contact," I yelled to Milford.

"Sorry," Milford apologized, "just can't raise him."

Spirits fell a little. Yet we were now sure we had not been forgotten. Perhaps we could count on support in the narrows ahead.

Complacency was again suddenly shattered. A strange blowtorch sound was coming over the water toward the boats from the south bank of the river. I jerked my head round just in time to see a black object approaching, fast. A red fireball at its rear trailed black smoke low over the water. It flashed past, only ten meters astern.

I croaked, "Some sonofabitch has fired a rocket at us." Ramming the throttles forward, I bellowed at the Marines, "Open fire. Get the launch site."

Nobody had even crouched. Cushing flung his cigarette over the side, pointing and bawling at the Marines.

Sergeant Kirchner ripped off a long burst from his M-16 rifle on full automatic. He had seen a patch of smoke on shore. Kirchner pulled out the empty clip and loaded a second. He took aim and blasted another full magazine at the shore. Laying down the M-16, he took up a snub-nosed M-79 grenade launcher, aimed it at the bank, and fired on a flat trajectory. The round exploded in the water only a short distance off to starboard.

Walt Heilman, watching, snatched the weapon, raised its trajectory, then fired a second round. A puff of dark gray smoke began to spread among the foliage hanging over the bank.

Sergeant John Moore was armed with the old-fashioned, yet highly effective BAR automatic rifle. He managed a single shot before the weapon jammed. This time it was Vice Consul Sciacchitano who grabbed the BAR, cleared it, and handed it back to the embarrassed Marine, who commenced textbook bursts of automatic fire under Sciacchitano's approving eyes.

Others, armed with a variety of weapons, started shooting at the riverbank. A Chinese Nung guard from the Delta Compound was pulling off good, steady, single shots with an M-16 rifle. He seemed to be aiming in the right direction. Retired army colonel Averill Christian, seeing this ragged fusillade, took charge at once, directing all fire at the bank near where a small stream fed into the Bas Sac. His sharp, experienced eyes had spotted the approximate launch site. It crossed my mind, vaguely, that the Nung should not still have a weapon.

The fire grew intense. Concentrated on three points of the riverbank, it had the desired effect—no more rockets. At my helmsman's perch, I grew mildly amused watching the Marines become instant veterans under the tutoring of civilians, who, almost to a man, were veterans of this and earlier wars.

I let the shooting go on for a couple of minutes. Then I yelled, "Cease fire! Knock it off! Cease fire!" Cushing, shaking with laughter, reached for a fresh cigarette.

As far as I know, these were the last shots fired by Americans in the Vietnam War.

The boats were now approaching the narrowest part of the river, where the channel wove between islands, often coming within yards of heavily foliaged banks. This was where I most expected trouble. Firing rockets from long range at a moving target was one thing. Firing at slow boats in a narrow channel was another.

Though our LCMs were armored to withstand small-arms fire and had concrete collars added to protect their engines, one chance hit by a rocket-propelled grenade in the well deck area could pierce the armor, wounding or killing many of the Vietnamese. Engrossed in worrying about these dangers, I barely noticed dark clouds forming.

A large splash of cold rain landing squarely on my nose brought me back to reality. In front, a gray wall was sweeping upriver; I could not quite believe our good fortune. A rain squall was more than any of us could have prayed for. At the place where the Bas Sac narrowed, where the boats were in most danger from either bank, driving rain engulfed the convoy. Soon the two LCMs were almost hidden from each other by murk.

The river's muddy surface seethed and writhed, pelted by millions of raindrops. Visibility closed to less than fifty meters. The din of rain and wind nearly drowned out the noise of the engines. The convoy seemed to enter a secret world—but one still harboring dangers. The channel followed a twisting course between dozens of islands, frequently taking us within a few meters of silent banks, densely covered by elephant grass, tangled with long, thick creepers, overhung by huge coconut trees. If ever the VC wanted perfect ambush country, it was here.

The Marines peered into the rain, alert, guns ready should enemy fire burst out from the banks. Hasty was on the port side. He sat huddled behind an M-60 machine gun, squinting over its barrel, with the rain dripping from his bush hat. I was somehow reassured by the reliable young NCO. Hasty was sharp. Had he not made certain that he was, after all, the last man to leave the shore, despite my efforts to best him? But then Hasty was a Marine.*

Thunder rumbled among the dark, tortured piles of cloud. Rain thrashed the Bas Sac. The black outfit that Hasty had commissioned a Can Tho tailor to make for him was soon soaked with cold water. Seeing Hasty shivering, I sent Sciacchitano with a field jacket to spread over his shoulders. From the sergeant's grateful expression, this obviously helped ease his discomfort.

Everyone in the boats was tense. I thanked fate that my mind was fully concentrated on steering. Despite a professionally piloted LCM leading the way, there was plenty to keep even an experienced sailor occupied. The channel was tricky under any conditions. Now I was steering a relatively large boat along it through a curtain of driving rain.

On the exposed well deck, improvised shelters were appearing. The Vietnamese are not usually stuck for solutions. All sorts of little tents sprang up within minutes. Ladies' umbrellas were being linked by ponchos and raincoats as I watched fascinated from my raised perch near the stern. Families huddled together as protection from the wet and cold in discernible separation from one another, even in that crowded space. This, too, was very Vietnamese.

The rain fell harder. Huge raindrops seemed to merge with the Bas Sac's muddy tide.

Milford, watched by Christian and Traister, had given up trying to contact the fleet by radio. I turned to Cushing: "If anyone was lying in ambush on the banks, this deluge should drive them indoors."

"Even a VC," mused Cushing, "is smart enough to get out of the rain."

"If not Americans." I grinned, looking up at the wooden roof over the stern. In normal days this provided shelter for the crew to sleep under. I stared ahead once more, eyes stinging from bullets of water, almost blinded. Suddenly, I remembered the helmet liner. The Marines' joke would be useful after all. Without taking my eyes off the river, I reached for it, shoved it on my head and felt warmer within seconds. More important, I could see more clearly. It shielded my eyes from the driving rain.

Two hours passed, then visibility slowly increased. The river began

---

* Hasty later became a lieutenant colonel of Marines, and his career continues as of this writing.

to widen as the rain ended, as abruptly as it had begun. A broad expanse of yellow water, a huge bay, lay off the port side. I remembered this place from my aerial reconnaissance flight. After studying the map, there was no doubt in my mind: the boats were through the narrows, not far from the mouth of the Bas Sac River. Out there, somewhere, was a U.S. Navy vessel waiting to greet the little flotilla. Milford tried the fleet emergency band. Still nobody acknowledged.

Late in the afternoon, C rations were handed round. Busy at the helm, I did not at first take much notice. The Vietnamese collected their cans and packages as families. Within seconds all had been spirited away under umbrellas, clothes, and luggage. The rations might never have existed.

Suddenly aware, I feared we had been shortsighted in allowing the rations to be distributed so early in the voyage. But, if the boats were sunk, at least each family might get ashore with some food. On balance I recognized we could survive for several days without eating. The children would, of course, need food. I had no fears about that. No Vietnamese family would willingly let its children suffer. I smiled to myself, staring from those empty cartons on the deck to the little clusters of poker faces. No pushing and shoving, no sharing outside the family either, a very effective technique for survival in a family-based culture.

Ever since entering the narrows, we had seen no other river traffic, not a sign of life on either bank. The rain had been so heavy that even riverside hamlets and houses were made invisible.

Suddenly, several hundred meters off, I saw a motorized barge coming upriver toward us. Nobody was visible on deck. The barge looked innocent, but one could never be certain. Four hundred meters, two hundred meters, suddenly we were passing less than thirty meters apart. I steered cautiously; the barge came abreast. A startled woman and two small children gaped at our strange vessels, heavily loaded with compatriots, crewed by armed foreigners. It was hard to imagine what those people thought as the pair of LCMs headed in the opposite direction, toward the South China Sea. Quite obviously, the boat was returning from fishing. My boats were clearly on different business.

I checked my watch and was amazed to find it was already six o'clock. The evening air was cool, clear after the rain. I saw fishing boats moored in the river, off a small village on the north bank. To the south, an island obscured our view of the other bank. I knew the South Vietnamese navy had a small base on the southern shore of the river near its mouth.

Though I no longer expected trouble from the South Vietnamese, I could not be sure. General Nam might have given Thang another direct order to stop our convoy. Thang would not have bothered to chase us. Rather, he would simply have radioed the local naval commander, or the local navy officer might just stop us on his own initiative. In any case, the next hour would answer such questions.

On the Bas Sac's shore, as we neared the sea, were mangrove swamps. As I looked at that long, thin line of lush green, I was reminded that this region had been under VC control for months. The lone village in GVN hands was the small district headquarters of the chief I had visited in February. I could picture the little major, with his splayed feet and raw hands, sitting with those Delta fishermen in that hot, stinking thatch house that passed for district headquarters, working in his underwear because of the heat. Where was he today? Fleeing through the thick groves? Dead?

I scanned the fast-approaching fishing village with a pair of binoculars. On this evening there was no sign of life. Well-tended boats were riding gently at their moorings. Either its inhabitants were staying indoors for some reason, perhaps fear of the VC, or they had run into the mangroves for safety.

I called to Hasty, "Keep the Marines alert," as I steered the boat away from that side of the river, as far as I dared. But the village remained peaceful. A thousand questions were left unanswered by that sight. Watching its tranquility reminded me of our own situation. The war from which we were fleeing could now have been on another planet. The horizon spread. A stiff wind gusted into our faces. Spray was blown over the flat bow as the landing craft struck into a light swell. The green South China Sea was opening before us under dark clouds. The little convoy had at last reached the river mouth.

Everyone began scanning the horizon, straining their eyes, searching for that promised U.S. Navy ship. The sea lay empty before us, peaceful, deceitful.

I wondered for a moment what to do. Then, partly out of optimism, I suggested to the others, "Maybe a large ship can't come in so close. The water's shallow around the Bas Sac mouth," I cheerfully reasoned. "We need to go some distance out to sea."

"Why don't we lash the boats together," proposed Averill Christian, "then tie ourselves up to that piling." Christian swung his arm in the direction of some old timbers breaking the surface just off the end of the last island at the river's mouth.

A light blinked from one of the posts. It probably marked the channel entrance. "What would you do then? Wait here? And if so, for how long?" I asked.

"We'd be safe," replied Christian, "until the navy comes and picks us up."

Christian's idea might seem a reasonable alternative, yet I doubted its wisdom. This must have shown on my face because Christian added, "It will be dark shortly, Terry. We have two, small open boats." To emphasize his point, the LCM began rocking in a steeper swell as we passed through the place where the Bas Sac's huge volume of water met the sea. "Two small boats, at night, Terry! Difficult to see each other and to navigate. In daylight at least we would know our position."

"I don't disagree, Averill. But these boats are more seaworthy than you think," I countered, glancing at my own LCM. True, it was an open boat. Small? Not really. Was I overconfident? I knew something of boats and the sea and felt certain our boats would stand up to fairly heavy weather. I concluded, on careful reflection, that we would be safer at sea.

The others waited. Cushing had no strong views. Neither did Heilman. Not wishing to dismiss Christian's proposal too abruptly, I acknowledged, "Your suggestion has merit, Averill. On the other hand, I want to put as much distance as possible between us and the VC, and the South Vietnamese navy. Moreover, we will be more visible on radar out on the open sea away from the 'clutter' close to shore. The boats are seaworthy, and the sea is relatively calm. I am confident that somebody is out there waiting."

Smiling, I reminded everyone of the Phantom jet that had passed overhead earlier in the day. "That guy saw us—he even did a barrel roll overhead. And don't forget the spooks."

"None of us will ever forget the spooks," growled Christian.

"We'll put to sea," I declared, ending the discussion. Collegiality could go just so far, I decided.

There was a general grunt of accord. I glanced at the stern. "Hasty," I yelled, "where's the flag? Mount the Stars and Stripes aft and the consular flag forward."

It was Walt Heilman who thought of fastening the flags to boat hooks. Thus the convoy left Vietnam with its ensigns flying. Heilman had a smile of pride on his face. I decided not to tell my companions that I had just noticed a small problem—brackets that normally held a compass were empty.

Yet I still felt confident. The worst was past. We would be on the open sea. Like most sailors, I felt safe and comfortable on the water. I retained a fair knowledge of seamanship. When consul in Danang, I had a small motorboat and made frequent trips along the coast. We had a recent military map, if not a chart, to guide us. This gave depth measurements along the coast. From them I could see that the channel swung southeastward as it went out to sea. Of most importance, the captain of the other LCM knew these waters like the back of his hand.

I knew that a destroyer drew too much water to risk the silt-filled Bas Sac channel. Perhaps the navy had sent one to stand off just over the horizon, I mused. Using the village as a navigational reference point, I swung the LCM roughly southeast. Although the channel might be shallow, it was fairly wide. This was the safest course.

I professed complete faith in our navy. Only a few days earlier, had I not been promised a ship? Convinced that once we cleared the shore and entered deeper water a patiently waiting destroyer or LST would pick us up on her radar, I pushed open the throttles. Even now some warship could be anxiously searching for us with all the aids that modern science can provide. The navy was absolutely reliable in times of crisis, I concluded, dismissing the others' fears as the worries of landlubbers. Any moment we would see a sleek gray hull knifing over the horizon.

The rest were far less confident. Why had nobody answered our repeated radio calls, they asked. But I glibly replied that it was probably the same sort of problem as with radar. We were too close to shore for clear signals. Once out to sea, really out to sea, all difficulties would slip away, I assured them.

Christian, in particular, remained skeptical. It was already eight hours since the CIA helicopter had flown overhead. The former colonel had little faith in that particular promise to alert the navy on our behalf.

Soon the eastern horizon was changing from gray to purple. Dusk was bringing an indigo sea. The light in the west began to fail swiftly. The shoreline grew fuzzy. I remembered many years before admiring the beauty of a sunset over that table-flat landscape. Now it was almost swallowed by the coming night. Was this to be the last time I saw a day finish across the Mekong Delta? It was a sad moment.

There seemed to be more overcast out at sea. But as the last traces of day went over the horizon, we began to spot lights on the water. Some were ahead, others to port. My growing worry was of losing contact with the other LCM. I asked Hasty to call over the radio and tell its captain to steer for the clusters of lights. At the same time, I ordered the Marines to fire off some flares. Milford, another professional optimist, kept up his efforts on his radio to contact anybody.

Hope slowly rose. Excited chatter came from those on deck. But the lights turned out to be attached to fishing nets anchored to buoys. On the rich spawning banks at the mouth of the Mekong, hundreds of such lights can be seen every night, warning ships to keep clear. As soon as we closed on the lights, I remembered what they were and changed course, slightly to the south, to avoid them without losing direction.

Hasty joined Milford on radio watch. They commenced repeating "Mayday" messages on all radio frequencies of every radio on board the LCM. At twenty-minute intervals, the other Marines fired rocket flares. Hope soared into the night with each distress rocket—and fell slowly, like the smoking red fireballs that floated down for a while before hitting the waves. On the radio, any monitoring ship was asked to fire a pair of flares in answer to locate its position. But nothing broke the total blackness. Clouds concealed the stars.

Four hours later, the wind increased. A light rain began to fall. For some time, the roll of our LCM in the offshore swell had been causing some of our passengers to become sick. We were in no danger, but the rougher seas increased the pitch of our flat-bottomed boats. Unfortunately, many of the Americans and Vietnamese had never been at sea before. Moreover, Vietnamese seem more prone to motion sickness than most other people.

Soon the stench of vomit from the deck below was impossible to escape. Children began to cry. The wind was cold, adding an edge to its bite. There was not much I could do to lessen their discomfort or the children's fear, save continue my self-assurance act, which was becoming harder each minute. I had been on my feet steering the boat for almost eleven hours. If this were all, perhaps I would have felt less tired, but the voyage was the tail end of many exhausting weeks, during which I had averaged only four hours' sleep a night. My legs felt worn out, heavy. It was a feat of strength to shift my feet on the steel deck. Not even the wheel gave me much support, while wind and sea conditions required constant alertness.

Reluctantly, I concluded that no rescue vessel would slide out of this night. Better to lash the boats together and lay to for the night. Otherwise, we risked losing one another during the hours of darkness.

There was one other reason. Holding the boats together would cut out some of the constant maneuvering as we fought to keep close in a rising swell. Fuel would be saved and strain on helmsmen reduced.

That brought another matter to mind. I had began worrying about fuel. The boats had been tanked up as part of our contingency planning. But I had been planning only in terms of a journey down the Bas Sac. I had never contemplated more than a few hours at sea. (Unknown to me, both craft had fuel enough to reach the Philippines, some seven hundred miles away.) I had no idea of our vessel's range, nor did it occur to me to ask the Vietnamese crew of the other boat. Fatigue may have been lowering my mental acuity.

Pitching and rolling, the two boats edged toward each other, lonely shapes through the blackness. Heilman and Christian strained into the night as the gap narrowed. They made ready to hurl lines. Short waves were throwing spray into their faces.

Heilman flung his line at the dark hulk rising and falling with the sea. Through the gloom I saw hands reach out and safely grab the line. Then Christian hurled his, far out toward the other boat, which was swinging away. For a second it looked like it would fall short, but again, hands could be seen, reaching into the night, seizing the line. By a combination of sweat and cautious steering, the boats drew closer. Then came a crash and thump. They had swung against each other.

I called to the Vietnamese captain, "Send over somebody who knows how to switch on our navigation lights." Within a minute a wiry Vietnamese scrambled on board from the other boat. Soon he was giving me a lesson. The purpose of some of the gauges came as a surprise. With the excitement of leaving and the downriver passage, I had taken little notice of their existence.

But while this training session went ahead, the boats were beating against one another with the frightening possibility of hull damage. Both crew and passengers were becoming unsettled. Nervous, tired children were crying, and the stench of vomit was growing stronger. I decided to separate the boats.

At 11:30, I transferred Averill Christian, armed with a radio, to the other boat. There was a quick, shouted conference, for wind and sea were still rising. It was agreed the Vietnamese skipper should lead.

Reluctantly, I admitted to Cushing that he had been right. There was little prospect of rescue by the navy for some hours to come. Thus, I saw no point in wandering about the ocean without navigation aids.

The Vietnamese captain agreed, suggesting that we tie up to a fishing buoy and heave to for the night. In the morning, if no rescue ship came, we could follow the coast northward and reach the main evacuation fleet off Vung Tau, some one hundred miles to the northwest. In daylight, we would be able to navigate following the coast on our port side as we moved toward the fleet. The captain shared my confidence that the U.S. fleet would lie close inshore off Vung Tau. Laying to for the night seemed wise. Our boats would be far enough out to sea to be well clear of danger from the land.

Swinging into line, the pair of LCMs headed cautiously back toward the buoy lights, faint pinpoints of yellow twinkling on the black sea.

To port, a big firefight was going on in eastern Vinh Binh Province. Every few minutes orange flares would rise into the night, revealing the thin silhouette of land. Then came white lines of tracers and flashes from explosions before the sky ahead returned to darkness. But again fighting would break out, with the red glows expanding and contracting. At times, the wind carried the sputter of small-arms fire. It must have been a ground attack, quite a big one, which could only mean the old major's district headquarters. At that moment, watching those fiery reflections on the low clouds, I felt desperately sad and ashamed. The poor devils ashore were trapped. Even if they drove off this attack, where could they go? With reasonable luck, I would be safely on board a U.S. Navy ship tomorrow or the next day. I still had a country.

Trying to take my mind off the battle on shore, I began calculating sailing time to Vung Tau while keeping the boat on course toward the buoy lights. Heilman estimated the LCMs were making seven or eight knots against the tide, which would soon swing round to flow toward the shore. The wind grew colder.

Suddenly somebody shouted from up forward. Far away in the night was a cluster of bright lights. Heilman wondered if it was a seaside town or village. I was unsure. Christian's voice crackled out of the radio. "The captain of our boat says those are the lights of a ship."

"Is he certain?" I asked. It was still even possible, judging from their direction, that we were watching something on land.

Christian's voice came again, but this time less fuzzy. "He thinks they are from a sizable ship."

"OK. Let's give it a try," I said, not daring to hope that rescue might be at hand.

As I turned the boat in the direction of the lights, I ordered more flares fired. We watched as the red fire trails curved into the night. There was no response. The distant lights remained steady, bright. But the source was still a mystery.

Part IV

The First Boat People

≡ 17 ≡

Rescue at Sea

I checked my watch: past midnight—twelve hours in the boats. Twelve hours of steering and controlling the engines. I could feel the strain in my shoulders and legs. But I was determined to stay at the helm until we found a ship or were lashed to a buoy for the night.

Visibility from any small vessel on the open sea is poor. You're too close to the surface to see very far. To this was added the difficulty of a dark and rainy night. Several times I thought that I had lost the other boat. There seemed nothing in front of us except blackness and endless rolling waves.

"Walt," I asked Heilman, "can you stand forward? When you spot the others, give me directions."

"Sure," replied Heilman.

Down on the deck, a steady stream of Vietnamese men, women, and children were taking turns hanging over the stern to relieve themselves. Some were less surefooted than others. For some time, the vice consul had been hanging on to people. Otherwise, several surely would have fallen overboard.

"Good God!" Hank Cushing exclaimed. "Look!"

I swung round. To my astonishment I saw, right below, a young Vietnamese girl suspended in midair, dangling over the waves, held in the firm hands of two young Marines. Her pants hung around her knees. From between her open legs a stream of water poured into the sea. Both Marines had delicately fixed their eyes toward the dark sky. When finished, she giggled nervously, tugged up her pants, then gasped, *"Cam on, ong"* ("Thank you kindly, sir"). Blushing, she was returned to her huddled family in the well deck.

"Now I've seen it all," muttered Cushing.

"Is that so, Hank," I quipped.

"That really does begin to look like a ship," said Cushing.

"Thank God!" I exclaimed gratefully. I could now see masts. It was an anchored freighter of some kind.

My first reaction was relief. But as we closed on the freighter's lights, I felt a growing sense of caution. The ship had not acknowledged us, despite the flares we had fired. Clearly, the vessel must be friendly. Why would a large cargo ship be lying at anchor at a time like this, virtually floodlit, off the coast of Vietnam—other than involvement in the evacuation? Perhaps it was the navy. Had they not promised to be waiting at the mouth of the Bas Sac?

It took an hour to come within hailing distance. My weary eyes took in steep black sides, a high white superstructure. Finally, I recognized on her smokestack the red, white, and blue bands of the United States Lines. At least the question of nationality was solved. We chugged slowly toward her, turning to pass close astern. Right above me, on her stern, I saw in white letters: *Pioneer Contender*—New York. By this time, Christian's boat was hard under her great black side.

I watched from a distance with the engines of my boat idling. I was worrying about Christian. During the last weeks Christian, who was no longer young, had kept going by dogged determination. Now the retired colonel was still out in front with no thought of sparing himself. I was thankful that Christian soon would be able to rest in a proper bunk. He could not go on much longer on willpower alone.

But as I watched, something seemed to be going awry.

I moved my boat closer to get a better look. Christian was shouting upward at a sailor on deck. As I drew closer, another head appeared over the rail of the freighter. This sailor began waving his arms vigorously, leaving no room for doubt. We were being told to get away from the big ship's side. My first response was one of disbelief. As the initial shock of this rude greeting passed, we began to react. Later, Christian explained to me that he had been trying to convince those leaning over the rail that he was not a Chinese pirate. Eventually, Christian did get his message across. Even then, the same sailor waved us off again. I began to lose my temper.

Angry at this treatment, I nonetheless circled slowly while the first boat rubbed against the freighter's side. The sea was getting rougher. As I approached the ship for the second time, Christian appeared to have settled things with those on board. Suddenly, rope slings were dropped into the first boat's well deck. To my astonishment, a dozen Marines appeared along the freighter's rail. They began to lower themselves into the LCM. Soon they were expertly whisking the Vietnamese into slings and up to the ship's deck.

With the first boat empty, mine was called alongside. When I reached the other LCM I saw it was completely deserted, guns lying abandoned on the deck. I told Hasty to organize a working party and throw all guns into the sea, apart from the Marines' personal weapons. At almost the same moment a Marine captain leaned over the freighter's rail and yelled down to us that "nobody with arms was gonna come on board ship."

Hasty screamed back, "We are Marines, sir! We do not throw our arms overboard."

The captain, with Hasty's words ringing in his ears, meekly retreated. I grunted approval of Hasty's principled stand. After fourteen hours steering a boat, I really did not care what happened to a few rifles. But I did sympathize with Hasty's anguished sense of honor. The boy had done his duty. Why should he be treated like an irresponsible teenager? I made a mental note to ask if the ship had experienced some ghastly incident. Little did I know, *Pioneer Contender* had been at Danang.

Walt Heilman lent a hand with the tricky job of bringing the LCM right up to the big ship's side. The hard part was to keep the LCM steady. However, with the help of Heilman, who gave clear, sound directions, I was able to keep the LCM close enough to the ship's side to ensure that our human cargo could be safely lifted on board *Pioneer Contender* in slings.

To his credit, the first man lowered in a sling into the well deck of our LCM was the Marine captain, Garcia, who introduced himself as assistant G-3 of the 9th Marines. Most of Garcia's men were from the communications detachment of regimental headquarters. His Marines and Hasty's, working as a team, cleared the boat of its passengers. Most of the Americans were sent up in the first batches. Heilman and I remained to maneuver the LCM while Cushing helped the Marines in the well deck.

I followed each person's journey through space to the safety of the big ship's deck. Once in the sling, whole families were winched upwards by the freighter's cargo booms until, high enough to clear the rail, they were swung inboard where more Marines waited with outstretched arms. It was about this time that I was informed the navy wanted my landing craft to be off Vung Tau by morning.

At first I thought it was a joke. I stared in disbelief at the face above that had delivered this incredible news as the wind blew salt spray in my eyes. I recall being conscious of the roll and thump of the LCM as it crashed against *Pioneer Contender*'s side and of noticing how the plates in the hull were welded together. When the message was repeated, with no trace of humor, I turned to Heilman and asked, "Like to volunteer, Walt?"

Heilman's reply was short and to the point. The officer up on deck yelled again, "They want you there by morning. All you have to do is follow this ship. The navy will probably put a man on board each LCM before running into the beach."

That message hinted of a lot more than just twelve more hours on an LCM. We could be involved in lifting hundreds of people, possibly thousands, off sandy beaches. I wearily shook my head to clear it before informing the messenger, "I will have to ask for volunteers." The Vietnamese crew of the first boat refused to stay with it.

Cushing and Heilman immediately offered to take charge of one boat. Hasty volunteered to help me handle the second boat. Kassebaum, Whitten, Sciacchitano, and the other Marines volunteered to stick with me.

With that settled, I showed Hasty how the boat controls worked. Exhausted, I collapsed into an abandoned stretcher that I found on the right side of the raised afterdeck of my LCM. Grinning up at Hasty I informed him, "Your lesson is finished, young man. Congratulations, you are now a fully qualified coxswain. Call me if there is any emergency. Otherwise, you and the other Marines take turns running the boat. I am going to sleep."

The prospect of an over-the-beach evacuation was daunting. We could be ferrying refugees off the shore for days. I doubted that anybody in the fleet had a clear idea of what had been taking place the previous day at Saigon or in Vung Tau.

Some time later, Hasty awakened me.

"What the hell is it now?" I growled.

"Christian made a deal with the spooks' Filipinos," the Marine sergeant explained cheerfully. "He offered them a hundred green each to stay on board our LCMs for the night."

"And?"

"They will drive the boats up to the evacuation fleet."

"We will take charge of them again for the run into the beach at Vung Tau," I said, nodding agreement.

"One of the spooks from Can Tho is on board. He told Christian it was no problem. He'd make sure the boats arrive at the evacuation fleet."

"Seriously?"

Hasty nodded.

"Well, that really is different."

"It's about time the spooks did something for us," Hasty added.

Hasty gave me a hand up from the stretcher. The others were already on board the ship, I was informed. Brushing aside a solicitous hand, I grinned at Hasty as I told him, "Get in the sling first!" There was no protest this time.

Once in the sling, a boom winch hoisted it upwards, swinging the net out over the restless sea, then back toward the ship, until our feet thumped onto the steel deck. For a second I found it difficult to walk on the solid steadiness of the freighter. Below, the LCM still rose and fell, bumping against the ship, riding to each fresh swell of the black sea.

"Where are the Vietnamese?" I asked.

"In one of the holds, sir," replied a Marine from the loading party. "Last time I heard they were all sleeping."

"And the Americans?" I asked gratefully.

"Crew's mess. I'll show you."

At this point young Captain Garcia came striding along the deck plates. He saluted, then, with some tiredness, told me that I could sleep in the cabin occupied by the CIA man who was now going on board an LCM. But, he explained, I would have to vacate the cabin when the Agency man came back. I decided to keep my mouth shut, preferring to take up the berthing question with the ship's captain in the morning. Welcome aboard, I thought, but realized the ship had probably been taking strange faces on and off, like a bus. The crew, these Marines, must be sick and tired of all this constant upheaval.

"Mr. McNamara," somebody shouted.

I spun round to see a figure silhouetted in the yellow light of a companionway door. The voice said, "Mr. Christian has collapsed."

Christian lay on the deck of the crew's mess. A small stream of coffee was making its way along a plastic-topped table from an overturned cup. We carried the retired colonel to a cabin with two bunks. He was placed in the lower bunk. Christian was breathing heavily, his face flushed. I feared the worst.

Christian was indeed a prime candidate for a heart attack. Overweight, midfifties, and currently subject to great physical and mental strain: a classic coronary candidate. I asked him how he felt.

"Oh, I'll be all right," came a weak reply. "Just need rest, I guess."

"Thanks for all you did today, Averill."

Christian rolled his head on the pillow so he could see me, then continued in a hesitant voice, "You were right."

I smiled, trying to hide my puzzlement.

"You knew we could make it by water."

"Oh that!" I nodded. "Get some sleep."

I then went to find Captain Garcia to ask if there was a doctor on board.

"No," was the blunt reply.

"Is there a corpsman then?"

"Of course," Garcia almost protested.

"Then get him to look at Colonel Christian." I threw in the rank out of desperation. "He may have suffered a coronary."

Assuring me that his corpsman would examine Christian immediately, Garcia sent for the medic. He then informed me that the ship's master wished to see the consul general and that he would escort me to the captain's cabin. Leaving Hank Cushing (who would make sure the corpsman arrived) watching over Christian, I set off to pay my respects to the captain. Cushing at least would know where to find me in case of an emergency. As we went through the ship, I was shown a bunk in a small stateroom with a shower and a toilet. Passing by the crew's mess, I stopped to see how the others were doing and to offer them the use of my newly acquired bathing facilities. At the same time, I had to break the sad news that they would be sleeping on deck.

With Captain Garcia leading the way, I climbed a series of near-vertical steel ladders into the superstructure. The captain's quarters were directly beneath the bridge. Garcia stood aside to allow me to enter a large cabin. Three men were in the room. The tallest was a broad-shouldered, relaxed man who wore the eagles of a captain on his collar. Having made the formal introductions, he waved me to a comfortable chair opposite his own.

"Would you like a cold beer, Mr. Consul General?"

"I would indeed, Captain."

An icy can of beer was thrust into my hand. I took it gratefully, feeling yet again that a huge weight was being lifted from my back. I carefully examined the label—Miller High Life. We all laughed. The captain's wry smile, in particular, made me realize how good it was to be once more among friends. I took a long swig from the can. The beer made my nose tingle and the malty flavor cleansed the lingering taste of the sea from my mouth.

"Thanks for picking us up, Captain."

"Anytime!"

"Had you been waiting for us long?"

The captain was surprised. "We weren't waiting for you—sorry."

"Really?" I had presumed otherwise.

The captain scratched his forehead. "Not this ship. We have been here for a couple of days. We came inshore with a helicopter-carrier and another ship"—the captain raised his eyebrows—"then suddenly our companions had to depart in great haste, leaving *Pioneer Contender* by herself. Now they want us to join the main evacuation fleet off Vung Tau. That's about seventy nautical miles northeast of here. So we will sail at daybreak."

I remained baffled.

The captain noticed. He said, "You were lucky."

"Very fortunate indeed," I replied. "What were you actually doing though? Anchored this close inshore with all those lights? You're a long way south of the fleet."

"Air America has been flying Vietnamese out of the Delta for several days," the captain began. Then he said curiously, "But you know all this surely, Mr. McNamara. We have a man on board from the CIA."

"Who receives the Vietnamese as they arrive on the ship?"

"Right."

Now I began to realize how little Downs had cooperated even at the very last. Although I knew they were flying people out to the fleet, I did not know that the CIA had a ship waiting out here just off the Bas Sac. During that final twenty-four hours in Can Tho, Downs never once mentioned its existence, despite knowing that I might well be sailing down the river with several hundred helpless people. Without intending it, the CIA's private arrangements, by pure chance, had served us well. I could not fully believe this extraordinary behavior.

As much to convince myself, rather than to confirm a sin, I asked the captain, "Do you know of any other navy ship in the area, searching for people coming out of the Bas Sac?"

The captain shook his head. "There are no other ships in our immediate area," he said. "Could be the odd merchant ship, but we have nothing on radar. Like we said, Mr. McNamara, you were lucky."

"Damn right." I silently finished my beer on the verge of falling asleep. The captain kindly suggested that I might wish to go to bed after such a busy day and night. After thanking the captain and his officers once more, I made my way below. First I went to check on Christian, who was groggy from the sedative the corpsman had given him. He repeatedly insisted that he "felt all right." As I started to leave the cabin, Christian called after me.

"What is it?"

"You were right, Terry," he repeated.

"That's OK, Averill."

"I was against it—going by river. But we never would have gotten out with our employees had you not organized the evacuation downriver. Even the Americans might not have made it."

"You need sleep, my friend," I interjected. "I am proud of you, Averill. You didn't agree but still went all out to ensure the evacuation worked."

Christian lay back and shortly was peacefully asleep.

My next stop was to make sure that the rest of my gang were OK. Besides, I was hungry. I knew that I would find them in the crew's mess. As expected, they were busy eating sandwiches and drinking coffee. It was not easy to wind down after the past weeks of tension. I sat with them, accepting a huge bologna sandwich while recounting what the captain had told me. Mustard dripped from the sandwich onto the table as I talked. It was the first solid food that had passed my lips since yesterday's breakfast in Can Tho.

Hasty and his Marines found bedding and C rations with their comrades from Garcia's unit, who were themselves sleeping on deck. The other Americans were treated to "fringe benefits" by the ship's crew. Boarding with Hasty and his detachment was like flashing a club card as they came over the rail. The Marines were soon plied with food and coffee. I found them in good spirits. Nobody seemed unduly worried about spending a night on deck.

The next morning I awoke to the ship's throbbing. When the *Pioneer Contender* took a slight roll I knew she was getting under way. As speed increased, the gentle pitch and roll became more lively. I luxuriated in drowsing in my bunk. My mind carried me back to another ship, some twenty-five years before, a similar awakening, but that was in the Sea of Japan. My destination had been wartime Korea.

I lay there for a while, noticing various possessions of the cabin's owner—a hairbrush, a photograph of a woman—as they slid back and forth along the steel locker top. *Pioneer Contender* was now shuddering into a swell. Still half asleep, I guessed she was making at least ten knots. Korea: that was a long time ago.

I was amazed at the resilience of my own body, for I could not have slept more than five hours. Perhaps it showed the difference between rest under tension and simply falling asleep through tiredness.

Lowering myself from the cramped upper bunk reminded me of how stiff I was. Maybe I wasn't so resilient after all. I looked out the porthole. The ship was plowing over blue-gray seas with a sad overcast obscuring the sky.

In the distance I could make out the dark line of the Vietnamese coast. We were heading in a northeasterly direction, toward Vung Tau; no other reason for that course. Through the haze lying low over the white-specked waves, I saw the squat shapes of our LCMs, following a few hundred yards astern, rising and sinking on the swell like toys.

As I watched, a great cloud of spray hid the leading LCM. I could imagine how wet it would be on her open deck. *Pioneer Contender's* bulk was comforting. There were goose bumps on my tattooed upper arm as I squeezed into the stall shower. Marine plumbing and tepid water were unexpected comforts. Already, we were a short, safe, distance from land. No VC or NVA were cruising at sea. For the first time I realized fully what we had done. All were safe without casualty.

A shave, the taste of toothpaste in my mouth, a fresh, clean shirt, washed jeans, and I was ready to greet a new day. Task number one was to find my staff. After a few minutes of searching, I came upon them, huddled together, waiting for breakfast in the crew's mess. For most, their night had not been comfortable or dry. Nevertheless, they were still in good heart. Kass had stretched out on a coil of rope on the open deck. He had been so tired that even light rain during the night had failed to awaken him. Christian was active, cheerful, with color back in his ruddy cheeks; a healthy sparkle had returned to his eyes. When I questioned him closely, for I was taking no chances with his health, I saw that he was obviously feeling much better.

Hasty explained briefly that *Pioneer Contender* was definitely on her way to join the main evacuation fleet off Vung Tau. "What about the LCMs?" I asked.

"They're following," said Hasty. "But I don't know what happens after we reach Vung Tau."

"If the navy wants them for taking people off the beach," suggested Christian, "that could mean days."

"Sure." I nodded. "In any case, we will transfer them to the navy when we get to Vung Tau. If need be, we will run them into the beach to evacuate people."

≡ 18 ≡

USAID Logistics to the Rescue—Again

At 9:30 I went to the bridge with Hasty. Closer to Vung Tau the sea had slackened. It was still hazy. The low hills near Long Hai were almost invisible. *Pioneer Contender* slowly commenced to thread her way among an armada of different types of ships anchored well out from the shore. The navy still seemed to think there was danger from long-range guns. The big freighter edged almost apologetically between neat lines of warships. It was some time before she found her allotted anchorage, tucked out of the way in the second-class berthing among a motley fleet of merchant ships that had been gathered for the evacuation.

The radio on the bridge gave a constant running commentary. In between crackles we heard ships reporting to the task force commander. Sometimes orders were issued to a vessel. Other ships were consulting each other. Most of this clipped radio chatter seemed to be about numbers of evacuees on board individual ships. The captain told me that the U.S. Navy had just pulled off the largest helicopter evacuation in history. All round, the South China Sea was littered with wreckage and flotsam. So many Vietnamese helicopters had come out to the fleet that some had been shoved overboard. There was simply no space for more aircraft on the command ships' decks.

I felt that I should now inform the navy of our safe arrival in the main fleet. *Pioneer Contender* was adequate in an emergency, but she was not equipped to cope with American castaways on a longer-term basis. No one should be forced to spend nights sleeping on an open deck when space was available on half the ships of this mighty task force.

The captain handed me his radiophone. "Call the task force commander," he said. "Go right to the top!"

Holding the radiophone a little gingerly, I called the flagship. Once in contact, I explained who and where we were, then requested transfer to another ship. Silence followed. After some minutes my message was acknowledged. Further silence. Then an irritated voice coldly instructed that I should await a reply. Time passed slowly. I grew impatient.

Yet I knew how much radio traffic was in the air. Several hundred evacuees were lost among thousands being scooped off the shore. Even so, there had been only four consulates general in Vietnam, which made one wonder whether anybody would have noticed if we had been left in Can Tho.

Hasty remarked cheerfully, "Military Sealift Command seems to be in confusion this morning."

While we waited, one of our LCMs picked up some refugees from a fishing boat. The LCM requested permission to come alongside and off-load. When the number was established, the captain gave Hasty permission to control this operation by radio. He added, "Sergeant Hasty, warn the Filipino crew this is it. No more."

No sooner had the refugees climbed on board *Pioneer Contender* than Garcia's Marines, armed with M-16 rifles, lined the rail, firing single shots into the water to keep all local boats away. By midmorning crowded fishing sampans were wandering among the gray steel ships of America's rescue fleet.

Fed up with waiting, I again called the flagship. This time I was less courteous. Suddenly, in the middle of this maddeningly impersonal radio chatter, a friendly voice broke in. It identified itself as the USAID chief of logistics at New Port.

But New Port was many miles up the Saigon River. The VC must have taken New Port hours ago. The same friendly voice went on to announce that a Japanese tug, on lease to USAID, would arrive at 1:00 P.M. She would pick us up for transfer to a Korean LST. The latter, much bigger than our LCMs, was built to put tanks onto a beach. It was a proper ship built for the high seas. The Vietnamese from Can Tho were to remain on the *Pioneer Contender* for the journey to a temporary refugee camp on the island of Guam.

I thanked the voice. It had brought a human dimension to the detached coldness of fleet radio traffic. As I stepped off the bridge, my ears were still tuned in to that eerie formality. I shuddered. But, I soon accepted that perhaps it was the only way to cope with such a gigantic human tragedy—to adopt a faceless, impersonal attitude, turn yourself into a sprocket of the big navy machine.

In the crew's mess, I quickly spread the word. In about one hour we would leave *Pioneer Contender*. I suggested that the Americans get their meager belongings together and say good-bye to their Vietnamese friends. But first one last task had to be carried out—discreetly. All Vietnamese employees were told to gather on the stern, away from other curious eyes. Christian, when lookouts confirmed all was quiet and safe, began handing each man his pay, in dollar bills. I had given instructions that all the American cash at the consulate general be brought with us—not left behind or unaccounted for.

This impromptu payday finished, I wished all good luck, thanked them for years of loyal service, and explained how the *Pioneer Contender* would take them all to Guam. From that island they would be flown to the United States. I added that I hoped we would all meet again in the United States. There was one last word from Hank Cushing. "Keep those dollars out of sight," he warned. "Keep your mouths shut. Otherwise, you could lose your money and maybe your life." Nobody disagreed.

Next, I went down into the poorly lit forward hold. Several hundred pairs of wondering almond-shaped eyes greeted my arrival. I wished to reassure these poor frightened people who faced an unknowable future. I moved among the little family groups, squatting or lying on the dark steel deck. Whenever I saw familiar faces I stopped, said a brief au revoir, then moved casually to the next group.

Not all those in the hold were known to me. I presumed that many were from upcountry or had worked in some capacity for the CIA. Unexpectedly, I came upon a familiar figure dressed in the uniform of an ARVN colonel. It was Nam's chief of logistics. As my eyes adjusted to the gloom in the ship's hold, I saw other ARVN officers with their families. It suddenly dawned on me why Nam had ordered the RVN navy to bring us back to Can Tho. He must have assumed that I was carrying deserting senior officers in my boats. Instead, these people had been evacuated in helicopters by the CIA. They were the reason the Can Tho CIA needed a navy ship laying off the Delta. Deserting ARVN officers could not have been sent to Saigon for regular evacuation from Tan Son Nhut. No wonder our CIA colleagues were reluctant to join us on the river.

At one point, I drew Bao Gia aside. Without anyone seeing, I shoved a fistful of dollars into the boy's trouser pocket. "Don't use them till you are off the ship, Gia," I whispered. The young man nodded, his aquiline features tired, sticky with sweat, yet with a gleam of determination filling his sad eyes.

A few feet away I saw Phuoc, whom I beckoned to join us. "Treat him like a younger brother, Phuoc." The driver nodded. "And stick together." The eyes of both confirmed they understood. "Now, here's my mother's name, address, phone number. The town is Troy. It's in a state called New York. That's on the other side of America, roughly 150 miles north of New York City."

Again both nodded that they understood.

"Once you get near a telephone," I said, "put a call through to my mother. Tell her where you are. She will help you, and I will contact you as soon as I can, OK?"

After visiting with others who had come out in our boats, I placed a foot on the bottom rung of the steel ladder, glancing round one last time to make certain that an adequate supply of drinking water and food was set out in the hold. But as I expected, all were being well cared for by the *Pioneer Contender*'s crew.

What would become of all these trusting people? They had trusted once and look where they had ended—in a ship's hold with no real idea of what the future held, armed with only those treasured possessions that they could carry with them. I knew that I could do no more for them under the present circumstances. They were safe, dry, and would be fed by the navy. The hold was primitive, but not uncomfortable or dangerous.

Emotionally spent, I began to climb the ladder. "Sir, oh sir, it is a small request please," a woman's voice called softly in fluent French. Turning once more I found myself looking down into the large eyes of Madame Duc.

"I wish to thank you," she said, her delicate features taut with emotions, "for saving me and my children."

I grunted politely, unable to put my thoughts into words. This was one conversation that I had hoped to avoid. Duc had stayed. And I knew that he would never leave Nam's side unless ordered.

The dreaded question came. "Have you any news of my husband—or the general?" The large eyes were full of charm and hope.

"Not since leaving Can Tho." I added honestly though kindly, "I'm afraid we don't know very much about what is going on ashore."

"Yes, it is early," she said with eyes now frightened, glistening.

I was momentarily at a loss. Then I asked, "Have you any friends or relatives outside Vietnam to whom you can go? What are you going to do once off the ship?"

"I have family in France. They are related to the Martinis whom you know from Africa."

"Of course." I remembered the Martini family at the French Embassy during my two years in Dahomey. That seemed a lifetime ago. "Well," I said with a wan smile, "please give them my regards when you see them." My words seemed to brighten her face. "Good luck," I added as I escaped up the ladder. There was no way I could assure her that her husband would survive. Indeed, I was convinced the man was either dead or a prisoner.

When I stepped on deck, a fresh wind was driving waves against the big ship. A small tugboat was alongside *Pioneer Contender.* Time to go, I realized, walking a little faster to gather my few belongings from the cabin. Having closed my small bag, I went back up to the bridge where I thanked the captain and his officers for rescuing us. Before leaving, I added my polite concern for the Vietnamese in the hold who, I explained, had loyally served the U.S. government for many years. The captain understood my concern and told me not to worry. "They will be safe and well cared for as long as they are on this ship."

It was a long climb down *Pioneer Contender*'s side to the tug's deck. Once we were aboard, the tug drew away quickly. I still suffered pangs of guilt. The voyage to Guam would be very long for the Vietnamese down in the hold. On the other hand, removing the eighteen Americans was probably the best thing I could have done. Our presence on board had simply further reduced the limited supply of rations and water. Besides, I was responsible for seeing that my American colleagues did not suffer unnecessarily.

The tug was modern with an odd, forward-leaning superstructure, a typical Japanese ship design. When her engines reached full speed, it was obvious they were extremely powerful. The skipper was a breezy Australian, his crew Japanese. *Pioneer Contender* began to shrink. Soon she was just one of the larger ships anchored in the midst of the fleet, merging into the haze, growing smaller every second.

A few minutes went by, then out of the mist came the low shapes of a pair of LCMs. Spray flew from their flat prows as the boats made a wide slow circle. I could see the CIA Filipino employees waving from the wheelhouse on each boat. I raised both arms to return their farewell. Across the open waters came the lonely wail of boat horns. The Filipinos were saying good-bye—and also thank-you. It gave me a feeling of having done something worthwhile during all this mess.

Just before leaving the *Pioneer Contender,* I had been informed the navy had decided not to use the LCMs in an over-the-beach evacuation. Thus we were relieved of the need to take back control of the LCMs. The *Pioneer Contender*'s captain told me not to worry; the boats would be taken aboard a navy ship to be returned to the United States. The Filipinos, he said, would rejoin their Vietnamese families and be taken back to their country. One hopes this did not complicate previous domestic arrangements when they all returned to the Phillipines.

On board the tug, I soon found familiar faces. Bob Lanigan from Saigon was in the pilothouse. So were others who had been towed down the Saigon River in barges. I began exploring the little ship. Below, I discovered the crew's mess and galley were like floating branches of the Cholon PX, crammed with cases of gourmet foods and quantities of hard liquor "rescued" from the New Port commissary.

Lanigan and I began comparing notes. "We had great difficulty," he said, "in persuading people that evacuation down the Saigon River was viable. I kept saying that it was the best means of coping with large numbers of evacuees." Bitterly he continued, "No attention was paid to us or to a water alternative. They just pressed on with evacuation by air. In the end, our barges left Saigon half empty."

I was surprised and saddened to find that others had been fighting similar battles with Saigon.

"We had an easy trip," he said. "Little bit of ineffective sniper fire directed from the banks—but that was all. Shit, one barge even ran aground on that real twister of a bend in the river. But these tugs are something else! Came off like a cork out of a bottle. We were out at sea well before dark. Choppers kept passing over our boats, lights blinking, the whole bit, most of the night," Lanigan recounted as he leaned on the tug's railing.

"Really?" I had not expected that. "I thought air evacuation was supposed to stop at dusk."

"Terry," Lanigan began sadly, "it was a mess. I get so furious just thinking about the whole damn thing. People on the evacuation lists were trapped in houses. People waited on roofs for helicopters that never came. The embassy was besieged by a desperate mob as the Marine helicopters took load after load off its roof. You could see it from the port! And we sat there for hours. At one point we thought the whole damn city might come crashing through the dock gates. For a long while, nobody came. Then a trickle. Finally we had to go—with one barge half full. Others were empty. As were some ships. In the end, we heard those big Marine choppers flying overhead until well past dawn."

"Jesus! I had no idea it was that bad," I murmured.

Lanigan yawned and asked, "How about you?"

"We started by getting arrested. Took two hours until we were released. Then about halfway downriver the VC fired a B-40. But they missed. Our radios never worked. We never raised anybody or anything during fourteen hours. We could not find a promised navy ship, then *Pioneer Contender* rose out of the night." Surprising myself, I concluded, "But it was a fairly uneventful trip, come to think of it."

Lanigan rubbed his eyes with both hands. Spray was being blown in our faces. "What are you going to do now, Terry?" he asked with a tired grin.

I couldn't think what to say. For the first time in weeks I had no responsibilities. Somebody else was charged with our safety. "Whatever I am told." I laughed and watched foam from the wake bubble up well astern.

I wondered what it was like in Can Tho that morning. At least I could say truthfully that those Vietnamese employees from the consulate general who were still there had made their own decision to stay. All who were on the final evacuation list and still in Can Tho had been given a fair opportunity to leave in the boats. The overwhelming majority had taken it.

I then went forward to where Kass and some of the others were half asleep, sitting with their backs braced against the curved gunwale of the bow, out of the wind and salty spray. I sat down with them. Within seconds I was sleeping, deeply, for the second time in a month. The first had been the night before on the *Pioneer Contender.*

When I awoke, it was afternoon. I checked my watch. It was four o'clock. The tug was still heading south. I asked Kass, "What's the latest?"

Kass shrugged his shoulders. "There's a Korean LST waiting for us somewhere out there. But you know that. Sorry—not fully awake myself, Terry."

"No problem. It's a USAID-leased ship, I guess."

"I think so."

"They were used to run supplies up and down the coast under charter."

Kass said, "The tug is going back to Australia."

"Then I hope we find that LST!"

Kass laughed. My run-ins with Australians were almost folklore. Then he quipped, "But I guess your principles fall short of declining an Aussie beer."

"You're right." I grimaced as I pulled myself to my feet and stretched.

We were opening cans of beer in the galley when someone on deck shouted: "LST in sight!" A quarter of an hour later the tug drew alongside, rocking severely with the swell, pitching clouds of salt spray as the gap narrowed. A wooden ladder was lowered from the much higher, rust-stained gray side of the LST onto the small tug's superstructure. Trying not to look down at the green water swirling below, we clambered warily up the ladder, clinging to our few belongings, staring only upwards into the curious faces of Korean deckhands waiting to haul us safely on board. Once on deck, as a man, we turned and waved farewell to the chubby little tugboat. She had heard our call and had come to the rescue.

The Korean LST was in much worse condition than she had appeared from the tug. Standing on the blackened steel deck, I could see dirt and rusting paint everywhere I looked. The Koreans had gotten her from the U.S. Navy, but being a hardworking and resourceful race, had immediately rented the vessel and a crew back to Military Sealift Command. Down through the years of war, she had carried military supplies from Saigon to Cam Ranh Bay, Nha Trang, Phan Rang, Danang. She had sailed up major rivers, too, which was why the ship had been in New Port. When final evacuation had been ordered, she was still under contract to the USAID logistics staff in New Port. Loaded with supplies and fuel, these gentlemen had very sensibly put to sea, having equally sensibly offered passage to dozens of Vietnamese officers with their families. The LST was crammed with people.

Cushing, Kassebaum, and I began a futile reconnaissance of the ship. The crew's living quarters were overflowing with American and Vietnamese logistics officers and their large families. Kass remarked wearily that salary, profession, and number of children were definitely linked in Vietnam. Many of the Americans also had large Vietnamese families. After half an hour, rather dejected, I led them back to the open deck where we bedded down. Fortunately, we found a clean space with a fair amount of room.

The Koreans were doing their best. Yet it would have been expecting too much, with all those well-heeled distributors of Uncle Sam's bounty on board as passengers, not to expect that self-interest would arrange cabin bookings.

That evening, leaving our gear on deck, my companions and I trudged below for supper. Elbowing our way into the packed crew's mess, we found a menu of watery soup accompanied by canned beans saved from the New Port Commissary. All was laced with fiery kimchi, as if the cook thought a reminder were needed of his nationality. I thought of that can of Australian beer on the tug. Maybe Australians were not so bad after all, I pondered remorsefully, as I drank glass after glass of powdered lemonade mixture trying to cool my mouth.

I next considered sending a message to Washington. Clearly our families back in the States must be reassured of our safety. Again, help came from the resourceful American logistics chief. He added his considerable weight to my request to the Korean captain. A short message was written by Mac Prosser, one of my officers, listing our eighteen names with the fact that the American consulate general at Can Tho had been closed and all personnel safely evacuated to the fleet offshore.

The Koreans would send the message through navy channels and have it receipted—which they said was very important—but apologized that it would not be transmitted until nightfall, when fleet radio traffic was less congested. To my knowledge, this message never reached the State Department. It seems the navy was again too busy to bother with a small group of lost Americans sending messages from a "foreign" ship.

With the setting of the sun, a stiff breeze picked up. Soon the temperature fell uncomfortably. My group, acclimated to years spent in the steamy heat of Cochin China, was unused to cool temperatures, nor did we have warm clothing. When we asked for bedding, no spare blankets could be found. For the second night running, my colleagues lay on a steel deck and slept under the stars. All we could do for warmth was to huddle together.

As the night became colder, several of us climbed onto some small rickety tables that had been left on deck. This at least got us off the cold, dirty deck. Hank Cushing and Kass had found a folding canvas cot and climbed in, each tucking his feet under the opposite man's chin. Wrapping themselves in flags saved from the consulate general, they slept. In the clean light of dawn, I woke to find a couple of bodies wrapped stiffly in the American flag. For a moment I had the terrible thought that a couple of passengers had died during the night and were ready for burial at sea.

Toward midmorning, a message came from the flagship. The USS *Blue Ridge* would send helicopters to take us off the LST. Hallelujah! We had not been forgotten after all, just temporarily misplaced. The choppers would arrive during the afternoon. With unmilitary lack of precision, no time was given. My band once more settled down to wait.

It was tedious, if not unpleasant, sprawling on the rusty deck plates enjoying hot sunshine and a cooling sea breeze while we listened to the groaning of the LST's anchor chain. We now lay some miles offshore with the coast only an indistinct shadow along the western horizon.

It was not hard to adjust to such peaceful and carefree living. Yet the sudden change of pace made us more impatient. Even the collected Hank Cushing was glancing at the sky. Finally, just before noon, the familiar clatter of helicopters was heard somewhere off to starboard. As the drumming beat grew louder, we strained into the glare. Soon two green Hueys were circling the lonely LST.

Dozens of Vietnamese surged on deck. Aided by Hasty's Marines, the Korean crew organized a clear space in the center of the deck. Hasty waved in the first helicopter, ducking as flakes of rust and paint were torn from the LST by the prop-wash. The helicopter settled, rotor turning, barely resting on its skids, while the first group squashed on board. There were too many Americans for all to be taken off in a single lift.

"Averill," I bawled over the din, "you go on this first flight." As I pushed Christian forward, I shouted to the helmeted crew chief that Colonel Christian was ill and should be seen by a doctor as soon as he arrived on the flagship. I then helped Christian into one of the canvas seats that faced each other in the crowded Huey. He was soon strapped in tight. Before they left I shouted up at those in the helicopter, "Make sure the navy doesn't forget us again!" Christian's reply was lost in a gale of wind and noise as the Huey thumped back into the sky. I stood with Cushing, Kass, and Hasty, watching for some time, before settling down once more to wait.

We were now part of the system, with all the imposed long waits and sporadic bursts of action. Our problem was compounded by the fact that we were civilians, outsiders, dealing with the military machine. My "do-it-yourself" evacuation did not help to regularize our situation. Nonetheless, our small group had finally penetrated the system and could no longer easily be ignored by it, avoided by it, or completely forgotten by it.

At 3:00 P.M. two small specks began to grow in the southern sky. The sound of rotors beating came faintly over the water. A few minutes passed and then the pair of helicopters noisily circled overhead. Down came the first Huey until its skids were resting lightly on deck. A crewman jumped onto the steel plates, his enormous green helmet making him resemble one of Darth Vader's villainous warriors from deep space. To us, he was a final guide on our trek to "the world."

I took a last glance at dozens of Vietnamese faces pressing in round the cleared space. I wished I could take them all with me. Clearly, this was not possible. In any case, the Koreans would do their best to care for their passengers. The Can Tho group's absence would make their task a bit easier. Watching as the first Huey took off, Hasty waved in the second. I shrugged my shoulders. There was nothing else to be done other than thanking the Koreans and the ever-helpful USAID logistics chief. I followed the last of my group into the helicopter. The aluminum deck of the chopper seemed amazingly new and shiny after the dirt and rust beyond the Huey's doors. A broadly grinning Hasty was seated opposite me.

I felt the surge of the lift, the nose dipping slightly, as the Huey slid forward and skyward. Faces below grew less distinct, the squat LST shrank into a model ship, unlovely, alone again, peacefully moored on the lazy blue surface of the sea. Then the Huey swung away as our most recent temporary home fell behind and beneath the skids, to vanish from sight.

With more altitude, the wind through the open doors grew cooler. It was less hazy up higher. I guessed that the Huey was flying at about two thousand feet. Within minutes we began to see other ships. For miles to both sides, vessels of every description lay anchored on the calm, flat sea. It was an incredible display of power.

I shook my head in dismay. How could a nation with so much strength end a war abandoning its allies and saving its own citizens in such ignominious circumstances? It would not be the last time I would ask that question in the months and years ahead. The sight of this huge fleet was a wound that would never fully heal.

═══ 19 ═══

"Terry and His Pirates" Join the Navy

The Huey banked and began to descend fast. Below was a big vessel painted warship gray yet resembling a merchant ship. As we approached, the image changed. She had landing pads for helicopters on the great open deck. Her central island was festooned with radar dishes and whip aerials. When the Huey began its final lineup, the full deck slid into view. Several silver and blue Air America helicopters were parked on the flight line. I wondered if some were from Can Tho.

What would I say to Downs? Dismay had given way to disgust. Nobody can predict how someone will react in the face of danger. It was a feeling of disappointment most of all. Downs—cool, tough-looking, athletic—fitted an American's best self-image. Nonetheless, it was he who had run away. Ironically, it was people like the seemingly mild, but tough Kassebaum, an ex–Peace Corps volunteer with no previous training for such a crisis, and Hank Cushing, the former college professor, who had put up a firm display of daily courage. What would I say if confronted with Downs? The idea that both of us might end up on the same ship had not, until then, crossed my mind.

The Huey landed with a firm bump at 4:05 P.M. on May 1. We were technically back in "America"; the odyssey was finished. A naval officer in light tan uniform helped me onto the deck. He then introduced me to the executive officer of the *Blue Ridge,* who courteously welcomed me aboard. Feeling in good hands, I followed the "exec" across the windy flight deck to a small office in the superstructure. Inside, sailors working under strong electric lighting were collecting guns. Without regret I handed over my pistol. I had no attachment to firearms.

A minor crisis developed: the sailors wanted my kukri as well. One rule for all, they insisted. I had a nagging fear that I might never see the knife again. After some discussion, the ship's executive officer intervened to say I could keep my treasured kukri. A receipt was given for the pistol with a promise it would be sent to my home. I never saw the pistol again.

The *Blue Ridge*'s large wardroom had been converted into a reception area for evacuees. Sailors, ready with neat piles of forms, sat at trestle tables waiting to welcome us back to the joys of bureaucracy. Soon I was writing out my life history, bit by bit, as I filled in the squares and question blanks on the forms. I looked up and grinned at the executive officer.

"Could we send a message to Washington?" I asked.

"Sure, write it out."

Having less than full confidence that the message sent by the Koreans had gotten through, I jotted down a few lines reporting again that the Can Tho consulate general had been closed and that its American, its third-country-national, and a large part of its Vietnamese staff evacuated. The evacuation was now successfully completed with no losses or injuries. I handed it to the executive officer.

After reading it swiftly, the officer said, "Fine. We've reported to CINCPAC your being on board. But I'll see if we can push this through to Washington a little faster. After all," he smiled in a wry way, "you're our celebrity guests, Mr. McNamara."

With usual naval courtesy, as a senior officer I was offered a stateroom. "That's very kind," I said, but I wondered where my companions would be berthed. "And will my colleagues be nearby?" I had no wish to appear ungracious, but I could not bring myself to leave the others completely cut off from whatever influence I could command.

"Well, they will go down to the empty troop sleeping compartment with the other evacuees," came the frank reply.

"Look, I'm sorry," I said with embarrassed protest, "but I can't accept better accommodation than my companions. You understand."

"But you're a senior officer, sir."

"Think how you would feel," I pleaded, wondering if I was making a fool of myself, yet convinced that fundamentally my reaction was right.

At any rate, the young officer in charge of billeting screwed up his face, studied his clipboard, then said with warmth, "We can fit them all into staterooms, sir, except your Marines. They belong to the Marines again—and that means the troop compartments with the other Marines."

At that moment Major Kean strode across the reception area. Kean commanded all Marine guards in the embassy security detachments throughout the Far East. He and his men were certainly the last official Americans to leave Vietnam. He looked exhausted, though in good spirit. "Well done, sir," he shouted, then shifted to congratulate Hasty and his Marines. "You did the good job we expected."

We shook hands warmly. "Congratulations yourself." I sighed and said, "I wouldn't have changed places with you for a ton of gold. It must have been awful at the embassy. How did you manage to organize any kind of order under those conditions?"

We had started to hear about those last hours in Saigon. Kean shrugged his shoulders, too modest for any explanation. One accidental shot could have started a massacre. To this day, I believe that Kean deserves more credit than he has been given. His men and their discipline did not fail under incredibly trying circumstances.

Another friendly Marine officer pushed through the gathering crowd. This was the colonel who attended Jacobson's evacuation planning session in Saigon. He wanted to apologize that no ship had been waiting for us off the Bas Sac. He was clearly angry with the navy, yet delighted that Can Tho had made it down the river on its own. There was a lot of talking and quiet good humor. Hasty and the other Marines were taken to see Brigadier General Carey, commander of the 9th Amphibious Brigade. Carey sat them down in his quarters, gave them glasses of iced tea—the first cold drink for them in three days—and asked questions about the evacuation. When they finished, the general congratulated them on a fine performance, then sent Hasty and his men back to Major Kean for billeting. This unusual courtesy by a senior officer was a Marine's way of recognizing young troopers who had performed in the best traditions of an exacting corps.

With Cushing, I set off to find the cabin assigned to us by the young naval officer. To our amused surprise, the young man had given us the chaplain's cabin. We pushed open the door. Two large bunks filled the far end of the room, with lockers and a writing desk built along one bulkhead. On the other bulkhead was a washstand and more lockers. Cushing whistled with pleasure.

The chaplain was on leave. Most of the lockers were full of his clothes and souvenirs. This was not inconvenient, as neither of us had much in the way of personal belongings. Cushing had only the clothes he was wearing, and I had few more. We each borrowed a towel from the chaplain's ample supply, took refreshing showers in the neighboring "head," after which we decided to have a nap. Those bunks were too good to ignore.

I awakened to the tinny blast of a bosun's pipe reverberating from speakers throughout the ship. I groped for my watch. I had slept more than an hour. Cushing was slowly stirring in the bunk above. I was hungry, for none of us had eaten properly since the morning we left Can Tho. I rolled myself off the lower bunk, woke Cushing, then went down the cabins waking the others. There was no difficulty in finding the crew's mess: you simply followed the stream of evacuees.

On the mess deck, we caught sight of Hasty and his Marines. While we stood in the chow line together under harsh strip lighting, Cushing and I studied the faces of evacuees from Saigon. It was a further shock for both of us. Almost nobody smiled. There was little conversation. Some seemed to be sleepwalking, in deep trauma. I passed the word down the line of my group, "There is a table free on the far side of the mess hall."

I did not want my people catching this depression. Apart from the normal wish to keep morale high, I was proud of the way my staff had performed. The big decisions had been made by others. Nobody in Can Tho was to blame for the collapse of South Vietnam. We had withdrawn in an orderly fashion, under difficult circumstances. Most important, we had kept faith with our Vietnamese colleagues when it would have been far easier to abandon them as so many others had done.

Ignoring the general air of gloom, I began asking members of my group if everyone was comfortable. They seemed to be the only ones among the evacuees able to exchange normal banter. The Marines enthusiastically described their interview with General Carey. In young voices that swelled with growing pride, stories poured back and forth over the table. Cushing and I ate steadily, exchanged amused expressions, sometimes chipping in a remark when a story became too far-fetched.

It began to dawn on me that, as long as I kept my people together, my group might still perform some useful service. People with their brains and wits intact were going to be in short supply I suspected—certainly among the civilians brought out of Vietnam.

Cushing poked me lightly in the ribs and whispered, "I think our guys are providing the entertainment tonight!"

I looked around the expansive mess deck to see what Cushing meant.

Our group had indeed become the center of a quiet circle of approving sailors and Marines from the *Blue Ridge*'s crew. Within minutes, the invisible barriers between crew and passengers broke down. A Marine sergeant leaned over and said, "You're easy to identify. You're the only close-knit group among all the evacuees we got on board, sir. You're the only ones who don't look like they've just taken a beating. You people have spirit."

I looked the sergeant in the eyes. "I'll tell you a secret," I said. "If anything, these guys are worse bullshitters than before we left Can Tho!"

A sailor sitting with the sergeant added quietly, "Sir, you people are the one bright spot in an otherwise sordid mess."

By this time the group at the table had expanded into an adjoining long mess table. Marines and sailors were shifting benches, climbing over tables, until we had an audience of some thirty or forty. I found myself next to a burly, red-haired first class quartermaster, who happened to be the mess deck master-at-arms, a position of some power on any navy ship. It might be described as a cross between a police chief and a straw boss.

The master-at-arms asked, "Err, tell me, General," in reverential tones, "this outfit is kind of special, I presume?" I listened with interest. This was a man of influence and power, who should be treated as such. He was responding to the easy informality of our group, though puzzled to the edge of awe at the way Marine enlisted men were joking with a "general." He sent for more coffee and ice cream (it was not on the menu that day), then asked the location of my cabin.

"I guess you're pretty tired, General," he consoled with a gruff smile. "You just stay in the sack tomorrow morning. I'll send one of my mess cooks along with coffee and donuts."

I accepted this generous offer with all the graciousness at my command. This was not merely the natural kindhearted hospitality of young sailors and Marines. This was the red carpet itself. I knew from experience that breakfast in bed is not a common practice in the U.S. Navy.

Next morning, having breakfasted on hot cinnamon rolls and fresh coffee, I ventured down to the crew's mess deck. My main purpose was to express my gratitude to our benefactor. But there was another reason. During the night it occurred to me that Can Tho personnel needed a focal point on board *Blue Ridge*, for we would certainly be on the ship for several days. She would soon head for Subic Bay in the Philippines, a voyage of about seven hundred miles.

Cushing and I were hoping the master-at-arms might extend his influence in helping us borrow somebody's office. A great deal of paperwork needed completing before the group scattered, as it almost certainly would on arrival in the Philippines or eventually in the United States.

I had one driving reason for wishing to get certain facts written down, witnessed, and properly recorded. I believed the wave of revulsion sweeping America about everything connected with Vietnam would one day give way to a growing interest. The normal pressure of human curiosity was bound to mean that, in future years, as passions cooled, Americans would wish dispassionately to examine the war, its outcome, and how it was conducted. To my thinking, it was essential that accurate, firsthand accounts be preserved for future historians. Memories of events have a way of dimming and distorting, so it is important to record events while memories are still fresh. Thus, I asked each man to write an account of our escape for the historical record.*

Furthermore, every Foreign Service officer is entitled to an annual efficiency report. We would be on *Blue Ridge* for some days, not a bad time for quiet reflection about other people's futures. The performance evaluation report is the only official evidence a State Department officer has of the quality of his work. His next assignment and his chances for promotion depend to a large extent on these annual reports. Loyalty is a two-way street. I knew my staff would soon be competing with their contemporaries throughout the world for posts in Europe, Africa, Asia, or Latin America. My officers had coped with a great deal more than was normally expected of Foreign Service officers. It was my responsibility to make certain that appropriate comments be included in their files.

When I again arrived in the brightly lit crew's mess, the master-at-arms was busy organizing lunch. When he saw me, he stopped what he was doing to inquire, "How is the general feeling this morning?" His eyes had that alert tiredness of men who spend a lifetime rising and working two or three hours before daybreak. With due humility, for I knew from my own days as an enlisted man in the navy that the senior petty officers on a ship normally keep it running with an informal system of swapping favors, I proceeded to work my way into that privileged circle on the *Blue Ridge.* Surely, the needs of such a small group as mine could be easily met.

"Big Red" listened with no expression. Not a flicker of encouragement passed from his somber eyes. When I had finished, he said in a matter-of-fact tone, "General, you need to see the chief. He may be able

---

* See the appendix to this book for Sergeant Hasty's account.

to liberate an office." Summoning one of his many subordinates, "Red" instructed him to "lead General McNamara to the chief." It was a long journey.

With the sailor leading the way, I passed through a labyrinth of companionways, climbed up and down vertical steel ladders, clambered through watertight doors, and finally found myself in a large, comfortable, air-conditioned compartment. It had teletype machines, metal desks on which stood typewriters, closed-circuit television, and a general air of luxury that was confusing, for the place was also half-filled with a collection of nondescript individuals dressed mainly in jeans and combat jackets. As my eyes grew accustomed to the scene, I began to recognize among the civilian outfits some of those peculiar bush suits cut by a generation of Saigon tailors. This was clearly the press center.

Near the door, a sailor sat at a small desk. He appeared to be a sort of majordomo. I approached him and politely inquired if it were possible to see the chief. My sailor escort swiftly intervened, introducing me as "the general" before repeating my request. At the word "general," the man at the desk straightened his back, grabbed the telephone, dialed a number, and waited. There was a click at the other end of the line.

The young sailor cautiously began, "Excuse me, Chief, there is a *general* who wishes to speak with you. He is now in front of *my* desk, Chief. Shall I ask the *general* if he would wait, Chief?" There was a second's worth of babble. The boy smiled widely, "The chief will be right along, sir." He lowered the telephone carefully onto its cradle.

A small, harassed man suddenly appeared beside me. He wore gloom and despair on his face as clearly as the many badges of rank and service on his sleeve. His eyes were red from fatigue, his uniform crumpled from too many hours without rest. He explained that he was the chief petty officer in charge of public information and waved an arm tiredly toward the crowd of journalists. "What can I do for you, General?" he asked without enthusiasm.

I guessed the man had been coping with obscure requests all night, each one of which had been of desperate importance to its originator. I decided to slow down the pace.

With a broad smile, I introduced myself as the consul general from Can Tho. The formalities done, I explained my need for an office. Carefully, I injected "Big Red's" name in my pitch.

The chief's attitude seemed to change. At the mention of Red's name, he became more relaxed, confiding in a nervous, high-pitched conspiratorial voice that he had been up all night organizing the press room and ensuring that the small army of journalists, who had just come on board, were well cared for.

I tried to listen with signs of sympathy. I nodded, shook my head at the breaks in the chief's monologue. I was probably the first civilian the chief had been frank with in years. When the chief paused for breath, I quickly asked, "Might there be some office space available, Chief?"

"The chaplain's," he replied without blinking.

"Seriously?" I was beginning to feel I knew the chaplain.

"He's on leave. There's a chaplain's assistant there, but he isn't busy. Follow me, sir."

We pushed open a steel door. Next to the press center was another compartment with several doors leading in different directions. The chief stopped at a smaller door on the right side of the compartment with the caption "Chaplain" stenciled above it. The chief pushed the door open with a clank.

Inside, a young sailor was seated behind a typewriter. The chief said, "This is Consul General McNamara. He requires this office space. Make yourself useful or scarce."

Without losing a second, the sailor gathered up a collection of pipes and several Mickey Spillane paperbacks, but left the typewriter where it stood. He had urgent business in another part of the ship.

I thanked the chief profusely and offered any help that my men and I could provide to lighten the chief's burdens. The chief grinned, said thanks but he had trouble enough, and departed chuckling.

I carefully locked the office door, slipping the key in my pocket, and set off to find the others. They were sitting in a lounge outside my stateroom.

"Gentlemen," I announced in triumph, "we have a home." I led them to the new "Headquarters of Consulate General, Can Tho—Somewhere at Sea."

Sergeant Hasty posted a sentry. Somebody produced a sign identifying the chaplain's office as "Consulate General, Can Tho." From that moment until *Blue Ridge* steamed into Subic Bay, this office was the pride and focal point of our group.

Hasty made certain that one of his Marines was always on hand to accept messages or to receive callers. Soon a regular and plentiful supply of baked foods and coffee flowed along the gangways from Big Red's galley to our office. Within a day or so, we had annexed the lounge next door and decorated it with the flags brought out from the consulate general, the same ensigns that had flown over our LCMs during the escape downriver. These decorations seemed to delight the chief. He stood admiring the flags for a moment before remarking, "General, you lend some class to this place."

It was our fourth day on board when I was summoned to see Graham Martin. I had known that the ambassador was on the ship, occupying the admiral's quarters, high up in the bridge superstructure. John Hogan, Martin's press officer, escorted me past stiffly saluting Marine guards to see the ambassador in his quarters. The cabin was large and comfortably furnished, with a further cabin for sleeping and a small galley. Ambassador Martin stood alone in the middle of the day quarters, waiting for Hogan and me.

He greeted me with a broad smile, said how good it was to see me. I was caught slightly off guard by his worn appearance. He congratulated me on our evacuation, praising me for what he described as "steady stewardship" during my time in Can Tho. I was becoming uneasy, not knowing where this eulogy might be leading.

Finally, things began to clarify. Martin suggested I give a press conference. The river escape was a good news story. It might show some of the "more positive side" of the evacuation to the press, the ambassador purred. I raised no objections. Some publicity, I thought, might help gain later recognition for my staff. The ambassador obviously had his own reasons for wanting me to speak to the press. Without further discussion, Hogan was instructed to set up a press briefing for later in the day.

That afternoon, Hogan told me to be ready for the briefing at seven o'clock in the evening. At the appointed time, I arrived at a large, open compartment next to the chief's press center. It was well lit and furnished as a lounge. Through the portholes along one side, I could see the last traces of tropical dusk. Some thirty or forty journalists were gathered in the room, some standing, most sitting. There was an air of polite boredom. Mostly the occupants were non-Americans or stringers from the United States who worked for local newspapers. From their point of view I had the perfect "human interest" story. My Marines and staff were good copy for the small-town press.

None of the American press superstars were in the room. *Time* magazine had already filed a story on the Can Tho escape. Perhaps the other big media, such as the *New York Times, Washington Post, Newsweek,* and the television networks, were too busy to attend or simply skep-

tical of an officially organized briefing. In any case, the collapse of
South Vietnam was a historic and sensational disaster for foreign
policy; the human story of one small group of Americans was unlikely
to attract the interest of busy editors of major papers in the United
States.

Hogan introduced me as the consul general from Can Tho who
had organized and led an evacuation of personnel from the Delta. I
briefly described the evacuation, explaining the reasons that had compelled us to make the journey by boat. I did not mention the unauthorized use of helicopters by our CIA colleagues, for there seemed no
point in opening wounds in public. In any case, I was not yet certain
of all the facts of the case, and my own feelings did not ensure objectivity. Today, under the same uncertain circumstances, I would probably still choose silence.

Once the *Blue Ridge* was well clear of the coast of Vietnam, the captain ordered a barbecue for all hands. It was a kind gesture. His crew
had been under tension and overworked for several weeks. They needed
a break. His cargo of evacuees required some kind of jolt to bring them
psychologically back from Vietnam into an uncaring world that
came closer with each revolution of the ship's screws. A menu of fried
chicken, hamburgers, and hot dogs was soon scenting the broad flight
deck with the aroma of hickory smoke and sizzling meat. My boys and
I were squatting on the forward end of the long deck, eating hamburgers and drinking beer when Ambassador Martin and his wife
appeared from among the scores of sailors and civilians. Walking toward
us, Martin asked if they might join our group.

Martin seemed much stronger. He was recovering from the pneu-
monia and exhaustion that had brought him to the point of collapse.
He seemed in good spirits. Mrs. Martin was introduced, and we all sat
on the deck, enjoying the sunshine spreading over lazy tropical waves
as we ate and drank.

Martin asked the others about their experiences. Hasty gave the
ambassador a lurid account. Inevitably, the subject of helicopters
and the CIA came up.

When Christian described the CIA seizure of the evacuation helicopters as "cowardly and criminal," I intervened, attempting to put
the action into some kind of perspective. But bitter feelings were still
running high. When I weakly suggested that the VC had planted disinformation and their small diversionary attacks might honestly have
deceived some into thinking communist strength in the Delta was

greater than it really was, Traister commented that such "analytical failure was difficult to justify after twenty years of deep involvement in the Vietnam War."

Martin asked that such criticisms, however deeply felt, not be voiced to the press. He promised to take up the case of events in Can Tho and any others in which individuals had performed badly when he got back to Washington.

For the benefit of all, I said that, personally, I had no intention of pursuing the matter in the press. My only concern was that those who had done well should be given appropriate recognition and not find themselves no better off for the experience than those who had behaved badly. I emphasized that it was impossible for me to stop my former subordinates from talking to the press. Soon they would all pass from my influence. Several of them, I quietly informed Martin, were incensed by the behavior of their erstwhile colleagues. If he tried to censor them, matters might grow worse. In any case, I did not feel that he or I had any right to order or even encourage their silence. Martin accepted this judgment with good grace.

≡ 20 ≡

Back in the World

The *Blue Ridge* plowed through a slight swell. Ahead lay the entrance to Subic Bay. Steep mountains covered in deep green tropical forest encircled the huge naval base. Soon the ship was passing into calmer water, royal blue, laced with delicate strands of silver foam. The seas grew lighter and flatter. Overhead, small puffs of cumuli sailed slowly westward in a delft blue sky.

It had been seven days since we scrambled onto the flight deck of the *Blue Ridge* after our last helicopter flight. Now we stared over the long ship's side, taking in a new feeling of peace, enjoying the grandeur of the bay. It had a strange softness that not even the presence of the anchored warships could harshen. These great gray ships lay brooding, silent, swinging on their anchor chains. For them, too, Vietnam's war was over.

Leaning over the rail, admiring those warships dwarfed by the mountains, I began to wander down the dangerous path of self-examination. I thought about the insignificance of men and most of what they make and do. I had just given almost five years of my life to America's involvement with Vietnam. Every second of that time had seemed desperately important then. Now I felt cynical and used.

In the end, I did not succumb to depression, as did many of the others who had been involved in the evacuation. I was impatient to get ashore. Yet even here, I was disappointed. The *Blue Ridge* was unable to berth until evening, which meant that we were forced to sleep one more night on board. By morning, my good cheer was restored. Arriving in a land at peace brought me to accept that for me, too, the war was finished.

Yet, as I stepped down the gangplank in the fresh light of early morning, I realized that even if the fighting was ended, the suffering was not. There might still be useful work for a group such as my consulate general staff.

When I walked into the gymnasium on the naval base, where the military was busy screening all evacuees, I once more fought and won a battle for my kukri. This time I had to threaten a sit-down strike. But again a senior naval officer listened to my appeal and allowed me to keep my treasured knife. Thus a beaming consul general arrived on the ramp of Subic's Naval Air Station.

An ancient C-47, the naval attaché's plane, was standing ready to fly us south to Manila. Looking at the twin-engine "Gooney-Bird" with its silver nose pointed at the almost cloudless sky, I mused that it was almost the same vintage as I was, or not much short of it. Perhaps we were both showing our age. I climbed on board sweating, though sitting by the open door. The aircraft trundled to the end of the runway. I felt the drumming roar in my stomach as she took off. The cabin cooled with altitude. Soon I fell asleep.

I awoke to a change in the engine pitch. The aircraft was turning slowly into the wind, much lower, about to line up with the runway of Manila International.

In the distance I saw the trees and rooftops of the capital. Now almost on the ground, white strips on the tarmac flashed below the wing.

A sudden hard gust of wind slammed the aircraft from starboard. It began to roll. The thought flashed into my consciousness: how ironic it would be to die in an aircraft accident after having survived the events of the last weeks. Then I felt the aircraft begin to right itself, and we were airborne again. Ten minutes later, after a perfect landing, I was in a bus heading downtown toward the American Embassy.

America's embassy in Manila is a handsome old building. It faces one of the city's most fashionable main streets, once called Dewey Boulevard. Its rear watches over the smooth waters of Manila Bay, where only some eighty years before Commodore Dewey had defeated the Spaniards. I stood looking out through those rear windows, admiring the view as I waited to hear what the State Department was going to do with me. The scene was more dramatic than mine in Can Tho, I thought, remembering wooden roofs wet and shining from rain, somehow less ugly as each day passed, and that filthy bar outside the back gate.

From the embassy windows I could see Bataan and the jungled hump of Corregidor, both very clear, over on the far side of the bay. I reflected on how few years had passed since Dewey first seized these islands and established an overseas empire for the anticolonial American republic. What would Dewey have thought today, watching America withdraw from Vietnam?

There had been high and low points before. Those windows had seen it all: the surrender on Bataan, the paratroopers' daring jump onto Corregidor only three years later.

After a few minutes I was escorted to the office where Ambassador Martin and Wolfgang Lehmann, his deputy chief of mission, were already installed. Lehmann seemed tired. Probably he was still drained from those last days in Saigon. He told me that we would be in Manila for a few days awaiting the arrival of orders from the State Department. I asked him whether we could have an office to use while in Manila. There was still paperwork to be finished. But Lehmann said the embassy was overcrowded, and besides we had no real need of office space. Disappointed, I sought out an old friend.

Frazer Meade was now political counselor of the Manila embassy. Three years earlier, we had been students together at the Naval War College at Newport, Rhode Island. Meade might be able to find us a temporary home.

With Can Tho luck, one of Meade's junior officers was on leave. Without hesitation, Meade told me to move in. Thus, once again, the consulate general, though in exile, still had a home. Cushing helped me finish the personnel reports and commendations. Kass typed, and Averill Christian wound up his accounts. Vouchers for all money spent were handed over with the remaining cash. Christian had carried all those papers, plus a considerable sum of taxpayers' money, from his safe in Can Tho. The others were free and went sightseeing.

The Marines were billeted with the embassy's Marine detachment and soon found themselves back in the Corps. But come evening, all the Can Tho gang would gather together and spend hours in Manila's neon-lit bars, where dark-skinned girls flash long fake eyelashes with a directness that has its own charm. In every bar and street, jazz blared deafeningly into the night.

Once our paperwork was finished, I set about purchasing the beginnings of a wardrobe. The navy had opened the enlisted men's clothing store on *Blue Ridge* to us, but I found only a dungaree shirt and some underwear in my size.

On the second day after our arrival, Whitten and Sciacchitano burst into the office. "Guess what we heard," they said almost in unison.

"What?" asked Cushing, although he did not look up from his work.

"Americans are needed to help with refugees on Guam. It seems that most Vietnamese evacuees have been landed there or are on their way to the island."

"That's interesting," I remarked. We began discussing the idea of volunteering as a group. It made sense. We were used to working as a team. Together we combined a number of useful skills, from technical abilities to speaking Vietnamese. Only those who were married regretfully pointed out that they must decline. I told them that they were not to feel guilty. Their first responsibility was to reassure wives and children. Cushing said that he must obviously first go to see his wife and daughter, but as they were living in Bangkok, he could easily meet the group later, joining us on Guam if I could obtain permission for us to work as a team on the island. As a bachelor, I had no such encumbrances.

Lehmann turned the proposition down cold. We were not needed on Guam, he insisted, at least not as a group. Some Vietnamese-speakers might be sent as individuals. Lehmann claimed that Norm Sweet, the hard-pressed USAID official in charge of refugee camps on Guam, had asked that nobody visit the island without his prior approval. Wasting no more time, I appealed directly to Ambassador Martin.

Martin gave me permission to go with those individual officers whose services had been requested. But though he thought the idea of working as a group an excellent plan, Martin was no longer in a position to give permission for the whole group to go as a unit.

I broke the bad news: it was the end of the Can Tho group. We were given separate orders. Some were to go to Guam, others were being sent direct to the United States. Most shameful, some USAID employees went home to be laid off. Thus, the short existence of the Can Tho consulate general drew to a close. We said good-bye to each other, making the usual promises to keep in touch, exchanging addresses that would perhaps be safeguarded for years, perhaps lost and forgotten.

Christian and I flew to Hong Kong together. Christian's wife was there waiting for him. After coping with an army of Chinese tailors, I had twelve suits made in three days. I was able to wander around the booming island colony, enjoying the relaxing atmosphere and paying calls on old friends.

At the white skyscraper that housed the Hilton Hotel, Cliff Frink, the USAID logistician who had sent us the LCMs, was busy attempting to recover blocked USAID shipments still en route for Vietnam. I thanked him for the LCMs with all my heart. Frink's boats had made the successful evacuation possible.

I also met another old friend, the now former mission coordinator, who had been in overall charge of evacuation from Vietnam, Col. George Jacobson. The colonel had saved his own life at Tet in 1968 when he caught a pistol thrown through his bedroom window as a wounded Viet Cong was already halfway up the stairs. Prior to that moment, Jacobson had been giving the press a running commentary over the telephone on the fight for the embassy garden. As the Viet Cong, in desperation, blasted his way through the bedroom door, Jacobson calmly shot him.

Now I was able to thank Jake in person. The wily old warhorse grinned when I walked into his hotel room. "It would have been your ass, Terry, if anything had gone wrong," he commented, still highly amused. Then Jacobson added, "You did the right thing."

"I know, Jake. I would have been crucified."

"You would have been accused of criminal foolhardiness or worse."

"I know. But it was the only way I had of getting out the remaining Vietnamese employees and their families."

Jacobson looked me in the eye. "Tell me the truth," he said. "Did you think it was as risky as I did?"

I thought for a minute before replying. "I considered the dangers very carefully, Jake. But in the end, I always arrived at the same conclusion. We had surprise on our side. Moreover, the VC could not fully block a river."

"Sure." Jacobson nodded and waited for me to go on.

"I knew the VC might ambush the boats. They might even have time to deploy troops with rockets."

"I hear they did," said Jacobson with a laugh.

"Maybe." I smiled, remembering the fiery trail and the Marines being taught fire discipline by civilians. "But the boats were armored. We had good protection, at least from small-arms fire. Hits by rockets or crew-served weapons, however, would have been another story. We made it. How can one argue with success?" I quipped with a smile. On balance, I would do the same thing again.

While Cushing was in Bangkok, he heard from a former member of the CIA Can Tho staff how Downs had been placed under great pressure by his own American subordinates. Cushing was told that CIA employees held meetings at which Downs was informed that nobody wanted to go down the river. Some went so far as to warn him that they would refuse to do so if ordered by Downs or anybody else. Cushing and I had no idea at the time that this was going on. Clearly, this represented a serious breech in CIA leadership and discipline.

On Guam, conditions were not as hard as I had imagined they might be. The bulk of the refugees were living in a tent city that the Seabees had thrown together in record time on an airfield the Japanese abandoned in 1945. The Seabees had cleared ground, built roads, and provided water and electricity within forty-eight hours of getting orders to set up the camp. By the time I reached the island, most of this basic infrastructure had been installed. Medical services were being provided on the spot. Sanitation and garbage disposal were watched over closely by the military. There was a Marine Corps police force, not just to keep unauthorized people from getting into the camp, but to prevent the Vietnamese multitude from swamping Guam's small population.

My friends and I set up our own ombudsman service to help smooth relations between the Vietnamese and the American military camp authorities. A small information booth was set up in the middle of the camp, run mainly by former Can Tho personnel and others who spoke Vietnamese.

Troubled Vietnamese came with all manner of problems and questions. It was like being back in a Delta marketplace. All day, under a hot sun, my colleagues tried hard to answer questions, solve problems, mend disputes. If a matter was serious enough, they would take it to the appropriate American authority. Theirs was a useful middleman service. Often the Vietnamese were just bewildered and needed the patient ear of someone who spoke their language. The military personnel were equally anxious to run the camp smoothly. They, too, appreciated the services provided.

After a week, I had tracked down as many former Vietnamese employees as seemed to be present on Guam. I had searched the island's three camps, making certain no former Can Tho employees had special problems, or, if they did, that something was being done to solve them. I could see there were more than enough Americans on Guam capable of dealing with the general run of refugee problems. I was not needed on the island and might be of more use in Washington. In any case, I had to complete the paperwork involved in closing my post.

After a brief stay in Hawaii, I flew to Los Angeles. A refugee center had been set up at Camp Pendleton, the Marine base situated between

San Diego and Los Angeles. Again, I searched for former employees. Luck was with me. The camp was supervised by an old friend, Nick Thorne, a Foreign Service Officer with long experience in Vietnam. With Thorne's backing, I persuaded the immigration officials in the camp to waive requirements for security checks for former staff of the American mission on the grounds that they had been given security clearance years earlier, prior to their employment in Vietnam. It made no sense to subject them to a time-consuming search of the woefully incomplete records available in the United States. Immigration accepted this argument and began to process former employees' official entry into the United States. Finally, I set off on the last leg of my long journey home.

Washington is a city of spring. The season grows into a long kiss after a dull winter. When I saw it from the aircraft window as we approached National Airport, the long Mall was a dazzling emerald with bright strokes of color. The white dome of the Capitol had a softness that seemed almost to blur its shape against a clear southern sky. A promise of summer, auguring better times, was in the air. After finding a temporary apartment, I settled into the easy comfort of life in America.

Not that I could do much else. Dozens of State Department officers were flooding into the capital from Indochina. It was a personnel officer's nightmare. Many of these unemployed diplomats were fairly senior. Seven major posts in Southeast Asia had suddenly ceased to exist. Those dealing with other parts of the world were hardly likely to welcome this influx competing for a limited number of positions. I joined the queue and waited.

In the meantime, I worked as director of operations for the interagency committee established by the president to resettle the incoming refugees from Indochina. Toward the end of summer, I was telephoned while on a temporary mission in the refugee center at Camp Pendleton. "Would you like to be consul general not far from home, Terry?"

It was not a bad idea. My mother was getting on in age, and she would enjoy having me nearby. But what exactly was meant? Compared with Southeast Asia, even Mexico or the West Indies was not far from home.

"Quebec will need somebody in October," came the reply. This was the last place I would have imagined being posted. Yet it was only a few hours by car from my mother's home in Troy, New York. The job seemed a bit remote from the more important centers of diplomatic interest. It could be dull and a career dead end. Moreover, the winters were terribly severe. Nonetheless, I accepted. The election in 1976 of a government in Quebec dedicated to separation from the rest of Canada ended my concerns about the post's possible dullness.

A year later I was sitting in my comfortable office on the ground floor of the American consulate general in Quebec, with its views out over the narrows where the Saint Lawrence River passes beneath the Heights of Abraham, when my secretary brought me a telegram from the State Department. It congratulated me on my selection to receive the Superior Honors Award, the department's second-highest medal for achievement.

"No, they don't," I growled to the poor girl's astonishment and dictated an immediate response, politely declining to accept any award until my USAID colleagues received those for which they had been recommended.

Ultimately, all those Americans who left Can Tho with me did receive some official recognition. The Marines were first to award medals to their own, in the best tradition of the Corps. The State Department, under the prodding of Ambassador Carol Laise Bunker, director general of the Foreign Service and wife of Ellsworth Bunker, gave suitable, if delayed, recognition to its employees. The director of USAID, however, resisted giving awards to those who had evacuated Vietnam in 1975. Finally, grudgingly, under pressure, he allowed awards to be given at a ceremony held in November 1977.

Only then did I accept my decoration from the hands of Ambassador Thomas Enders in Ottawa. As he pinned the medal to my suit coat, my thoughts went back to those days of our evacuation from Can Tho. Many Americans had done their duty. In doing the right thing by our Vietnamese employees, we had escaped with some honor.

Epilogue

For me, Maj. Gen. Nguyan Khoa Nam, the IV Corps commander, is the hero of this sad story. When the end came, though he wanted to carry on the fight alone, Nam obeyed the new president's order to lay down his arms. Nam was a soldier who accepted the discipline his profession demanded.

Certainly, Nam must have struggled with his decision. The general's thoughts may finally have turned to Phan Thanh Gian, a heroic figure in Vietnamese history who faced a similar dilemma a hundred years before. This great mandarin, too, commanded the defenses of the Mekong Delta, when the French, seeking to extend their control over the rich rice-growing lands, pushed southwestward from Saigon. To avoid further bloodshed in a cause Phan Thanh Gian assessed as hopeless, he ordered his troops to surrender. But Phan Thanh Gian escaped the indignity of surrender himself. He took his own life.

Nam came to a similar conclusion. It was impossible for him to flee and desert his troops as others had done. He was not made that way. Equally, he could never have suffered the loss of face certain to follow in the wake of surrender to his lifetime communist enemies.

After releasing his subordinates from their solemn commitment to stay at their posts, Nam took the only course his sense of honor permitted. He shot himself in the head at his desk in his headquarters. I hope he will be remembered, as Phan Thanh Gian is remembered, as a man of honor.

Appendix*

MARINE SECURITY GUARD DETACHMENT
American Consulate General, Can Tho, Vietnam
(Aboard U.S.S. Blue Ridge at sea)

BSH:bsh
3000
1 May 1975

To: Consul General
From: Noncommissioned Officer in Charge
Subj: Evacuation of Consulate General, Can Tho, Vietnam
Ref: (a)   Verbal Orders of Consul General
Encl: (1)   Statement of Staff Sergeant Boyette S. HASTY
                253 82 51 49/3421 USMC

1.   In accordance with reference (a), Enclosure (1) is hereby
submitted concerning my actions and observations during the
period 0001 29 April 1975 through 1700, 1 May 1975.

Boyette S. Hasty

Boyette S. HASTY
Staff Sergeant
United States Marine Corps

cc: Commanding General, 9th Marine Amphibious Brigade
        Commanding Officer, Marine Security Guard Battalion
        (State Department)
        Commanding Officer, Company "C", Marine Security Guard
        Battalion

---

* This account is transcribed verbatim, except for corrections to occasional misspellings.

Statement of Staff Sergeant Boyette S. HASTY
253 82 51 49/3421 USMC

"At approximately 0515 on the morning of 29 April 1975 I was
awakened by the sound of explosions several blocks away. Through
radio transmissions from various stations on the emergency radio
net I discovered that VC/NVA forces had fired four (4) 122mm rockets from across the river in Vinh Long province into Can Tho city.
I immediately dressed and drove to the Delta Compound where Corporal JOHNSON was manning an emergency post at the boat docks to
check on his safety. I found him to be alright. I then drove to
the Consul General's residence to check for damage and found none.
I drove a block North to the bank of the river near the marketplace, which was crowded with people and ambulances. Two (2) 122's
had landed on an island on the river, and two (2) 122's near the
international hotel, causing an unknown amount of casualties. I
drove back to the Marine House, took a shower, and then checked
post at the Consulate. After discovering everything to be in order
I went to the Delta Compound for chow. At approximately 0745 I
arrived back at the Consulate. I knew that we would be evacuating in the next few days, so I dispatched several of my Marines on
various errands to locate or stockpile gear we would need. At
approximately 0840 I went to the Consul General's Office to check
for special instructions. While I was present we discovered that
the EAC phone was malfunctioning. During the meeting the PES(CIA)
chief came down and informed us that Ton Son Nhut airbase ·had been
rocketed and shelled early in the morning and two (2) Marines
had been killed. During the staff meeting it was decided that
Mr. TRAISTER would take his Vietnamese ARVN Sergeant-Interpreters
to the Delta Compound to live on board the boats. Since the
emergency radio link to Saigon and other posts was being overpowered by TCU transmitters, I said that Marines would open up the
alternate station at the Delta Compound and monitor it on a 24-
hour basis, until we left. At approximately 0905 I took Sergeant
PATE to the compound to stand the first radio watch to monitor
radios and the EAC phone. The telephone at that location was
malfunctioning also. I picked up the receiver to see if I could
hear anyone when Mr. JACOBSON, the Ambassador's Special Assistant, came on the line. After I identified myself he asked to speak
to the Consul General. I informed him that the Consul General
was at another area but that I would locate him and inform him
to call Saigon, which I did. I returned to the Consulate at approximately 1030. As I got out of my car my Assistant NCOIC, Sergeant
MOORE, came running up to me and said that the Ambassador had called
and told us to evacuate immediately. I told him to inform the other
Marines in the Detachment to prepare to move out. I then went immediately to the Consul General's office to obtain confirmation. He
in essence said the same thing, and that we would be going by helicopter. I went down to the Marine Guard on Post Number One in
the lobby, Corporal KILLENS, and informed him of the situation. I
asked him to notify Sergeant PATE at the Delta Compound to cease
monitoring the radio and report back to the Consulate. I then
got Sergeant MOORE and told him to have the Marines bring only
their weapons and one small bag. I ordered him to have the Marines
leave behind their flak jackets and helmets as there would be a

difficult weight factor on the helicopters to contend with. I then returned to the Consul General's office, where I discovered that Saigon had ordered our four (4) Air America helicopters back to Saigon to help them evacuate. We would now have to go [out] by the two (2) LCM's that the Consul General had acquired from the Alaska Barge and Tug Company a couple of weeks before, and the rice barge that we had bought and fixed up. I then went below to the C&R vault and removed the frequency crystals from the radio. I put the crystals in my pocket and went into the Marine Office to collect my men's passports, shot cards, and personnel records. I placed them into special waterproof pouches that I had had made for this purpose several weeks before. As I was doing this Walt MILFORD, the TCU communicator, ran into my office and begged me to help him destroy his Top Secret Crypto material. As it turned out all the PES(CIA) personnel had bugged out, leaving him to destroy everything by himself. I ran back with him to the C&R area and into the TCU vault where we started rolling out burn barrels and ripping the tops off with bolt cutters. After we got them open we found that they were of a type we had never seen before, but we decided that we had to try and use them anyway. While Mr. MILFORD took out the cypher components, I filled the regular incinerator full of classified files and lit it off. At this time Mr. CUSHING, the Deputy Consul General, came down the hall and offered to help. We got the burn barrels full of material and Mr. MILFORD and Mr. CUSHING started tying down the covers on the burn barrels. At this time the Consul General called me on the radio and told me to get to the boat docks ASAP. I sent Sergeant KIRCHNER with Mr. SCI-ACCHITANO, the Vice Consul. I then called the Consul General on the radio and asked permission to remain behind to cover Mr. CUSH-ING and Mr. MILFORD as the crowds were starting to get somewhat hostile. He gave his approval, and I then ordered Sergeant MOORE to take the remaining Marines to the dock and start loading the weapons and radios aboard the boats that I had stockpiled there earlier. I returned to the TCU vault where Mr. MILFORD told me that the barrels were not lighting off properly. I went to my office and located ten (10) incendiary grenades and returned to the vault with them. At this moment the barrels finally caught and went up in flames. We dumped the grenades and made our way out the front entrance to Mr. CUSHING's car, and had his driver take us to the Delta Club. When we arrived the Marines were just finishing load-ing the boats. Moments later all the Americans were accounted for and we boarded the LCM. Myself, Mr. CUSHING, and the Consul General were the last to go on. The rice barge cast off and moved out into the river. Aboard the LCM we had trouble getting underway, as the tide was out and we were stuck on the mud flats. At that moment we saw three (3) PES(CIA) Filipino employees and their fam-ilies running down the dock. Sergeant MOORE and myself jumped ashore and started throwing them aboard. Local Vietnamese started pouring through the compound gates so the Consul General ordered us to embark and we got underway. A few minutes later we halted to take the rice barge into tow and to wait for the LCM from the Shell docks to catch up with us. It was loaded with Vietnamese refugees, and when it came alongside we got under way again. The crew for our LCM had deserted several days earlier, so the Consul General, a former Naval Officer, took the helm and steered us out. At approximately 1245 two (2) armored "Mike" boats of the Vietnamese Navy halted our LCM's by firing across the bow. We halted, but they refused to come alongside us. Shortly afterwards four (4) more "Mike" boats arrived on station and joined the others. One of the boats came alongside the LCM with an English-speaking officer on board. He explained that he had orders from Commodore THANG, through the IV Corps Commander, to halt us until he arrived, which would take about a half an hour. We asked for and received permission to transfer our people from the rice barge to the LCM's so that we could consolidate our force. We also discovered at this point that the PES(CIA) people had retained control of at least one helicopter because we saw them flying overhead. We made radio contact with them and told them of the situation, and [asked] them to try to contact the U.S. Navy to liaison with the Vietnamese to see if they could help us get free. They gave us a "roger" and flew off into the sky, never to be seen again by us up to the time of this writing. At approximately 1410 Commodore THANG of the Vietnamese Navy came alongside. He informed us that General NAM, the IV Corps Commander, had ordered us stopped and searched for ARVN and draft age military males. We had some on board, but they were U.S. employees who would be in danger of their lives if the NVA took over, and we didn't want to lose them. Fortunately the Consul General had foreseen a problem like this and had made arrangements earlier to get the Commodore's wife and children to safety. In return, the Commodore took our word that there were none aboard, and allowed us to depart. We headed down the river and at approximately 1450 started receiving B-40 rocket fire from VC/NVA on the South bank of the river. Earlier I had asked for and received permission to have my Marines open fire immediately if fired upon without having to wait for permission. When we began receiving fire the Marines and some civilians immediately opened up with M-16's, M-79's, and various other weapons, suppressing the enemy fire. Consul General McNAMARA remained standing behind the wheel and increased the RPM's until we hit maximum speed. We took no casualties and we do not know if we inflicted any. As far as I know this was the last Marine combat action of the Vietnam War. (Note: Earlier in the month Colonel SILVA, the Assistant Army Attache from DAO in Saigon, and other personnel had come to Can Tho to get our available radio frequency list and to help make arrangements for our evacuation if needed. They had promised us air cover and a Navy Destroyer Escort to pick us up at the mouth of the Bassac river if we evacuated by sea.) At approximately 1500 a jet tentatively identified as an F-4 Phantom flew overhead and circled us once. We attempted to make radio contact but could not raise it, and it soon flew off. This was the only friendly air we saw during the entire trip. Moments later we were deluged by a tremendous cloudburst, which continued for almost an hour. This rain obscured us from sight by the VC/NVA along the banks of the river. The rain was extremely cold, and what I remembered most clearly was lying in the open behind an M-60, shivering. A few minutes later Mr. SCIACCHITANO, our Consular Officer, came over and covered me with a field jacket, which helped a great deal. We continued down the river as fast as possible, with the Marines remaining on alert in case of further attacks. Several times we went to battle stations when we were approached by suspicious Vietnamese small craft. Once they saw our display of weapons though, they veered off and left us alone. We reached the mouth of the Bassac river at approximately 1830, and continued out into international waters. We could not spot the Destroyer Escort that was supposed to be there to pick us up. I commenced calling "Mayday" on every frequency of every radio we had. (I continued calling for the next eight hours, but never received an answer.) As darkness fell we continued out to sea. We had no compass, so all navigation was by dead reckoning. At varying intervals we fired off flares, and I repeated my "Mayday" messages continuously, asking any monitoring U.S. ship to fire two flares to help us locate them. We still could not raise anyone. At approximately 2400 we were about to turn around and head back to shore for the night when we spotted what looked like a ship's lights in the distance. We immediately changed course and headed for it. Several times we fired flares, but could receive no answer. At about 0110 on the morning of 30 April we finally got close enough to identify the ship as the U.S. Lines "Pioneer Contender". The sea was extremely rough, and we experienced some difficulty in moving alongside for off-loading. After we came alongside the "Pioneer Contender" the Consulate MSG's caught lines thrown over by the ship and after several tries we were able to secure our LCM to the side of the vessel. Marines from the HQ's (Communications) Detachments of the 9th Marines (under command of Captain Garcia, the Assistant S-3) came down in a cargo net and helped the Consulate Marines load our refugees in and hoist them aboard. The Marines worked quickly and accurately and by 0200 the off-loading was completed. During the off-loading we received word that the LCM's were needed to help carry refugees from Vung Tau, and we were requested to leave a volunteer crew aboard them. The Consul General, although he had been at the helm for 14 hours, volunteered to stay, as did Mr. HEILMAN, Mr. CUSHING, and myself. A few moments later however a Mr. PARKER and several Filipinos who had been on the ship came down to take over. At 0200 we came up the cargo hoist, the last personnel on board. At this time we discovered that the "Pioneer Contender" had not been expecting us, knew nothing about us, and that it was pure luck that we had found them. Several Marines on board the ship had seen our flares and reported them to the crew, who ignored them. The Marines assigned to the ship were living in atrocious conditions, with only two (2) C-rations per day per man, and were sleeping on the open decks with no blankets or cover. Although they had little to offer they shared it with us in the traditional Marine manner. We slept on the deck with them that night and the next morning we were attached to them to assist in processing refugees. Shortly afterwards I accompanied the Consul General to the bridge where we attempted to find out from Military Sealift Command by radio when the volunteer LCM crews would be relieved. The result was utter confusion on the part of MSC and the Navy as to what to do with us. Finally they told us to stand by and we didn't hear from them again. At this time one of our LCM's had picked up some refugees from a fishing boat and requested permission to come alongside and unload. At the instructions of the Ship's Master I controlled the transfer operation from the bridge by radio. After the off-loading was completed I ordered the LCM's to pull back and not to let any Vietnamese board them, since the ship refused to

take any more. At this time Marines aboard the ship were firing
into the water to keep the local boats away. At approximately 1130
the tugboat "Chitosa Maru" came alongside with instructions to
transfer all evacuees aboard. My Marines were detached from the
ship's Marines and reassigned to the Consul General. I was the
last to leave, after having discovered my mother-in-law and three
small brothers-in-law in the hold of the "Pioneer Contender". We
were forced to leave all our Vietnamese employees behind [on the
"Pioneer Contender"]. We remained aboard the tug for several hours
as it steamed toward a rendezvous with LST 117, the "Booheung Pioneer". We boarded the LST at approximately 1800. That night we
again slept on the decks. The next morning (1 May) we began preparations for transfer operations to a U.S. Navy ship. Shortly afterwards some internal trouble occurred amongst the Vietnamese refugees
aboard. I volunteered to remain aboard with my Marines to provide
shipboard security, but the Consul General explained that no Americans would be remaining on board, and the Korean crew was armed
and could probably handle any trouble. At approximately 1130 we
started transferring Americans to the Command ship "U.S.S. Blue
Ridge" via Huey helicopters from Marine HMM 165. During the transfer I and my Marines remained on deck and moved to the fantail
to secure it for operations and to prevent the Vietnamese from
rushing the helicopters. It was approximately 1530 when the last
helicopter containing the Consul General, Mr. CUSHING, and myself
landed on board the "Blue Ridge." Once aboard we were frisked, our
weapons were confiscated, and we were herded down to a wardroom
for processing. Down below I met our Commanding Officer, Major
KEAN, and reported to him that the Marine Security Guard Detachment, American Consulate General, Can Tho, Vietnam was all present or accounted for, and that we had come out with all our
accountable weapons intact, plus four (4) extra M-16's and one (1)
extra M-79 grenade launcher. A few minutes later as we were processing through, a Marine Colonel came up to Sergeant MOORE and
myself and asked if we were U.S. Marines. We told him we were, and
he replied that we didn't need to process through. He took us to
another compartment where we met the Commanding General of the 9th
Marine Amphibious Brigade, Brigadier General CAREY. He asked us
to sit down and asked us some questions concerning our evacuation.
What I remember most is that he offered us a glass of iced tea,
the first cold drink we had had in three days. Following this we
talked again with Major KEAN, and then were taken below to the 9th
MAB G-4 office to make billeting arrangements."

The above statement is true and correct to the best of my
knowledge.

Boyette S. Hasty

Boyette S. HASTY

Index

About the Authors

Francis Terry McNamara was on active duty in the U.S. Foreign Service for thirty-seven years, retiring in 1993. In his three diplomatic postings in Vietnam, he served as provincial adviser with the CORDS program, first principal officer in Danang, and consul general in Can Tho. An experienced Africanist as well, he served in seven African posts and was ambassador in Gabon and São Tomé and Príncipe and in Cape Verde. Other posts included Beirut and Quebec. Earlier, he served in the U.S. Navy's Submarine Service.

McNamara is the author of *The French in Black Africa* (Washington: National Defense University Press, 1989), a standard work in English on France's unusually close relations with its former African colonies. He is working on a history of the Foreign Service in Vietnam from 1955 to 1975.

Adrian Hill is a British writer and former diplomat. His first novel, *The Tiger Pit* (London: Whydown Books, 1992), is a thriller set during the Olympic Games in South Korea. A forthcoming novel, *River of Stars,* is set in war-torn South Vietnam. He has also written for newspapers, magazines, and the *Royal United Services Institute Journal.* Hill's career in the British Diplomatic Service lasted from 1963 to 1991 and included service in Vietnam.